Being Philosophical

Being Philosophical

An Introduction to Philosophy and Its Methods

Stephen Hetherington

polity

Copyright © Stephen Hetherington 2024

The right of Stephen Hetherington to be identified as Author of this Work has been asserted in accordance with the UK Copyright, Designs and Patents Act 1988.

First published in 2024 by Polity Press

Polity Press
65 Bridge Street
Cambridge CB2 1UR, UK

Polity Press
111 River Street
Hoboken, NJ 07030, USA

All rights reserved. Except for the quotation of short passages for the purpose of criticism and review, no part of this publication may be reproduced, stored in a retrieval system or transmitted, in any form or by any means, electronic, mechanical, photocopying, recording or otherwise, without the prior permission of the publisher.

ISBN-13: 978-1-5095-5457-7
ISBN-13: 978-1-5095-5458-4 (pb)

A catalogue record for this book is available from the British Library.

Library of Congress Control Number: 2023945911

Typeset in 11 on 13pt Sabon
by Fakenham Prepress Solutions, Fakenham, Norfolk NR21 8NL
Printed and bound in Great Britain by CPI Group (UK) Ltd, Croydon

The publisher has used its best endeavours to ensure that the URLs for external websites referred to in this book are correct and active at the time of going to press. However, the publisher has no responsibility for the websites and can make no guarantee that a site will remain live or that the content is or will remain appropriate.

Every effort has been made to trace all copyright holders, but if any have been overlooked the publisher will be pleased to include any necessary credits in any subsequent reprint or edition.

For further information on Polity, visit our website:
politybooks.com

Contents

Detailed Contents vi
Preface and Acknowledgements xi

Introduction 1
1 Who Are You? 5
2 Philosophical Reading and Writing 72
3 What Do You Know? 91
4 Philosophical Reasoning 163
5 How Should You Act? 181
6 Philosophical Viewing 241

Index 265

Detailed Contents

Introduction	1
1 Who Are You?	5
1.1 Selves	5
1.1.1 Upaniṣadic impersonal selves	5
1.1.2 Buddhist no-selves	8
1.1.3 David Hume's no-inner-substantial-selves	12
1.1.4 Patricia Churchland's brainy selves	13
1.1.5 Ifeanyi Menkiti's socially created selves	15
Readings for 1.1	16
1.2 Souls	16
1.2.1 Plato's immortal soul	16
1.2.2 Wang Chong's nature	19
1.2.3 Avicenna's flying man	21
1.2.4 René Descartes's mind-meets-body	23
1.2.5 Martha Kneale's stories	27
Readings for 1.2	29
1.3 Self-reflection	29
1.3.1 Christine de Pizan's Reason	29
1.3.2 Mary Midgley's Beasts	31
1.3.3 Harry Frankfurt's wantons	33
Readings for 1.3	35

1.4	Personal identity	35
	1.4.1 Buddhist demons	35
	1.4.2 Vasubandhu's persons-as-collections	37
	1.4.3 John Locke's memories	39
	1.4.4 Derek Parfit's Teletransporter	41
	Readings for 1.4	43
1.5	Personal essence	44
	1.5.1 Karl Marx and human nature	44
	1.5.2 Frantz Fanon and race	47
	1.5.3 Sally Haslanger and gender	49
	Readings for 1.5	51
1.6	Personal will	52
	1.6.1 Aristotle trapped by the future	52
	1.6.2 Alexander of Aphrodisias trapped by the past	54
	1.6.3 Philippa Foot's explanations	57
	1.6.4 Edna Ullmann-Margalit's big decisions	59
	Readings for 1.6	61
1.7	Personal significance	61
	1.7.1 Lucretius living with death	61
	1.7.2 St Anselm living with faith	64
	1.7.3 Albert Camus living with absurdity	67
	1.7.4 Susan Wolf living with meaning	68
	Readings for 1.7	71
2 Philosophical Reading and Writing		72
2.1	Wondering what it is to be philosophical?	72
2.2	Reading	74
	2.2.1 Selfless philosophy (and Āryadeva)	74
	2.2.2 Self-philosophy (and John Perry)	76
	2.2.3 The Way of Truth (and Parmenides)	78
	2.2.4 Forms of Truth (and the *Mahābhārata*)	84
	Readings for 2.2	87
2.3	Writing	88

3 What Do You Know? 91
3.1 What is knowledge? 91
  3.1.1 Plato's knowing beliefs 91
  3.1.2 Nyāya's knowing episodes 93
  3.1.3 Bertrand Russell's stopped clock 95
  Readings for 3.1 98
3.2 Doubts 98
  3.2.1 The *Zhuangzi*'s puzzling questions 98
  3.2.2 Sextus Empiricus' competing appearances 101
  3.2.3 Nāgārjuna's empty words 103
  3.2.4 Abū Ḥāmid Muḥammad ibn Muḥammad al-Ghazālī's dreams 109
  3.2.5 Francisco Sanches's unknowing words 112
  3.2.6 René Descartes's demon 115
  Readings for 3.2 118
3.3 Knowing a physical world? 119
  3.3.1 René Descartes's dreams 119
  3.3.2 George Berkeley's ideas 121
  Readings for 3.3 125
3.4 Knowing other minds? 125
  3.4.1 Dharmakīrti's idealist reasonings 125
  3.4.2 John Stuart Mill's realist analogies 128
  3.4.3 Edith Stein's empathy 132
  Readings for 3.4 134
3.5 Knowing in action 135
  3.5.1 Wang Yangming's knowledge-action unity 135
  3.5.2 Gilbert Ryle's knowledge-how 137
  3.5.3 Elizabeth Anscombe's practical knowledge 139
  3.5.4 American Indian questioning-knowledge-how 142
  Readings for 3.5 145
3.6 Knowing's rights and wrongs 145
  3.6.1 Maria Montessori's methods 145

	3.6.2 Linda Zagzebski's intellectual virtues	148
	3.6.3 Helen Longino's feminist sensibility	150
	3.6.4 Miranda Fricker on epistemic injustice	154
	3.6.5 Charles Mills on white ignorance	156
	3.6.6 Vrinda Dalmiya's relational humility	159
	Readings for 3.6	161
4	Philosophical Reasoning	163
	4.1 Elements	163
	4.2 Uses	164
	4.3 Examples	167
	4.3.1 Revisiting Plato's *Meno*	167
	4.3.2 Revisiting the *Zhuangzi*	168
	4.3.3 Revisiting Longino's feminist sensibility	170
	4.3.4 Revisiting al-Ghazālī's dreams	172
	4.4 Philosophical reasoning as rhythmic gymnastics?	175
5	How Should You Act?	181
	5.1 Towards yourself	181
	5.1.1 Confucius' Way	181
	5.1.2 Aristotle's substantial happiness	184
	5.1.3 Yaḥyā ibn 'Adī's complete man	188
	Readings for 5.1	192
	5.2 Towards other people	192
	5.2.1 The Confucian *Great Learning*	192
	5.2.2 Immanuel Kant's ends-in-themselves	194
	5.2.3 Mary Wollstonecraft's early feminism	198
	5.2.4 John Stuart Mill's greatest happiness	201
	5.2.5 Nel Noddings's caring	204
	5.2.6 Martha Nussbaum's capabilities	207
	5.2.7 Charles Mills on the racial contract	210
	Readings for 5.2	214

5.3	Towards non-human animals	215
	5.3.1 Śāntideva's sentient beings	215
	5.3.2 Peter Singer's liberated animals	217
	5.3.3 Christine Korsgaard's fellow creatures	221
	Readings for 5.3	224
5.4	Towards nature	225
	5.4.1 The Stoics' cosmos	225
	5.4.2 Wang Yangming's one body	228
	5.4.3 Arne Naess's ecosophy	230
	5.4.4 Holmes Rolston's environmental ethic	233
	5.4.5 James Lovelock's Gaia	237
	Readings for 5.4	239
6	Philosophical Viewing	241
6.1	Why be philosophical?	241
6.2	Viewing the world philosophically	243
	6.2.1 Contents	243
	6.2.2 Attitudes	245
6.3	Viewing views philosophically	247
6.4	Views, views, views	249
6.5	Philosophy as experiment	253
6.6	Philosophy forever	257
6.7	Philosophical progress	259
6.8	Xenophanes' opinion	260
	Reading for 6.8	262
6.9	Living philosophically	262
Index		265

Preface and Acknowledgements

Being philosophical, even briefly, is special. Yet everyone can do it. *You* can do it. Reading this book can *help* you to do it. The book takes – and reflects upon – some initial philosophical steps.

Not all steps, of course; what would 'all' philosophy be? Is there just one way to be philosophical? Perish the thought. 'Philosophy' is a vague term – usefully so. It can bend and stretch. It can retract yet refresh and expand. All the while, it seems to mean *something* persisting – something clear *enough* – to get it under way. Philosophical *questions and ideas* have appeared, disappeared, reappeared, here and there, now and then, across the world and through the centuries, within socially and intellectually diverse traditions. So have many *methods* for engaging with those questions and ideas.

Yes, philosophy has methods. Even so, it is not merely methodical. It can be inspired. It embraces ideas appearing from … anywhere and nowhere. It welcomes previously unasked questions about ideas old or new. Philosophical moments can occur without warning. This is part of their charm. You might be browsing in a bookshop, a library, online. Watching the ocean. Walking. Opening books and articles, almost at random. Fun titles. Odd words. Puzzling sentences. Noticing philosophical thoughts within yourself might be unsettling, even overwhelming. Scattered ideas could be difficult to blend. Doing so might feel *too* difficult. But it is not. Well, sometimes it is, for a while. Persistence helps, though. When confused, don't panic. Never give up. Take a silent moment, or three, allowing what is not clear to *become* clear. Struggle with your thoughts. Then do not. Worry. Then do not. Think. Then do not. Then think again. And follow your thoughts wherever they lead. Will you discover answers? Perhaps. Will the effort be personally valuable? Hopefully so.

This book revisits and re-creates many such moments. Can we see and feel 'from within' *what it is* – even how it might *feel* – to begin being philosophical, in different ways with different authors on different topics? Not *all* ways with *all* authors on *all* philosophical topics; five lifetimes would be too brief for that. Philosophy can be *big* – big ideas, big challenges, big opportunities. It might arise anywhere at any time. It is ancient. It is now. It is the future. In this book we encounter, I believe, a representative sampling. There is a variety of philosophical styles and traditions, philosophical cultures and concepts, from diverse areas of the world, spanning more than two thousand years. We meet much, even if more awaits.

So, the book might fairly have been titled *Beginning Being Philosophical*. It could not justly have been titled *All That There Is to Being Philosophical*. That would have been misleading. Does philosophy possess an unchanging core, a potentially calcified heart, a single outer appearance? No. No. And no. It is many and more; it is here and there; it is now and then. Yet somehow it was, and still is, *something* – something definite *enough* to be recognised and appreciated, at least mostly so. This book's aim is to assist you in that respect, too.

How is the book structured? Chapter 1 is about metaphysics, chapter 3 is on epistemology, and chapter 5's topic is ethics. Those chapters introduce philosophical *ideas* of (in turn) reality, knowledge, and moral action. We also have three chapters – 2, 4, and 6 – that reflect upon *methods*. The 'ideas chapters' provide data that may be discussed in those 'methods chapters'. The 'ideas chapters' *show* some philosophical thinking in action. The 'methods chapters' *think about* such thinking. These chapters *explain* something of how such thinking works. The 'methods chapters' do this in three stages (interweaving with the 'ideas chapters'). Chapter 2 is on some aspects of how to *begin* thinking philosophically. Chapter 4 highlights how to build upon that base in *developing* philosophical reasoning. Chapter 6 concerns how to *evaluate* such reasoning, asking especially what larger lessons we may learn about the *nature* of being philosophical – including its potential for progress.

The book has many sections within those chapters, each focused upon a particular author or approach or idea. I will quote often from those authors. This is so that you experience something of *their* thinking, their own words and phrasing.

You will not experience the *full* richness of their thinking, since I will convey just one or two or three, say, of each author's ideas. You will also not always experience their thinking's full *complexity*. This could be welcome, since at times the complexity obscures a key idea. When reading philosophy, it can be difficult to chart and follow its reasoning and main ideas. I will select and commentate, imparting a sense of what is at stake, and what is being proposed, within a specific instance of philosophy.

Already that points to my first piece of advice for how to read philosophy. Always try to *find* the main ideas. This makes it easier to chart how an author claims to have *reached* them – her reasoning *for* them. And it will be easier to chart how she *uses* her ideas – what reasoning she generates *from* them. This might include clarifying or explaining those main ideas, imagining and defusing objections to them, extending or applying them, and so on. It might include ... well, whatever is thought to be *needed* for introducing, understanding, and communicating a philosophical idea. Be receptive. Be alert. Be adaptable.

All the more so, given how *varied* philosophical thinking can be. If philosophy is to make progress, it might wish to build on awareness of what, if anything, it has already achieved. This means not overlooking or undervaluing philosophy's enticing past, its diversity of language, ideas, topics, and ways of thinking. No single shortish book will encompass all of that. I wish it could. I have genuinely enjoyed travelling even a little distance along that intricate path, meeting elements of that past and that diversity. You might choose to journey even further along that path. (In this book's travels, I am an enthusiastic and inquiring tour guide – also learning as we wander, visiting some laneways and neighbourhoods that are as new for me as for you.)

The book's path, by the way, is not intended to mirror, or be constrained by, a formal and traditional university or college course. This is not written as a standard textbook, in content or structure. I *can* picture an imaginative introductory philosophy course being taught around the book. In no way, though, is this a *rules* book – rules for being philosophical. (I do not think that there are such rules.) It is more of a *welcoming* book – showing visitors around an exciting country. It might easily *complement* a first philosophy course. It could certainly help someone to *prepare informally* for such a course, even to read further – for fun, I hope – *beyond* the course's official boundaries. So, to anyone about to study philosophy (especially for the first time), unsure as to what kinds of intellectual experience await, welcome! Even if you are not enrolled in a philosophy course, if you are simply wondering what philosophy might involve, also welcome!

The invitation to write the book came from Pascal Porcheron, then at Polity Press. It was an intriguing idea. This is not my first introductory book. Even so, writing in this way remains an adventure. It is different to writing 'philosophy research'. I have never liked the word 'research' for what philosophers do in their 'serious' moments. Is it better to say 'search', not 'research'? And is philosophy as much creation as discovery, as much art as science?

Anyway, with genuine appreciation, I now thank several reviewers, who provided excellent criticisms and advice during preparatory stages when the book was being proposed and planned, along with two reviewers who read the completed manuscript, also offering helpful and perceptive comments. Pascal was encouraging and constructive – an editorial exemplar. After Pascal left Polity, Ian Malcolm continued in that vein – encouraging and constructive. And I thank Peter Adamson, David Bronstein, Waldemar Brys, Jonardon Ganeri, Karyn Lai, and Sophia Vasalou for great advice on some of the book's readings and sections. I learnt a lot in writing this book. Hopefully, you will learn much in reading it.

Introduction

Introductions can be cursory: 'Hello Xanthe, this is Xavier.' 'Hello, Xavier. Nice to meet you.' Then Xanthe glides onwards, maybe to meet someone else. This book's introduction – here and now – is not *that* fleeting. But it *is* like meeting a new person. 'Hello, this is philosophy, an old friend of mine.'

And I encourage you not to hurry onwards. Why not tarry for a moment, spending time with philosophy? I think that you will enjoy her company. She is distinctive, curious, lively. She can be surprising, creative, intelligent. She might question some of your ideas. But she will do it constructively, aiming always to understand. Will you become friends with her? There is a chance – with care, respect, and thoughtfulness. *That* is the encouraging spirit in which this book introduces you to philosophy.

I should mention two of the book's related features.

First, this is not an exhaustive 'life memoir' or biography for philosophy. When meeting someone new, an extended story is generally not what you need to hear. A few episodes from her life? Yes. Some hopes and concerns? Gladly. Will you then be motivated to learn more about her? If so, a friendship might have been born. Now think, analogously, about meeting philosophy. It has been 'alive' for *so* long, encompassing *vastly* many issues, questions, ideas, and so on, across *much* of the world. Almost any book introducing you to philosophy describes only a little of that vastness. But might you, upon experiencing philosophy's presence even to that tip-of-an-iceberg extent, be motivated to discover *more* about her? If so, another friendship – this time with philosophy – could have been born.

What form might such a friendship take? It will probably be reflective, chatty, and thoughtful – features with the potential to deepen a friendship. What are you doing well in how you relate to philosophy? What can you do better? How can the friendship be strengthened? Such questions underlie the book's 'methods' chapters (2, 4, 6) – *reflecting on* the 'ideas' chapters (1, 3, 5). The 'methods' chapters are being philosophical *about* some notable instances of philosophy, such as those in the 'ideas' chapters. The combination of those two kinds of chapter is like two friends taking a moment to reflect on their friendship and on experiences they have shared as friends. They reflect in that way to *understand* the friendship better, strengthening it in *that* way. This book's 'methods' chapters function in that way. They are opportunities to strengthen your friendship with philosophy, by *understanding* better the relationship that you have been developing with it by reading the 'ideas' chapters.

I will expand on that point, using a rough analogy.

The 'ideas' chapters are like outings and adventures that you might share with a friend: 'See that view. Let's go to that game. That was a great concert. Look at that painting. We should listen to that speaker.' And so on. The two of you are experiencing, together, aspects of the world 'out there'. Shared moments like that can be at the core of a friendship, obviously with a person *but also with philosophy*. For philosophy offers you plenty of ideas to savour and evaluate, as if talking back and forth in philosophical ways.

In which case, the book's 'methods' chapters are like occasions on which the two of you – philosophy and you – pause to discuss the friendship, seeking a mutual understanding that *itself becomes part* of the friendship. Think of how easy it is for two people to share experiences – going to a sports event, visiting a park together, and so on – in a *less mutually understanding* way. This is not a problem, so long as each enjoys being with the other. Yet maybe something more – *in addition to* the enjoyment – is possible, and would be welcome. Could the friendship be strengthened by both people *also sharing an understanding* of its nature and further potential? Taking a moment to discuss this with each other in a genuinely reflective way might help. What if there is no obvious problem needing to be discussed? That does not change my point. Knowing *that* there is no problem, after having thought together about this, could be reassuring, enriching the relationship. Doing this even occasionally could still be empowering. It might even uncover a previously overlooked weakness – a possible risk – within the friendship. I realise that not everyone wants to engage in such discussions. (I myself do not always want to do so.) There is even a contrary risk, of undermining what had been good about the friendship: thinking too much about a feeling might weaken or remove it. But sometimes a thoughtful conversation about the friendship, say, *can* strengthen it. The conversation could make the friendship more fully and thoroughly honest, for a start.

It is no coincidence, then, that chapter 1 is about *selves*. This book is a first meeting with philosophy, potentially the start of a friendship. And philosophy is like a *highly self-reflective* person. Becoming friends with philosophy is like coming to know someone who can fluently direct your attention, from the outset, to features of *both* you and her, *as* selves, that might be significant for developing a friendship with her. She has *already* been seeking to understand such matters – for thousands of years, we will find. That is commitment. That is substantial. Philosophy is like *that* person. Philosophy is like someone who has thought a lot about her self (and beyond) – not in a narcissistic way, but in a constructive 'What-am-I?' way. Her efforts are constructive also by thinking about *others* – in a 'What-are-they?' way. She tries to understand everyone, as far as possible – in order to understand even a single one of us. What, if anything, do all of us have in common as selves? Can philosophy help you, *as* a potential friend, to answer that question?

The good news is that she will try, beginning in chapter 1.

1

Who Are You?

1.1 Selves

1.1.1 Upaniṣadic impersonal selves
There is no single perfect place or time for taking one's initial philosophy steps – *starting* to be acquainted, let alone friends, with philosophy. But here, now, is an excellent place to begin, by meeting one of the *earliest* steps ever taken, in the Upaniṣads. These were philosophically religious literary writings on ideas from four earlier sacred Vedic texts, grounding what became Hinduism. Religion and philosophy are not always so separate. That is evident in these Upaniṣads (the term 'Upaniṣad' means 'hidden connection', maybe 'hidden teaching'). All were written in Sanskrit, in northern India, seemingly over several centuries, possibly starting around 700 BCE. (By whom? We do not know.) Let us sample a few of their ideas about *selves* (a beginning focus explained a moment ago in the book's introduction).

What *is* a self? I am one. You are one. Or so we say. But what do we mean? What *should* we mean? Can we find self-understanding in the Upaniṣads?

In the *Bṛhadāraṇyaka Upaniṣad* (Great Forest Upaniṣad; the oldest Upaniṣad; probably pre-Buddhist), a sage, Yājñavalkya, spoke with his wife, Maitreyī, about selves (4.5.12–13).

> It is like this. As the ocean is the point of convergence of all the waters, so the skin is the point of convergence of all sensations of touch; the nostrils, of all odours, the tongue, of all tastes ... the mind, of all thoughts; the heart, of all sciences; [and so on; followed by the next paragraph].
> It is like this. As a mass of salt has no distinctive core and surface; the whole thing is a single mass of flavor – so indeed, my dear, this self has no distinctive core and surface; the whole thing is a single mass of cognition.

Yājñavalkya seems to have been saying that the self within any *one* of us is somehow the same within *all* of us. There is no difference in *that* respect between my self and yours. Dramatically, this does not mean 'the same in nature'; it means 'the very same self'. My personal self *is* your personal self, and vice versa. Neither of us has a distinct personal self. It is as if all of us *partake in*, or *share*, a self – the same self, a common self. Yājñavalkya says this (4.5.15): 'When ... the Whole has become one's very self, then who [= what more specific self] is there for one [= one's self] to see and by what means?'

Does that make sense? Here is one way in which it might. Each of us *is* different. But is that because each of us has a fully individual *self*? Or might everyone be *the same thing* in whatever makes us persons at all? You and I would be *one* – somehow literally one self. People often say that we are all connected, really or fundamentally the same. Is that the picture here? We would be the same, in a way, by sharing a single universal self. Might we differ only in other details, such as how we look and what we think and feel? How I look is not how you look; yet our different appearances would be superficial: they would not be what makes either of us a *self*, let alone a distinct self.

Consider these lines from the later *Kaṭha Upaniṣad* (5.9–10):

> As the single fire, entering living beings,
> adapts its appearance to match that of each;
> So the single self within every being,
> adapts its appearance to match that of each,
> yet remains quite distinct.
>
> As the single wind, entering living beings,
> adapts its appearance to match that of each;
> So the single self within every being,
> adapts its appearance to match that of each,
> yet remains quite distinct.

Those analogies extend Yājñavalkya's one about the 'mass of salt'. The 'single wind' (the general power of breathing, I think this means) circulating within each of us 'adapts its appearance to match each of us'. Our *two* selves would be *one* self, in that way (these analogies suggest).

Here is a more subtle way to make the point. In the also early *Chāndogya Upaniṣad* (5.18.1), Aśvapati talked of 'this self here, the one common to all men', and said that, when one knows the self 'as somehow distinct' (as *not* a single universally shared self), one 'eat[s] food'. What did Aśvapati mean? It is explained by this contrast, with which he continued:

> when someone venerates [the self] as measuring the size of a span and as beyond all measure [= when one *does* think of the self as universally shared], he eats food within all the worlds, all the beings, and all the selves.

This seems to be saying that when thinking of one's self in that universal way, as *everyone's* self at once, one is engaging with the Whole: one 'eats food' among all the selves at once, so to speak; one does this in 'all the worlds', as 'all the beings' at once.

Maybe. I am trying – cautiously – to interpret some ancient writing, asking what may emerge. It feels like something important is being suggested. These Upaniṣads are poetic and complex, though. I am focusing on one idea that can arise when reading them. It seems like a philosophical idea. We have begun being philosophical.

1.1.2 Buddhist no-selves
Or might there be *no* selves? (No I? No you? No one else?)

That question is sparked by another of the world's oldest organised ways of thinking – Buddhism, whose distinctive ideas include *the no-self view*. Meet King Milinda (he was real – the Greek king Menander) and the sage Nāgasena (perhaps not real) in a northern Indian dialogue, *The Questions of King Milinda* (from around two thousand years ago).

> Milinda the king ... addressed [the venerable Nāgasena] ... 'How is your Reverence known, and what, Sir, is your name?'
> 'I am known as Nāgasena, O king, ... But although parents, O king, give such a name as Nāgasena, or Sūrasena, or Vīrasena, or Sīhasena, yet this, Sire, ... is only a generally understood term, a designation in common use. For there is no permanent individuality (no soul) involved ....'

Thus Nāgasena, almost immediately, imbued an ordinary meeting with a philosophical tone. He acknowledged the *name* 'Nāgasena'. But he denied that a real self was being named. King Milinda responded by paraphrasing Nāgasena's thesis and wondering, aloud, whether it is true. 'This Nāgasena says there is no permanent individuality (no soul) implied in his name. Is it now even possible to approve him in that [= to agree with him]?' Whereupon Milinda reached for rhetorical questions that, in his view, showed why Nāgasena's no-self view *cannot* be true.

> 'If, most reverend Nāgasena, there be no permanent individuality (no soul) involved ..., who is it, pray, who ... lives a life of righteousness? Who ... devotes himself to meditation? [Moreover, if there is no Nāgasena,] we are to think that were a man to kill you there would be no murder.'

Nāgasena was being asked, by Milinda, *who* is doing 'his' meditation if not really him (he who is named 'Nāgasena')? What *would* the imagined action of aggression be, if not murder of Nāgasena him*self*? Milinda persisted with such questioning, trying to *locate* the person Nāgasena:

> 'your brethren in the Order are in the habit of addressing you as Nāgasena. Now what is that Nāgasena? Do you mean to say that the hair is Nāgasena?'
> 'I don't say that, great king.'
> 'Or the hairs on the body, perhaps?'
> 'Certainly not.'
> 'Or is it the nails, the teeth, the skin, the flesh, the nerves, the bones, the marrow, the kidneys, the heart, the liver, ... or the brain, or any or all of these, that is Nāgasena?'
> And to each of these he answered no.

Thus, Milinda asked about physical *parts* of Nāgasena. If *they* are not Nāgasena, what is?

> 'Is it the outward form ... that is Nāgasena, or the sensations, or the ideas, or the [constituent elements of character], or the consciousness ...?'
> And to each of these also [Nāgasena] answered no.

Milinda was asking whether Nāgasena is constituted by a general appearance – an outward form. No? Then what of something 'behind' the appearance, a capacity for thinking or some actual thoughts? Still 'no', said Nāgasena.

Hence, Milinda felt that he had asked about all aspects of Nāgasena, the 'outward' appearance and the inner mental life. But there is this further possibility.

> 'Then is it all these ... combined that are Nāgasena?'
> 'No! great king.'

Really? Milinda seems to have asked about all of the parts, outer *and* inner. Now he was being told that, even when they *combine*, still no Nāgasena-self results.

> 'But is there anything outside [these] that is Nāgasena?'
> And still he answered no.
> 'Then thus, ask as I may, I can discover no Nāgasena. Nāgasena [= the name 'Nāgasena'] is a mere empty sound. Who then is the Nāgasena [= the actual person] that we see before us? It is a falsehood that your reverence has spoken [= in advancing the no-self thesis], an untruth!'

Milinda concluded, we see, that Nāgasena's original thesis is false. Is that the end of the discussion?

No, replied Nāgasena. He argued that the name is *more* than 'a mere empty sound', even if *less* than perfect evidence of a full self. He did this by applying Milinda's form of argument to the example of a chariot. The aim was to show that Milinda's form of argument is *too strong*: it is not to be trusted, because it *too readily* makes its criticism (such as of the no-self thesis). Mimicking Milinda's questioning, Nāgasena asked about the chariot's parts – axle, wheels, ropes, etc. None is the chariot, it is clear.

'Then is it all the parts ... that are the chariot?'
'No, Sir.' [This is Milinda answering.]
'But is there anything outside them that is the chariot?'
And still [Milinda] answered no.
... [So, infers Nāgasena,] Chariot [= the word 'chariot'] is a mere empty sound. What then is the chariot [= the actual chariot] you say you came in? It is a falsehood that your Majesty has spoken, an untruth! There is no such thing as a chariot!

Milinda bristled. Should he therefore stop using the word 'chariot'? No. He claimed to be using the word simply as a 'designation in common use' – hence not as something that needed to pass the strict test that Nāgasena was applying.

Yet Nāgasena replied that he was *also* entitled to that sort of standard, even when using his own name. It can be used in a looser way, as 'chariot' is. His appearance, his thoughts, and so on, can be designated *loosely*, with the name 'Nāgasena'.

Very good! Your Majesty has grasped the meaning of 'chariot'. And just even so is it on account of all those things you questioned me about – the thirty-two kinds of organic matter in a human body, and the five constituent elements of being – that I come under the generally understood term, the designation in common use, of 'Nāgasena'.

I have no decisive immediate reply. When I *say* that I am a person, a self, I use words. (I just did so.) Might they be mere conveniences – handy *tools* for interacting socially, denoting loosely? The name 'Nāgasena' was one of many names that could have been bestowed on the baby Nāgasena. Are other words equally arbitrary in that same way? The name 'Nāgasena' reveals nothing of the baby's real nature. Must we treat the non-name word 'self' as revealing part of his real nature? Surely not. It is *only* a word.

1.1.3 David Hume's no-inner-substantial-selves

We might test those questions arising from Nāgasena and Milinda (section 1.1.2) by travelling across the world and the centuries to eighteenth-century Scotland. There, we meet the philosopher (and historian) David Hume (1711–76) – plus a *further* question about selves. Do I have an easily discoverable *'inner'* self that is definitively me? Here is Hume.

> There are some philosophers, who imagine we are every moment intimately conscious of what we call our SELF; that we feel its existence ... and are certain ... both of its perfect identity and simplicity.

People often talk in that way of having a *soul*. Hume doubted that they should:

> when I enter most immediately into what I call *myself*, I always stumble on some particular perception or other, of heat or cold, light or shade, love or hatred, pain or pleasure. I never can catch *myself* at any time without a perception, and never can observe anything but the perception.

Hume was testing an hypothesis (as philosophers often do, I expect to find in this book). This one concerns whether there are 'inner' selves. Is that what a self needs to be? Is each self knowable only by its 'owner' when she is 'looking within' (this is called *introspecting*)?

Imagine *trying* to know one's self in that way. Hume tried. But he inferred that he could not succeed. All that he could find were *other* things – mental events, say (he called them 'perceptions', we see). These are 'inner happenings' (we might say).

But how do they happen? Are they being overseen by a self 'behind' them? Is there a self 'inside', *having* those experiences? Hume would dismiss that as empty talk – *mere* words – since we can never 'find' that self.

'*There* it is, having and owning these mental events of mine. It is *how* they are literally mine!' No, says Hume, since he cannot 'look behind' the inner experiences. They are all that he can find within, by introspecting. On his thinking, we should conclude that there is no inner personal substance – no inner *thing* that is a self.

1.1.4 Patricia Churchland's brainy selves
Must we agree with Hume (section 1.1.3)? Or can we find a further hypothesis still as to what selves are like? Can recent science help us with this?

For instance, maybe a self is only a *body*. Is it just *part* of a body? Philosophers often consult relevant areas of science. Will neuroscience help here? Can *brain*-science be *self*-science? Patricia Smith Churchland (b. 1943), a Canadian philosopher, might think so:

> modern neuroscience and psychology allow us to go beyond myth and introspection [= what we saw Hume using] to approach the 'self' as a natural phenomenon whose causes and effects can [instead] be addressed by science.

Churchland is alerting us to what she thinks is the proper *method* to use when reflecting on selves. We must look to science's methods. After all, think of what *progress* has been made in brain research.

> Neurobiology is beginning to reveal why some brains are more susceptible than others to alcohol or heroin addiction, or why some brains slide into incoherent world-models. ... Perhaps some questions will forever exceed the neurobiological reach, though it may be hard to tell whether such problems are just 'as yet unsolved' or whether they are truly unsolv*able*.

So, Churchland is confident, it seems, about neuroscience being self-science.

> As I watched [on an MRI machine, after stepping out of it] the computer monitor showing my brain tilted at various angles and cut at various slices, what stirred me was the idea that I might come to know my neuroself at least as well as I know my psyche-self. Or, at least, someone in the next generation might.

Churchland's hope, apparently, is that neuroscience will reveal what a self literally is. Neuroscientists may propose and test *hypotheses* as to the nature of a self. Might this even prompt us to focus less on selves as such, and more on functionally apt and usable self-*ideas*?

> The best hypothesis is that [this] involves a complex idea (representation) that the brain generates through activity in various different regions, including the regions representing the body and a representation using memory of the past. The brain activity that we know introspectively as 'myself' is probably part of a set of larger patterns of activity the brain deploys for making sense of and getting by in the world.

Do neuroscience's advances suggest that we would profit by *reframing our question* of what a self is? Centuries of philosophy have focused on 'looking within', introspectively 'seeking' one's self (as Hume tried to do: section 1.1.3). Does science now provide a *better* method?

Even if questions about selves *feel* as if they could be answered by 'looking within', and by listening to how people use the words 'I' and 'me', maybe we *need not* proceed in those ways. Why not welcome what science says about brains — especially how a brain helps its 'surrounding person' to function, including her having mental representations *saying* that she is a self? She could *link* these with words such as 'I' and 'me'.

And might that be *all* there is to having a self?

1.1.5 Ifeanyi Menkiti's socially created selves

We may wonder, though, whether brain-science (section 1.1.4) would do justice to *social*-selfhood. That matters if being a self includes having a kind of social reality. Am I a self only by being socially deemed to be so, socially treated as such?

That idea is portrayed by Ifeanyi Menkiti (1940–2019), a Nigerian philosopher who taught in the USA. He distinguished between 'most Western views' and 'the African view' of 'the person'. The latter view (I do not know if there is 'the' African view; I bypass that question in order to understand Menkiti's suggestion) 'denies that persons can be defined by focusing on this or that physical or psychological characteristic of the lone individual. Rather, man is defined by the environing community.' This concerns how a person *is an I at all*: 'in the African view it is the community which defines the person as person.' A person is a person *due to* a community's treating her as one.

Philosophers often aim to test ideas before accepting them. And (as this book will show) there are many possible ways to do this. One approach is to examine an idea's *implications*. Menkiti's thesis has an implication that could feel odd. He said that 'persons become persons only after a process of incorporation ... into this or that community.' That process takes time, which allows the person – the self – to become *more* a person – *more* a self – along the way:

> full personhood is not received as simply given at the very beginning of one's life, but is attained after one is well along in society ... [So] the older an individual gets the more of a person he becomes. ... One does not just take on additional features, one also undergoes fundamental changes at the very core of one's being.

As a child, was I *less* of a person or self? Menkiti offered some linguistic support for that idea, *against* the view 'that either an entity is a person or it is not':

an acquisition of personhood [= an acquisition of this status over time, not simply having it from the outset] is supported by the natural tendency in many languages, English included, of referring to children and new-borns as *it*.

I am not sure what this shows. Menkiti was resting his case partly on facts about human language use. Do all socially widespread ways of talking embody insight into reality? This question arose with urgency for King Milinda (section 1.1.2); it still does.

Readings for 1.1

For the Upaniṣads, see *Upaniṣads*, trans. P. Olivelle (Oxford: Oxford University Press, 1996); quotations from pp. 70–1, 146, 243–4. For *The Questions of King Milinda* (the *Milinda-pañha*), see the translation by T. W. Rhys Davids (Oxford: Clarendon Press, 1890), Bk II, ch. 1, pp. 25–8 – available at www.sacred-texts.com/bud/milinda.htm. For Hume, see *A Treatise of Human Nature* (1739–40), Bk I, part IV, sec. VI. For Churchland, see 'The brain and its self', *Proceedings of the American Philosophical Society* 155 (2011): 41–50; quotations from pp. 42, 43, 45. For Menkiti, see 'Person and community in African traditional thought', in *African Philosophy: An Introduction*, 2nd edn, ed. R. A. Wright (Washington, DC: University Press of America, 1979), pp. 157–68; quotations from pp. 157, 158, 159.

1.2 Souls

1.2.1 Plato's immortal soul
We can be motivated to think about our selves (such as in section 1.1) because they would be making *us*

whatever and whoever we are. But should we add to that motivation the conviction also that people (such as us) are *special*, within reality as a whole? Some believe so, by thinking that we – and only we – have *souls*. How might we argue for that picture?

We may begin in ancient Greece. The Athenian philosopher Plato (428–348 BCE), in his dialogue *Phaedo*, portrayed his teacher Socrates (470–399 BCE) as envisaging personal immortal souls. Socrates argued for this while waiting, with friends, for the hemlock poison that would kill him, by official order. Would Socrates' soul survive his death? That was the question of the moment.

Here is one of those Socratic arguments (a sequence of questions, some of them rhetorical).

> What sort of thing ... would naturally suffer the fate of being dispersed [= broken up and destroyed]? ... Would you not expect a composite object or a natural compound to be liable to break up ...? And ought not anything which is really incomposite to be the one thing ... which is not affected in this way? ... Is it not extremely probable that what is always constant and invariable is incomposite, and what is inconstant and variable is composite?

Socrates was approaching the specific topic of a *soul*'s nature via something more general – the nature of *anything's being composite*. He was not saying that every 'composite object' is fragile in an everyday way, breaking easily upon contact. He asked about an *underlying* capacity to be divided, perhaps within extreme situations, into parts. Even a solid object can be like that. But are there things that *cannot*, in *any possible* circumstance, decompose or be divided?

We can see where Socrates was heading with that questioning: are *souls* among those fundamentally indivisible things? How did he reach this question?

First, he explained that indivisible things will not be 'concrete objects you can touch and see and perceive' – physical bodies. This is because being physical brings with it an underlying *divisibility*, at least in principle. Physical things have parts – *bits* or potential *pieces*.

One of his companions, Cebes, therefore agreed that physical things 'are never free from variation' – *unlike*, however, 'absolute equality or beauty or any other independent entity'. The variations might be potential, not actual. But 'absolute equality or beauty' lack even that potential for being varied: they are 'always constant and invariable'. Physical bodies can undergo changes, exhibiting variety. Absolutes cannot. This is a basic difference.

Still, *where* are absolutes? We use words for them (we think). But can we *see* them? Seemingly, no. We see only physical things. Socrates continued:

> So you think that we should assume two classes of things, one visible and the other invisible? ... The invisible being invariable, and the visible never being the same?

Socrates applied that thinking, involving those distinctions, to the immediate issue:

> are we not part body, part soul? ... Then to which class [= of the visible and the invisible] do we say that the body would have the closer resemblance and relation?

To which, Cebes replied: 'the visible' (since we see bodies). Socrates then made a key move: 'the soul, is it visible or invisible?' Cebes said that it is 'Invisible to men' (people); from which he inferred, 'the soul is in every possible way more like the invariable than the variable.' In contrast, the body is more like 'the variable'. Hence, 'the soul resembles the divine, and body the mortal.' Socrates concluded: 'in that case is it not natural for body to disintegrate rapidly, but for soul to be quite or very nearly indissoluble?' A dramatic result!

Yet I wonder: where does my soul exist, *while* I am alive – *before* my body disintegrates? Hume's worry (section 1.1.3) suggests that I cannot find my soul by 'looking within'. Later in the *Phaedo* (105c), however, Socrates called soul 'what must be present in a body to make it alive'. Does this mean that, when watching another living body, we know that *something* inside it – a soul – is keeping it alive?

That idea is intriguing (and will be revisited in section 3.4). But does it apply to all living bodies, not only humans? Should we *extend* our conception of souls in that way? Earlier (70d), Socrates claimed to be discussing 'not only ... human beings but ... all animals and plants'. Even then, he said (105d) that 'soul is immortal': once a soul is within a body, it cannot 'admit death' (= itself succumb to death). The body can; the soul cannot. The body can disintegrate; the soul cannot.

How should we evaluate this striking Socratic story? I will neither accept nor reject it quickly. I will hold it in mind as an hypothesis while encountering further ideas. (Holding something in mind as an idea, without having decided on its truth, is starting to feel like a necessary skill for reading philosophy.)

1.2.2 Wang Chong's nature
I will now travel from Athens to China for an alternative view about people and souls. A few centuries later than Socrates, Wang Chong (27–100?) boldly 'followed his own path'. From his *Balanced Inquiries* (ch. 62) comes this reasoning.

> People today say that when men die they become spiritual beings [*kuei* or *gui*: ghosts], [and] are conscious .... Let us try to prove by means of the species of

creatures that the dead do not become spiritual beings, [and] do not possess consciousness ... We do so by means of other creatures. Man and other creatures are all creatures. When other creatures die, they do not become spiritual beings. Why should man alone become a spiritual being when he dies?

Wang reacted differently than Socrates did (section 1.2.1) to the idea of a spiritual being's invisibility. Socrates thought that something's being invisible would accompany its *not* being diffused or dispersed. Wang did not: 'When the vital forces [*ch'i* or *qi*] have left man, ... [the whole body] decays and disappears. It becomes diffused and invisible.'

> The vital forces produce man just as water becomes ice. As water freezes into ice, so the vital forces coagulate to form a man. When ice melts, it becomes water. When a man dies, he becomes spirit again.

That final sentence sounds promising: I will become 'spirit again'? But Wang then defused that idea, continuing in *materialistic* terms (that is, talking of physical aspects of reality):

> He is called spirit just as melted ice changes its name to water. As people see that its name has changed, they say that it has consciousness, [and] can assume physical form ... But they have no basis for saying so.

What about when a person is still alive? Is she activated *then* by a soul, a spirit? It seems not for Wang, who claimed to understand our mental aspects in terms of our physical natures.

> Man is intelligent and wise because he possesses the forces of the Five Constant Virtues (of humanity, righteousness, propriety, wisdom, and faithfulness). The five

forces are within him because there are the five internal organs in his body (namely, heart, liver, stomach, lungs, and kidneys, which correspond to the five virtues). If the five organs are unimpaired, he is wise. If they become diseased, he becomes hazy and confused. ... When a man dies, the five organs rot and decay. ... The body needs the vital forces in order to be complete, and the vital forces need the body in order to have consciousness.

1.2.3 Avicenna's flying man
We might call Wang's (section 1.2.2) approach *deflationary*: it claims to understand our selves in terms of *less*, not more – describing just our bodies, adding nothing non-physical to them. But not everyone has followed that physicalist path. Might some philosophical flights of fancy – imaginative leaps – take us 'out of our bodies' when trying to understand our selves?

Here we may engage with what philosophers call a *thought experiment*. This one is from the medieval Islamic philosopher Avicenna (980–1037). (That is his Latin name, by which he is generally known in the West. His Islamic name was Abū ʿAlī al-Ḥusayn ibn ʿAbd Allāh ibn Sīnā.) He was born of Persian heritage, in what is now Afghanistan, near Balkh. Mostly, he wrote in Arabic (although one major work was in Persian). I will quote from 'On the Soul', in *The Cure* [or *The Healing* – 'al-Shifā']. This work was offered '[f]or the purposes of establishing the existence of the soul belonging to us':

> it has to be imagined as though one of us were created whole in an instant but his sight is veiled from directly observing the things of the external world. He is created as though floating in air or in a void but without the air supporting him in such a way that he would have to feel it, and the limbs of his body are stretched out and away from one another, so they do not come into contact or touch.

That was Avicenna's first step, inviting us to imagine this odd circumstance. He then asked what this imagined person, floating freely, could know about their self.

> He has no doubts about asserting his self as something that exists without also [having to] assert the existence of any of his exterior or interior parts, his heart, his brain, or anything external.

We are not told why the imagined man 'has no [such] doubts'. Maybe Avicenna was thinking that the man can have an 'inner' sense of self without needing to *verify* it, say, by checking his body and its 'parts'. The verifying would *add* to what he was already asserting. But this would not be *needed*. That is why, for example, the imagined man 'will ... be asserting the existence of his self without asserting that it has length, breadth, or depth.' That seems to be implied by the previous step, since length, breadth, and depth *are* only aspects of his physical 'parts': 'and, if it were even possible for him in such a state to imagine a hand or some other extremity, he would not imagine it as a part of his self ...' I assume that Avicenna says this because he thought that his reasoning had *already* established that the man has sufficient sense of his self without having needed to verify anything *further*, such as physical 'parts'. The man could assert 'I exist' and feel that he had asserted a complete thought, without needing to add anything about physical 'parts' or aspects. In which case, the man will infer, his existence as a self is not also bodily: 'what [the reader] has been alerted to is ... the existence of the soul as something that is not the body – nor in fact *any* body ...'

That is Avicenna's 'flying man' thought experiment (sometimes called the 'floating man'). It concludes that the flying man 'can assert the existence of his self'. (I have also seen this use of 'his self' translated as 'his essence', which seems to add power to the term 'my self'. Section 1.5 will discuss the idea of personal essences. For now, we may read Avicenna's challenge as follows.)

Should we adopt Avicenna's own interpretation of his thought experiment? The potential assertion that he mentioned would be silently 'inner'; otherwise, the flying man could hear it 'out loud' – physically. Avicenna sought to imagine an adult's being created instantly in a state of complete sensory deprivation – nothing bodily being felt! Yet could this flying adult feel his reality as a *person*, as a self, while lacking any bodily sense?

I cannot be sure.

Even if I was sure, how would I use my confidence? Avicenna was asking whether the flying man and his self-knowledge were imaginable. He did not offer his thought experiment as a conclusive argument that *must convince everyone*. It was 'a pointer that serves [both] as alert and reminder by hitting the mark with anyone who is at all capable of catching sight of the truth on its own.' Still, regardless of whether one is like that, either Avicenna's answer is correct or it is not. If it is, what would this show about *us* – who are clearly not 'flying people'? Should we infer *anyway* that each of us has a non-physical soul – knowable in the 'flying man' way, 'from within', not using knowledge of one's body?

1.2.4 René Descartes's mind-meets-body
It is difficult to answer that question directly, by 'thinking away' one's body so as to imagine being Avicenna's flying man (section 1.2.3). I will consider an account that does not 'set aside' the body even while focusing, in a way akin to Avicenna's, on the mind. This account is from the French philosopher René Descartes (1596–1650). For him, each of us is a mind *and* a body – non-physical *and* physical.

We look to his 'Meditation VI' (in his *Meditations on First Philosophy* of 1641): 'there is a great difference between mind and body, inasmuch as body is divisible and the mind is entirely indivisible.' That 'inasmuch as' is effectively a 'since': Descartes's conclusion ('there is ... and body') was being derived from a premise about divisibility/indivisibility ('body is ... indivisible'). This premise reminds me of section 1.2.1's Socratic distinction between divisibility and indivisibility. Again it is being used to contrast mind (for Socrates, 'soul') with body:

> when I consider ... myself inasmuch as I am only [= only in my role as] a thinking thing, I cannot distinguish in myself any parts, but [I do] apprehend myself to be clearly one and entire ...

This is like Avicenna's flying man, but it is Descartes's supposedly *being* like that imagined man. Descartes was confident that, when he focuses on himself-thinking, he cannot find 'parts': even specific thoughts are not *parts* of a mind. Thoughts can be lost; this does not *divide* a mind, by removing a part. Descartes thus experienced himself-thinking as 'one and entire'. (Close your eyes. You *can* try this at home.)

> [A]nd although the whole mind seems [= in his everyday experiences] to be united to the whole body [= a single mind relating to the whole body], yet if a foot, or an arm, or some other part, is separated from my body, I am aware that nothing has been taken away from my mind.

So, the mind *remains* whole – hence, always a whole mind being linked with a body – even when the body itself does not remain whole:

> it is quite otherwise with corporeal [= bodily] or extended [= having spatial dimensions] objects, for

there is not one of these imaginable by me which my mind cannot easily divide [= also in imagination] into parts ...; this [teaches] me that the mind or soul of man is entirely different from the body ...

Actual body-part removals are not needed; we can *imaginatively* divide any bodily object into parts. I can do this for my own body. And *losing* a body-part (even in imagination) would make the body smaller (at least in imagination). Again, though, to lose a thought is not to make one's mind literally smaller. Body and mind are distinct and different, concluded Descartes.

Is each of us therefore composed of two *kinds* of thing – a physical body plus a non-physical mind? Body is divisible, while mind is not? Is each person a *duality*, in that Cartesian way ('Cartesian' is the adjective from 'Descartes')?

We might test that dualism – asking how likely it is to be true – by comparing people with (non-human) *animals*. In his 1637 *Discourse on Method*, Descartes insisted that animals ('brutes')

have no reason [= no rationality] ..., and ... it is nature which acts in them according to the disposition of their organs [= such as their senses], just as a clock, which is only composed of wheels and weights[,] is able to tell the hours and measure the time more correctly than we can do with all our wisdom.

In one way, Descartes was praising animals: we *want* a reliable clock (not 'all our wisdom') when seeking to know the time. If we could 'get inside' an animal's mind, might we know what they know, as they know it? Was that Descartes's view?

Not exactly, since he was belittling those animals. They lack 'reason'. Like clocks, they do not *have* minds. What was Descartes's evidence for this? It is that people use language, while animals do not:

> there are none [= no people] so depraved and stupid ... that they cannot arrange different words together, forming of them a statement by which they make known their thoughts ...

That is, any person has the capacity to communicate with words. In contrast,

> there is no other animal ... which can do the same. It is not the want [= the lack] of organs [= senses] that brings this to pass [= that causes this], for ... magpies and parrots are able to utter words just like ourselves [= as we do], and yet they cannot speak as we do, ... so as to give evidence that they think of what they say [= using words in more complex ways].

Descartes wrote that around 400 years ago. Yet many animals, we now think, do seem to use language. Descartes said that

> we ought not to confound [= confuse] speech with natural movements which betray passions [= feelings] and may be imitated by machines as well as be manifested by animals; nor must we think, as did some of the ancients, that brutes talk, although we do not understand their language.

If animals could talk, 'they could communicate their thoughts to us just as easily as to those of their own race.' Really?

Interestingly, some of those 'ancients' interpreted animals *more* generously than Descartes did in this respect. Do we now regard animals as more *like* us in this way, as using language? I do not feel forced to follow Descartes here. But was he correct about people – each of us being a body *and* a (non-physical) mind – even if not about animals?

1.2.5 Martha Kneale's stories

Many will be tempted by Descartes's mind–body dualism (section 1.2.4). I often hear people talking of their mind and their body as different *kinds* of thing. ('Welcome to the Mind and Body festival!') Is such talk coherent?

Descartes realised that he needed to explain how a non-physical mind would *interact* with a physical body. Where would they meet? In physical space? Yet a non-physical mind is not *in* physical space. We talk of a thought *causing* a bodily reaction or movement, or vice versa. But how can something non-physical literally affect something physical, or vice versa? Where would this happen?

That is the 'mind–body problem'. It threatens Descartes's mind–body dualism (by pointing to a potentially large gap in what dualism could explain). Can we save the dualism by showing that the apparently large problem is *not* a problem? Here is an indication of how Martha Kneale (1909–2001), an English philosopher, approached that challenge.

She imagined four ways to tell a story describing an *action*. (For simplicity, I ignore the fourth, the 'psychoanalytic' one.) The main three are 'commonsense', 'phenomenal', and 'physical'. Here are elements of each (in that order; with 'phenomenal' denoting 'subjectively experienced phenomena', such as sensations).

> [Commonsense] The sight of his face roused Louise to a sudden fury which drove her to clutch the knife.
> [Phenomenal] In series L there occurred a visual field in which was prominent an ovoid pinkish patch. Simultaneously ... there occurred a feeling of intense anger. These were succeeded by kinaesthetic sense-data ['data' is the plural of 'datum' – each is Latin – they refer to 'inner' experiences seemingly linked to a bodily sense capacity] and a smooth roundish tactile datum.

> [Physical] The light reflected from a considerable area of human skin fell on the retina and stimulated the optic nerves. Brain cells in the optical area were excited. ... An efferent current passed to the muscles in the right arm ...

Are those stories useful? Are only some correct?

The commonsense story seems to lack *precision* and *detail* possessed by the others – the phenomenal ('inner' felt experiences) and the physical (physiology and physics). But do the others lack something vital when compared with the commonsense story?

> The traditional mind-body problem is the problem whether the physical and mental [= phenomenal] stories can be combined and, if so, what sort of combination is permissible.

(That word 'combined' is functioning here as the word 'interact' did at the start of this section, introducing the mind–body problem.)

Kneale suggested that the terms for (respectively) physical details and mental details used by the other stories are permissible partly because the commonsense story is itself permissible. We should not be *too* impressed by the physical story's scientific nature. Maybe this science cannot ever be completed. Maybe it will ultimately need some of the commonsense story's physical terms. By analogy,

> any ordinary text-book of physics or chemistry will contain statements which correlated items in the commonsense story with items in the physical story ... 'liquid' belongs to the commonsense theory, and 'particles' to the physical story, but the physical scientist has no difficulty in bringing them into the same sentence in order to state ... a causal connection between a state of the liquid and a state of the particles.

Should we feel relaxed when telling a commonsense story about persons even if we *also* seek a scientific story? Can we, as people, be viewed accurately from *all* of those viewpoints?

Readings for 1.2

The *Phaedo* quotations are from H. Tredennick's 1954 translation, in *Plato: The Collected Dialogues*, ed. E. Hamilton and H. Cairns (Princeton, NJ: Princeton University Press, 1961): see pp. 53, 61–3, 87 (for 70d, 78b–80b, 105c–e). For Wang Chong, see *A Source Book in Chinese Philosophy*, ed. W.-T. Chan (Princeton, NJ: Princeton University Press, 1963), at pp. 299–302. For Avicenna, see *Classical Arabic Philosophy: An Anthology of Sources*, trans. J. McGinnis and D. C. Reisman (Indianapolis: Hackett, 2007); quotations from pp. 178–9. For Descartes, see *Meditations on First Philosophy* and *Discourse on the Method of Rightly Conducting the Reason*. Each is in *The Philosophical Works of Descartes*, vol. I, trans. E. S. Haldane and G. R. T. Ross (Cambridge: Cambridge University Press, 1911); quotations from 'Meditation VI' at pp. 196, 198, and from the *Discourse* at pp. 116, 117. For Kneale, see 'What is the mind-body problem?', *Proceedings of the Aristotelian Society* 50 (1949–50): 105–22; quotations from pp. 105–6, 114, 116–17.

1.3 Self-reflection

1.3.1 Christine de Pizan's Reason
Section 1.1.5 described the idea of selves being socially created. Is there a possible danger of some selves being socially misdescribed, even overlooked?

In medieval France, in 1405, appeared a striking book by the intellectually wide-ranging writer Christine de Pizan (1364–1431?). *The Book of the City of Ladies* was an allegorical tale in which Christine (as philosophers often call her) imagined meeting three virtues (Reason, Rectitude [= rightness], Justice) and building, in words, a 'City of Ladies'. It would be free from male misogyny, with 'ladies' no longer dismissed and undervalued by men. Some early passages, from Christine's conversation with Reason (speaking here), convey a sense of the book's aim.

> Dear daughter, ... we have come to bring you out of your ignorance which so blinds your own intellect that you shun what you know for a certainty and believe what you do not know or see or recognize except by virtue of many strange opinions.

Which 'strange opinions' are those? Men's. Not all men's, as Christine recognised, but ones advanced by many famous male writers – dismissive and badly inaccurate claims about women. Even someone as intellectually accomplished as Christine was subjected to such claims, ones able to shape her self-representation. Correcting that is her book's mission. Lady Reason resumes:

> consider whether the greatest philosophers who have lived and whom you support against your own sex have ever resolved whether ideas are false and contrary to the truth. Notice how these same philosophers contradict and criticize one another ... [and then focus on] those passages where they attack women. ... Come back to yourself, recover your senses, and do not trouble yourself anymore over such absurdities.

Wise words. Bold for those times; still apt for ours. I like Reason's advice to 'Come back to yourself.' We can read that as 'to your self' – Christine's capturing how a sense of one's *self* can be lost by listening to misleading voices. This can happen in everyday life (and is deeply unfair, as section 3.6.4 will explain). Reason guides Christine through centuries of male writing in that vein, not always about flesh-and-blood people, yet often in sweepingly dismissive ways, belittling most or all women. Are those writers to be believed? Of course not, but not *only* because they are mistaken in specific claims. 'Notice [advises Reason] how these same philosophers contradict and criticize one another.' That is already excellent evidence against their being reliable authorities. If one is to be reliable, one's thinking must be *at least* consistent.

That moral feels timeless. When reading current philosophy about … anything, we must read with reason – and acuity and fairness. (We learn also from Christine's two other Ladies: be right and just.) Throughout this book, we will find those Christine-morals *mattering*. As Reason also says,

> these attacks on all women – when in fact there are so many excellent women – have never originated with me, Reason, and … all who subscribe to them have failed totally and will continue to fail. So now throw aside these black, dirty, and uneven stones from your work, for they will never be fitted into the fair edifice of your City.

Selves, then, are not only men's selves. This sounds so obvious as not to need stating. But history suggests that it does need to be said. Christine's was an early philosophical voice for women's selves being *accepted* as selves.

1.3.2 Mary Midgley's Beasts
Reason helped Christine (section 1.3.1). Is reason the key to selves? Is it the most significant feature of being

a person? Mary Midgley (1919–2018), an English philosopher, doubted so.

> Had we known no other animate life-form than our own, we should have been utterly mysterious to ourselves as a species. And that would have made it immensely harder for us to understand ourselves as individuals too. Anything that ... shows us as part of a continuum, an example of a type that varies on intelligible principles, is a great help.

Am I the *person* I am, partly by being an *animal*?

> [I]t is invalid to compare suicide in lemmings or infanticide in hamsters *on their own* with human suicide or infanticide. But when you have ... considered the whole nature of the species, comparison may be possible and helpful.

Which comparisons, then, are needed for understanding ourselves?

Philosophers have long welcomed pictures of ourselves as including a distinctive capacity for reason. We saw Descartes (section 1.2.4) denying that animals even have minds. Midgley continued:

> In the philosophic tradition, Reason ... has usually been sharply opposed to Feeling or Desire. This has determined the attitude of most respectable philosophers to the related subjects of animals and human feelings. They have usually just dismissed animal activities from all comparison with human ones, on the general ground that, in man, decision is a formal, rational process, while animals have only feeling, ... a kind of wholly contingent slop or flow ..., so that its analysis cannot concern philosophy.

Yet consider wolves, say:

The whole pack is bound together by affection. But this affection too is not 'blind impulse'; it has a *backbone*, a structure that keeps it steady through variations of mood.

Is the wolf pack therefore not *so* dissimilar to us? When wolves hunt, intelligence is manifested, as surely as when I plan a journey. Should I infer that my self is not *so* different to a wolf's self, if reason is a feature of each? How much can I learn about my self by studying Beasts – as Midgley called them, her word evoking how others might talk (such as Descartes did) when claiming to find a deep chasm in natures between Us and animals who are Not-Us?

1.3.3 Harry Frankfurt's wantons

Still, is there *something* distinctive about us, compared to 'other creatures'? Harry Frankfurt (1929–2023), an American philosopher, suggested so: 'one essential difference ... is to be found in the structure of a person's will. Human beings are not alone in having desires and motives, or in making choices.' Animals, like us, have wills – 'desires and motives'. But do we *use* our wills differently to how animals do?

Among desires, said Frankfurt, some are 'first-order', while some are 'second-order'. (He is imagining a *structured ordering*, starting with 'first', where higher-numbered orders build upon lower-numbered ones.) First-level ones are 'normal' desires: I want (that is, I desire) a sandwich now. Second-order ones are *directed at*, or *about*, actual or possible first-order ones: I want to not be wanting a sandwich now (since I want to be concentrating on work). That 'want to not be wanting' is second-order; the other wants (to eat a sandwich; to concentrate on work) are first-order.

How does that distinction illuminate a *person's* will?

> Someone has a desire of the second order either when he wants simply to have a certain desire or when he wants a certain desire to be his will. In situations of the latter kind, I shall call his second-order desires 'second-order volitions' ... [I]t is having [these] that I regard as essential to being a person.

How informative is that? It depends. Who – or what – is *not* like that? Frankfurt reached for a colourful term – 'wanton' – denoting any being with 'first-order desires but ... no second-order volitions'. The adjective 'wanton', dating perhaps from the 1300s, means 'undisciplined', in the sense of 'ungoverned'. Frankfurt used it also as a noun. He applied it when, in a specific respect, there is a lack of *self*-governing. Someone could look like a person – yet really be a wanton!

> The essential characteristic of a wanton is that he does not care about his will. His desires move him to do certain things, without its being true of him either that he wants to be moved by those desires or that he prefers to be moved by other desires.

Frankfurt's main example concerns 'two narcotics addicts'. 'One ... hates his addiction and always struggles desperately ... against its thrust. ... He is an unwilling addict, helplessly violated by his own first-order desires.' At least that addict is a person: he 'wants to take the drug' *and* 'wants to refrain from taking it'. He also *cares about* this inner clash. He *wants* the wanting-to-refrain part of the clash 'to constitute his will', rendering inoperative the wanting-to-take part of the clash.

The second addict might, or might not, share that inner clash. But he lacks something significant: 'he does not prefer that one first-order desire rather than the other should constitute his will.' In this respect, he is a wanton – 'no different than an animal'. He is not caring enough *about* his will (even if the clash is present). He is not caring enough to make his will a *person's* in this respect. Unlike the first addict, he is being a wanton.

Like others, I am probably a wanton in many respects. I lack time and motivation to reflect on all actions that I might, or might not, pursue. Hence, at most I am a person in *some* respects, on Frankfurt's story. Should that worry me? I am unsure.

Readings for 1.3

For de Pizan, see *The Book of the City of Ladies*, trans. E. J. Richards, rev. edn (New York: Persea Books, 1998); quotations from pp. 6–8, 18. For Midgley, see *Beast and Man: The Roots of Human Nature* (London: Methuen, [1978] 1980); quotations from pp. 18, 24, 256–7, 279. For Frankfurt, see 'Freedom of the will and the concept of a person', in *The Importance of What We Care About: Philosophical Essays* (Cambridge: Cambridge University Press, 1988); quotations from pp. 12, 16, 17, 18.

1.4 Personal identity

1.4.1 Buddhist demons

When asking whether and how selves include *reason* (section 1.3), we might also wonder how selves exist *over time*. For reasoning takes time, as do lives in general. So, how does one *stay* a single self – a single person – *across* time? This question matters also because we might wonder whether I am a person *at all* today only if I am the *same* person – still me – on other days. Am I not really a person right now, unless I exist across time, such as from a birth (or earlier) to a death? Those questions reflect the apparent fact that this apparent-person writing these words *differs* in various ways from anyone who existed yesterday – having new thoughts and experiences, for a start. How can there be literal identity – *just one* person – surviving and even uniting those changes?

Such questions worried some early Buddhists. Here is part of a story, from the Madhyamaka tradition (the 'Middle Way'). We have this story courtesy of a translation from Sanskrit into Chinese around 400 CE (the Madhyamaka school, still prominent in Tibetan Buddhism, is a form of Mahāyāna Buddhism).

> [A] man ... was sent afar as an envoy. He spent the night alone in an empty house. In the night a demon ... put [a man's corpse] in front of him, and then there came another demon chasing after and shouting at the first demon angrily: 'The corpse is mine. ...' The two demons then fought over [it] ... The first demon said: 'There's a man here whom we can ask.' ... [The man] said ...: '[The corpse] was carried in by the first demon.' The second demon was terribly angered. He grabbed the man by the hand, ripped [one arm] from his body and threw it on the ground. The first demon then took an arm from the corpse and immediately attached it to the man .... In this way both of his arms, both feet, his head, two sides, and in the end his whole body was replaced. The two demons then devoured together the body that had been replaced, wiped their mouths and departed.

Dramatic. Nor did it end there. The man's consciousness had apparently survived this total replacement of his body.

> This man thought: 'I've seen my body born of my mother has been eaten up by the two demons. Now this body of mine [= the one of which his consciousness is now aware] consists completely of the flesh of another

person [= the corpse that had been carried into the room]. Do I truly have a body now? Or do I have no body? If I think I have a body, what I have is completely a body of another; if I think I have no body, now I actually do have a body.' ... [Upon arriving home, he said to a Buddhist monk:] 'I don't even know myself if I'm a person or not.'
[Conclusion:] So there are times when the body of another is also conceived [= felt, in consciousness] as I. One cannot say that there is an I on the grounds of the distinction between other and I.

This tale, although fantastical, feels relevant. The man says 'there are times' when this sort of challenge might arise. I hope not, at least in this confronting form. But we can change his 'there are times' to 'there could in theory be times'. Then we can consider the *idea* of a body's parts being replaced by another body's parts. And we can apply this to realistic cases. For a replacement-of-body-parts seems to happen, subtly and slowly, from one day to the next during our normal lives. Today's body cells are replaced by ... new body cells, continually. Over time, might *all* of today's body cells be replaced?

In which case, how is someone the same person – some *one* person – at those different times? And how is an apparent-person today a real person at all today, if few-if-any of his body cells will remain in place, so that a *stable* body is now present?

1.4.2 Vasubandhu's persons-as-collections
There have been many Buddhist strands of thought. The monk Vasubandhu (c. 350–430), from north-west India, co-founded the Yogācāra ('yoga practice') tradition. He rejected Madhyamaka doubts (such as from a moment ago, in section 1.4.1) about there being persons. Discussing someone called 'Devadatta', Vasubandhu suggested that

he is not just one thing, but [a collection of phenomena] causally conditioning [other] phenomena [within the same continuum of the collection] to which this name ['Devadatta',] has been given. It is to these [phenomena] that we refer when we say that Devadatta moves or apprehends [an object].

What did Vasubandhu mean? A little earlier, he responded to the question 'If a self does not exist, ... who remembers?' and the claim that there must be an *agent doing* the remembering. Vasubandhu's response focused on the *nature* of that agent. Must it be *a separate self*? No:

is [an agent] grasping an object [in this case] anything other than [the occurrence of] a memory [in a continuum of consciousness? Surely it is not. No separate act of grasping is required, and consequently no self as the agent of this act is required, to explain the occurrence of a memory of an object. ...]

Vasubandhu's point seemed to be that even a memory-moment's occurring does not prove that *a separate self is having* the experience. Instead, we can say this: there is a succession of consciousness-moments, some of them memory ones, some not; and *that sequence is the person*.

Yet (we might reply to Vasubandhu) how do we explain our usually talking as if the person *has* the sequence of consciousness-moments – which sounds different to saying that she *is* the sequence? If we are to make sense of what is happening, do we *need* the person to be a separate self whose continuing existence links those moments?

Not according to Vasubandhu: the moments are linked because each *causes* the next. He argued for this interpretation with an analogy.

> We figuratively apply the term, 'flame' [of a butterlamp], to the continuum of flames and say that the flame moves to another place when a flame [at a later moment in its continuum] arises in another place.

We talk of 'the flame', perhaps thinking that our phrase denotes a separate entity. But we are denoting just a sequence of flame-moments. The sequence has a structural integrity (which leads us to talk of 'the flame') – yet it has this *because* each of its moments causes the next. Hence, we *need* not talk of 'a flame' in any way that refers to a separate entity.

Vasubandhu continued, expanding his analogy.

> In the same way, we figuratively apply the expression, 'a consciousness,' to the continuum of consciousnesses, and say that a consciousness apprehends an object when an apprehension of a different object arises [at a later moment in the continuum].

We talk of 'a consciousness', perhaps thinking that our phrase denotes a separate self. But we are denoting just a sequence of consciousness-moments. The sequence has a structural integrity (which leads us to talk of 'a consciousness') – yet it has this *because* each of its moments causes the next. Hence, we *need* not talk of 'a consciousness' in any way that refers to a separate self.

Incidentally, Vasubandhu's picture of a person's existing *over* time could be combined with Hume's worry (section 1.1.3). Hume was sceptical about a separate self's existing within a person even at a *single* time.

1.4.3 John Locke's memories

Centuries later, the English philosopher John Locke (1632–1704) also offered some thinking that could blend with Vasubandhu's (from section 1.4.2). How does a person exist from one moment to another? Vasubandhu talked of memories. So did Locke.

> *Person* ... is a thinking intelligent Being, that has reason and reflection, and can consider it self as it self, the same thinking thing in different times and places; which it does only by that consciousness, which is inseparable from thinking.

Like Vasubandhu, Locke highlighted the role of consciousness: 'in this alone consists *personal Identity*, *i.e.* the sameness of a rational Being.' His word 'sameness' means 'sameness from one time to another'. So, the specific role (for consciousness) being highlighted was that of *constituting a single person from one time to another*. (But notice Locke's word 'rational'. This will soon matter.)

> And as far as this consciousness can be extended backwards to any past Action or Thought, so far reaches the Identity of that *Person*; it is the same *self* now as it was then; and 'tis by the same *self* with this present one that now reflects on it, that that Action was done.

The key is Locke's phrase 'consciousness ... extended backwards'. This denotes memory. Locke thought that it allows him to treat 'person' and 'self' as identical. Personal identity 'reaches' back in time only as 'far' as memories do: 'the same *self*' does likewise.

Yet Locke was not treating selves as *substances*. For him, 'self' was more like Vasubandhu's 'continuum of consciousness'. Locke used the term 'Animal' to denote a body, including one that might accompany a person (a self). A body's identity is a substance's identity and is not the same as a person's identity. 'The Question being what makes the same *Person*, and not whether it be the same Identical Substance ...'

Why did Locke distinguish persons from substances? He claimed to be able to imagine a person's existing, over time, in *different* substances (bodies). These need not even be 'full' bodies, as this example shows:

Upon separation of this little Finger, should this consciousness go along with [= accompany] the little Finger, and leave the rest of the Body [= leave it behind], [then] 'tis evident the little Finger would be the *Person*, the *same Person*; and *self* would then have nothing to do with the rest of the Body.

Is this 'evident'? Locke was testing his idea by applying it to an extreme case. He interpreted the case as he did, because he regarded the term 'person' as playing the following *role* for us. '*Person* ... is a Forensick Term appropriating Actions and their Merit; and so belongs only to intelligent Agents capable of a Law, and Happiness and Misery.' A Law? Merit? Yes, Locke thought that, if a self lacks *memory* of doing action X, no 'Reward or Punishment, on the account of any such Action' applies to that self. Thus, for Locke, 'person' was a term reflecting *moral/legal responsibility*. Do I *deserve* to be held accountable for X if I cannot bring to mind having done X? No, said Locke. ('Forensick' is his spelling of 'forensic', by the way. The *Oxford English Dictionary* mentions its being used in 1647. Locke's 1690 use is also cited.)

Was Locke turning 'person' into a technical term? Maybe so, as we saw Frankfurt doing (section 1.3.3). Each assigns a carefully chosen meaning to the word, aiming to capture something of why we *care* about the term. What *matters* in being a person? Can that question reveal how we *should* use the word 'person' – hence something of what a person *is*?

1.4.4 Derek Parfit's Teletransporter

How might we continue testing Locke's idea (section 1.4.3) that retaining memories matters to personal identity over time – but that keeping the same physical substance or material does not? Derek Parfit (1942–2017), an English philosopher, helped us by entering his Teletransporter.

> I have been to Mars before, but only by the old method, a space-ship journey taking several weeks. This machine will send me at the speed of light. I merely have to press the green button. ... Will it work? I remind myself what I have been told to expect. When I press the button, I shall lose consciousness, and then wake up at what seems a moment later. In fact I shall have been unconscious for about an hour. The Scanner here on Earth will destroy my brain and body, while recording the exact states of all of my cells. It will then transmit this information by radio. Travelling at the speed of light, the message will take three minutes to reach the Replicator on Mars. This will then create, out of new matter, a brain and body exactly like mine. It will be in this body that I shall wake up.

Our hero hesitates. But he is reassured by his wife: 'As she reminded me, she has been often teletransported, and there is nothing wrong with *her*.'

Hopefully so!

That is another *thought experiment*. (We discussed Avicenna's, in section 1.2.3.) Parfit said that even such far-fetched stories

> arouse in most of us strong beliefs. And these are beliefs, not about our words, but about ourselves. By considering these cases, we discover what we believe to be involved in our own continued existence, or what it is that makes us now and ourselves next year the same people. We discover our beliefs about the nature of personal identity over time. Though our beliefs are revealed most clearly when we consider imaginary cases, these beliefs also cover actual cases, and our own lives.

A story such as Parfit's is thus an intellectual *tool*. If his final sentence is correct, then, although the story concerns a fanciful notion of teletransportation, we can be prompted to reflect on 'actual cases' – what is involved in *actually* existing from one time to another.

We begin reflecting by engaging critically with the story itself, testing 'internal' details (before trying to extend its reach, applying it to 'actual cases'). For instance, what of those three minutes while the message is travelling to Mars, prior to the replication's occurring? Is the person *dead* during that period? Is a person *brought back* to life by the Replicator on Mars?

Parfit moved from this story to others, always testing philosophical theories. For example, can we use his story to evaluate Locke's 'psychological criterion' (involving memory) of personal identity? Does the Replicator preserve psychological continuity – while a new substance (Locke's term) arises? Parfit thought so, before arguing that such continuity is what *matters* in personal survival. It is why we *care* about surviving.

So, in general, we should care more about our psychological than our physical continuity. More generally still, we can accept that important psychological continuity is not *only* memories 'looking back'. It includes intentions 'looking ahead'. The Replicator supposedly re-creates a rich 'inner life' in those respects.

Parfit saw his argument as supporting some Buddhist views. He cited, approvingly (p. 502), Nāgasena (section 1.1.2) and Vasubandhu (section 1.4.2). (And his Teletransporter looks like a modern version of those Buddhist *demons* in section 1.4.1.) This does not guarantee that Parfit was correct, or that they were. But it is evidence of various philosophers giving voice to a way of thinking (about persons) that can travel – even without a Replicator! – across centuries and cultures.

Readings for 1.4

For the Madhyamaka 'demon story', see Jing Huang and Jonardon Ganeri, 'Is this me? A story about personal identity from the *Mahāprajñāpāramitopadeśa*

/ *Dà zhìdù lùn*', *British Journal for the History of Philosophy* 29 (2021): 739–62; quotations from pp. 756–7. (The second name inside that article's title is the Chinese translation of the initial Sanskrit one, the first name appearing there.) For Vasubandhu, see J. Duerlinger's translation, in *Indian Buddhist Theories of Persons: Vasubandhu's 'Refutation of the Theory of a Self'* (London: Routledge, 2003); quotations from pp. 97, 99, 100 (including the material in square brackets). For Locke, see *An Essay Concerning Human Understanding*, ed. P. H. Nidditch (Oxford: Clarendon Press, [1690] 1975), Bk II, ch. 27, secs. 9, 10, 17, 26, at pp. 335, 336, 341, 346–7. For Parfit, see *Reasons and Persons* (Oxford: Clarendon Press, 1984); quotations from pp. 199, 200, 204.

1.5 Personal essence

1.5.1 Karl Marx and human nature

Personal identity over time – being a single you from one time to another – was the overall topic of section 1.4. Section 1.4.1 began by mentioning being-a-person-even-at-one-time. I will now focus on that. What makes *you whoever-you-are* even at a single time?

This is not about anything trivial, such as standing in a particular place at a particular time. Can we describe something more like a *personal essence* – vital features making you you? They need not be features only of you. But they are informatively and definitively you. For instance, what of *being human*? Are you definitively human? You are not the only human. Still, is there such a thing as *human nature*, shared by you with the rest of us?

One of many philosophers whom we might read here is Karl Marx (1818–83), the German philosopher most famous for his ideas about political and economic shapings of society. I will mention a few of his earlier remarks.

In *Theses on Feuerbach* (1845), he gave us this notable thought (Thesis 11): 'The philosophers have only *interpreted* the world in various ways; the point is to *change* it.' That can sound like an invigorating call to action. Yet interpretive care is needed. Presumably we want the actions, any changes to 'the world', to be good. This occurs more reliably when flowing *from* good interpretations of 'the world'. So, if good changes are to be made to societies, good interpretations of those societies' people are needed – incorporating, at the very least, good understanding of *what a person is*. One question to be answered, maybe before contemplating potential changes, is this: do we have a shared human *nature*, an *essence* as people?

What did Marx say? At this pivotal stage (1845) in his philosophical development, his Thesis 6 (on Ludwig Feuerbach's criticisms of religion) included these remarks.

> Feuerbach resolves the essence of religion into the essence of *man*. But the essence of man is no abstraction inherent in each single individual. In its reality it is the ensemble of the social relations.

Marx's *Theses on Feuerbach* were posthumously published notes, not a finished article. We have some freedom in interpreting him. He seems to have meant something along the following lines.

If there is a human nature, 'an essence of man', it is not a Special Thing existing apart from us, abstractly – yet then implanted wholly in each of us. For Marx, 'the essence of man' is a grouping (an 'ensemble') of *ways in which we relate to each other*. Those details somehow add up to ... human nature. That is how we share a human nature. We share *in* it, by jointly creating it, through our socially manifested interactions. It *is* however we are arranged within society. It *is* our relationships, intermeshing, distancing, dominating.

I will mention two further passages from Marx's earlier writings, clarifying that picture. The first is from *Contribution to the Critique of Hegel's Philosophy of Right: Introduction* (first English trans., 1926).

> *[M]an* is no abstract being encamped outside the world. Man is *the world of man*, the state, society. ... Religion is the *fantastic realisation* [= imagined description or projection] of the human essence because the *human essence* has no true reality.

So there *is* man, as 'the world of man'. Is there then a human essence? Yes, and no. *No*, in one sense: what lacks 'true reality' is 'the *human essence*' (Marx's emphasis) as an 'abstract'. But *yes*, in another way: there is a human essence in a looser sense, not as something abstractly pure. Man is a living *'world of man'*. Being human is *actually acting as* a human – as one among many, along with everyone else being human, everyone else putting into practice this *opportunity* to be human.

Even more clearly in that spirit, this is from *Comments on James Mill* (1843).

> Since *human* nature is the *true community* of men, by manifesting their *nature* men *create*, produce, the *human community*, the social entity, which is no abstract universal power opposed to the single individual, but is the essential nature of each individual, his own activity, his own life, his own spirit, his own wealth. Hence this *true community* does not come into being through reflection, it appears owing to the *need* and *egoism* of individuals, i.e., it is produced directly by their life activity itself. ... Men, not as an abstraction, but as real, living, particular individuals, *are* this entity. Hence, *as* they are, so is this entity itself.

Marx ended Thesis 6 of his *Theses on Feuerbach* with this: 'Essence, therefore, can be regarded only as 'species', as an inner, mute, general character which unites the many individuals *in a natural way*.' We thus reach Marx's idea of a *species*-essence or -nature, as what each of us *has*, even if it is not *fully enclosed within* each of us. It is more that each of us is fully enclosed within *it* – within our shared social reality.

1.5.2 Frantz Fanon and race
We met the idea, from Menkiti (section 1.1.5), of selves being created socially. We have now met Marx's concept of a species-essence or -nature that would be constituted socially (section 1.5.1). So, we should also ask whether a *personal* essence is determined at all socially. Could others' actions impose, in effect, a species-essence upon one? If so, it could matter greatly, even for *what one is* at a time, how others act towards one. For example, how might that idea interact with a person's *racial* aspects?

I do not often consciously have a *sense* of being 'white' (not an ideal term, but a standard one). Yet could that reflect my living in a country (Australia) where I belong to the largest single racial grouping? What if I was to live in a country where, every day, I would feel a racial separateness or distinctiveness? Could that make me feel 'trapped' in my race – forever conscious of it?

That psychological question raises this metaphysical one: is my race *essential* to me? Maybe I take it for granted, since people rarely insist on my being aware of it. But what if they *were* doing so (even non-aggressively)? Would this make me feel divided – Australian yet not-Australian?

That question gains added force when we listen to Frantz Fanon (1925–61), a philosophically minded psychiatrist, originally from Martinique in the Caribbean, who worked in several countries, including France. 'In the white world the man [= person, more generally] of color encounters difficulties in the development of his bodily schema.' Fanon allowed readers inside his personal experiences. First, though, he reflected on a kind of *self-locating*. He described various everyday movements:

> these ... are made not out of habit but out of implicit knowledge. A slow composition of my *self* as a body in the middle of a spatial and temporal world – such seems to be the schema. It ... creates a real dialectic between my body and the world.

What Fanon found was that his body is not *just* a body. It has a social reality:

> the white man ... had woven me out of a thousand details, anecdotes, stories. I thought that what I had in hand was to construct a physiological self, to balance space, to localize sensations, and here I was called on for more.

Fanon seems to have meant that, as a black person, he was called upon for *much* more than some of us will ever be – much that was deeply unwelcome:

> assailed at various points, the corporeal schema crumbled, its place taken by a racial epidermal schema. ... I existed triply ... I was responsible at the same time for my body, for my race, for my ancestors. I subjected myself to an objective examination [meaning: thinking of himself *as* an object, looked at by white people], I discovered my blackness, my ethnic characteristics; and I was battered down [by many unfair stereotypes applied in how white people were 'seeing' him, how they were unfairly describing him]. ... [C]ompletely dislocated, unable to be abroad with the other, the white man, who unmercifully imprisoned me [in his

case, with words and presumptions], I took myself far off from my own presence, ... and made myself an object. ... I wanted to be a man, nothing but a man.

Fanon wanted not to be looking at himself from that 'other' (white) perspective. Yet he was not allowed to be simply a man, free of imposed-by-the-other self-gazing: 'My body was given back to me sprawled out, distorted, recolored, clad in mourning in that white winter day.' Powerful words. Difficult to write, I expect. Difficult to read, I know. I am glad that I have done so.

Seemingly, Fanon was feeling as if being black was, in those respects, *being made socially* essential for him – socially *inescapable* for him. He was always seen by whites as black (and not in a kindly or understanding way), even though this was never essential: he could have been regarded, surely most of the time, purely as a man, not a black man. Fanon could have been allowed by white people, in how they acted towards him, to *forget* his being visually black. For them, however, he was always so, and not in an appreciative way. He was thereby inescapably – essentially – wearing others' prejudices and stereotyping. Yet those harsh, ignorant, unfeeling responses to his being black never *had* to exist.

1.5.3 Sally Haslanger and gender

What, now, of essence and *gender* – another feature (in addition to race: section 1.5.2) that has often resulted in people being treated unfairly? What role does gender play in the literal *identity* of a person? For example, would I have been literally *me* if not male? What, if anything, is essential to a person in being male, say? Is it purely biological? Is it genetically determined, beyond social 'creation'? Or is one's gender identity – in my case, being male – created either wholly or partly by choice? If so, whose choice? Mine? A social group's? I do not remember making a conscious choice. Might I have been unconsciously making one? Or has a choice been made *for* me by others (maybe consciously; maybe not)?

Do I feel male? I am not sure what that means. Does the following analysis help? It is from Sally Haslanger (b. 1955), an American philosopher.

> *S is a man* iff$_{df}$ [= 'is defined by what follows'] S is systematically privileged along some dimension (economic, political, legal, social, etc.) and S is 'marked' as a target for this treatment by observed or imagined bodily features presumed to be evidence of a male's biological role in reproduction.

Haslanger's definition takes us beyond the purely biological, talking of systematic privilege enjoyed by males as a group. That privilege is a social fact, present in many eras and societies. Is Haslanger therefore charting what the term 'man' has *meant*, even if implicitly-because-in-practice, within those eras and societies? (I should mention Haslanger's also offering a similar definition for 'is a woman' – highlighting systematic subordination, not privilege. I expect that her thinking could be adapted for further genders.)

Already Haslanger's definition raises a powerful question: do I not know that I am a man if I do not know the relevant history of privilege that has, in effect, helped to *create* men (in line with that definition)? It would not be enough for me to know my body. It would not be enough to be called a 'man' by others. Haslanger's definition does mention 'bodily features', 'observed or imagined', 'presumed to be evidence' of a potential reproductive capacity. But notice the qualifiers in her description. She is being careful, given the vagueness in all of this – even in *being* a man, say.

Such vagueness could be important. Since Haslanger offers a definition, everything that follows her 'iff$_{df}$' is supposed to be clear, helping us to *learn* about 'is a man' (on the definition's left-hand-side): we do this by using our good understanding of those terms used in the defining (on the definition's right-hand-side). And we do seem to learn something. I have heard people say that 'male' refers to something biological, while 'man' denotes something social. I became a man somehow, somewhere, in my life; I have always been male. That is the suggestion. Yet where, exactly, would a biological *dividing line* be between male and not-male? Must there *be* a biological dividing line? Maybe all of this is inherently vague, so that there is *no* biological dividing line – no definitive *Here*-Is-The-Exact-Biological-Difference line.

Is biological classification always simple anyway? Whales were long regarded as fish; now they are deemed mammals. Is the idea that all people are either male or female – 'and that is that, being purely and precisely biological!' – similarly outdated, awaiting replacement by a more accurate description, taking into account more details, applying a better theory? We need improved understanding and social acceptance of *all* genders – where in principle we may allow this 'all' to be open to 'possibly more than two'.

What might emerge? Can a person change gender without ceasing to be that same person? Or is one's specific gender essential to personal identity? I have no simple answers to these questions.

Readings for 1.5

For Marx's *Theses on Feuerbach*, see *The Collected Works of Karl Marx and Frederick Engels: General Works 1844–1895*, vol. 5: *April 1845–April 1847* (New York: International, 1976); quotations from pp. 4, 5. For Marx's *Contribution to the Critique of*

Hegel's Philosophy of Right: Introduction, see again *The Collected Works*, vol. 3: *March 1843–August 1844*; quotation from p. 175. For Marx's *Comments on James Mill*, see also vol. 3; quotation from p. 217. For Fanon, see *Black Skin, White Masks: The Experiences of a Black Man in a White World*, trans. C. L. Markmann (New York: Grove Press, [1952] 1967); quotations from pp. 110, 111, 112–13. For Haslanger, see 'Gender and race: (What) are they? (What) do we want them to be?' *Noûs* 34 (2000): 31–55; quotation from p. 39.

1.6 Personal will

1.6.1 Aristotle trapped by the future

When I think about what might be essential to me (as I was doing in section 1.5), I often find myself wondering whether I have a *free will*. This question is not about me especially. Does *everyone* have – maybe essentially – a free will? (In section 1.3.3, Frankfurt argued so, adding a structural detail.) This would be a power at least to think, decide, choose. I often *feel* like I have this power.

But is that feeling always misleading? Am I never really free in how and what I think?

That question can take shape with a philosophical challenge from Aristotle (384–322 BCE). Born in Stagira, he was later Plato's pupil in Athens, later still the tutor of Alexander ('the Great'). This challenge is from his *De Interpretatione* (On Interpretation, ch. 9).

It began with a thesis about truth, specifically *future*-tense truth (notice Aristotle's using 'will'):

> if one person says that something will be and another denies this same thing, it is clearly necessary for one of them to be saying what is true – if every affirmation is true or false ...

To say 'X' about the future is to deny 'not-X' of the future. At least one of those is true, 'if every affirmation is true or false'.

Aristotle then included *more* tenses in his argument, adding 'now' and 'earlier' (discussing an example):

> if it [= any given thing] is white now it was true to say earlier [= at any earlier time] that it would be white; so that it was always [= at any earlier time] true to say of anything that has [= now] happened that it would [= later] be so.

The key to this reasoning is the initial 'if it is white now'. If the 'it' *is* white now, this – its now being white – cannot be undone: what's done is done! Even if, earlier, we did not know whether the thing in question would be white now, the fact is that, *given its being* white now, *even earlier it was* true that – as *has* occurred – it *was going to be* true: 'it could not not be so, or not be going to be so. [In which case,] it is impossible for it not to happen; [in which case,] it is necessary for it to happen.' That implication was then rephrased by Aristotle, talking of a *necessity* in how things occur. 'Everything that will be, therefore, happens necessarily. So nothing will come about as chance has it or by chance; for if by chance, not of necessity.'

Was Aristotle really saying what he seemed to be saying? He seems to have presented an argument for a *fatalism*. Its conclusion implies that whatever *does* happen *therefore had to* happen. In that way, whatever happens was *fated* – bound – to happen. For instance, will I travel next year to Mexico? I have no current plans to do so. But suppose that it happens: at that later time, it *is* happening. On Aristotle's argument, it is *already true* that I *will* make that journey: that future-tense truth is true now.

I called it 'Aristotle's argument'. But he was not endorsing it. He presented it in order to understand it. Now that we have it in plain view, can we find a way to set it aside? That was what Aristotle wanted to know. So do I.

For a start, does this fatalism imply that my life is *already* 'taking me towards' outcomes that 'await' me, even if I have no sense of what they are? No matter what I do now, is it *already* true that I will be going to Mexico? Can nothing that I now do *prevent* my travelling there, even if I currently intend never to go?

Maybe I cannot ensure that my future will be as I hope or intend. Is that a problem? Perhaps not. If fatalism is correct, at least there *are* future facts – 'awaiting' me, so long as I stay alive. That sounds like seeking hidden treasure. Will I *find* my future – almost literally?

1.6.2 Alexander of Aphrodisias trapped by the past

Aristotle's fatalist argument (section 1.6.1) asked whether we are somehow 'trapped' by the *future*. Are we even more clearly 'trapped' by the *past*?

I can expand that question: has the past – not merely mine, but the entire world's (with its causal laws) – put in place *so* much detail as to fully constrain everything about me, even my 'private' thinking, deciding, and choosing?

That is the question of whether, in a *causal* way, whatever is already in place determines – produces, controls, limits – whatever will follow. The fatalism discussed by Aristotle was a *semantic-logical* determinism, building on ideas about meaning, truth, and logic. What of the world's *causal* details? We function within their boundaries, at times feeling limited by them: 'I cannot do that. It's beyond my physical capacities.' But do causal laws also hinder us *without* our noticing it? Can we think that we are acting freely, choosing among available options – when really we are following a predetermined path, as characters in a world-story that we had no part in writing?

Here is one way to clarify those questions.

Picture reality as composed of a series of whole-world stages, each following almost immediately from the previous one. Each is a millisecond (time-slice) of the entire world's history, say, followed seamlessly by the next. Is everything about you *now* determined by everything about and around you from one millisecond ago? Was everything about and around you a millisecond ago determined by everything about and around you from a millisecond before that? And so on, all the way back in time, to your first millisecond of existence – which was also determined, by whatever was in place a millisecond before that. And so on, and on, and on. Where does it end? How could you break free of all *that*? Those questions arise for me, for everyone, for everything.

I mentioned causal laws. The idea of causal determinism long pre-dates modern science. The early Stoic Chrysippus (c. 280–207 BCE; born in what is now Turkey, moved to Athens) apparently initiated such talk. Here is a later version, from a *critic* of Stoic thinking, Alexander of Aphrodisias (c. 200 CE; also born in what is now Turkey before moving to Athens). Once more, we see a philosopher presenting an argument, as well as possible, in order to evaluate it critically – and fairly.

Alexander began, on the Stoics' behalf, in this way: 'they say that ... [n]othing comes to be in the universe in such a way that there is not something else which follows it with no alternative and is attached to it as to a cause ...' This proposes that everything leads ('as ... a cause') to something else, 'with no alternative' outcome being possible. Anything that *is* will *bring about* something else.

Alexander continued, still presenting Stoic thinking (I add hyphens for clarity):

> nor ... can any of the things which come-to-be subsequently be disconnected from the things which have come-to-be-previously, so as not to follow some one of them as if bound to it.

I assume that Alexander's term 'disconnected' means 'disconnected in imagination' – that is, imagined to have come-to-be-*without*-being-caused-by-something-prior.

So far, Alexander has provided two Stoic points: everything causes something, and everything is caused by something. Combining these gives us ... what? This: the world is *tightly* and *fully* structured, with a chain, a pattern, of linkings – of everything that has happened or will happen – everything!

And those linkings are strong. They need to be so.

> For [otherwise] the universe would be torn apart and divided and not remain single for ever, organised according to a single order ..., if any causeless motion were introduced; and [this would happen] if all the things that are and come to be did not have causes which have come to be beforehand [and] which they follow of necessity.

Alexander was drawing a Stoic picture of *the universe's being structured by causation into a unified whole*. 'The organisation of the whole, which is like this, goes on from infinity to infinity evidently and unceasingly.' Is it therefore a whole, a universe, without beginning or end? Does it stretch backwards, and forwards, forever – infinitely? That *is* the idea: causation never began and will never end.

> Fate itself, Nature, and the reason according to which the whole is organised, [the Stoics] assert to be God; it is present in all that is and comes to be, and in this way employs the individual nature of every thing for the organisation of the whole.

Does this imply that, on the Stoic approach, I should think of myself and my actions as oh-so-tiny pieces of an infinitely extended whole? Am I *that* insignificant? Maybe. Will this be a personal problem? I hope not.

There are various ways to formulate the idea of one's life being shaped by cosmos-sized influences, even forces, over which one has no control. Think of astrology. Widely respected in many places and periods of history, it talks of one's nature and future, linking these through a causal story. Whether that astrological-causal story is reliably accurate is not my point. I mention it as an instance of what a causal determinism, true or not, *could* look like.

1.6.3 Philippa Foot's explanations

Causal determinism (such as the Stoics' version: section 1.6.2) says that everything is shaped – controlled – by the past, given how the world works in general. That means being controlled by *the past plus reality's laws*. But what if those laws reflect physical reality yet our minds are not physical? Would this give us an 'inner' freedom? Thinking might not *feel* physical. Do laws of physics, biology, etc., leave each mind free to act 'in its own world'? Or are we still controlled through laws of *psychology*?

I will consider a discussion by Philippa Foot (1920–2010), an English philosopher.

> We cannot ... take it for granted that whenever the word 'determined' or the word 'cause' is used this [= the overpowering role of natural causal laws] is ... implied, and what is intended may be in no way relevant to the question of free will. For instance, an action said to be determined by the desires of the man who does it is not necessarily an action for which there is supposed to be a sufficient condition.

Why did Foot talk of 'a sufficient condition'? She was denying (with 'cannot take it for granted') that, when we deem an action 'determined' by something (such as 'desires'), we are highlighting something that was *itself enough* (sufficient) to cause that action. We might say that someone's desires caused him to act as he did; we might even use the word 'determined'. But this would not commit us to meaning that those desires *fully sufficed* for causing his action. And since 'the question of free will' *is* asking whether actions are caused in a wholly constraining way, this is why Foot suggested that what we say about the person's desires 'may be in no way relevant to the question of free will'.

> In saying that [his action] is determined by his desires we may mean merely that he is doing something that he wants to do, or that he is doing it for the sake of something else that he wants. ... [I]t is wise to be suspicious of expressions such as 'determined by desire' ...

Foot's use of the word 'merely' was vital. Her point was that we need not seek anything further, such as *fully sufficient* conditions, in explaining the agent's action. Foot then applied her point about 'determined by desire' to a related phrase – 'determined by the agent's character'.

> One might suppose that an action was so determined if it was *in* character, for instance the generous action of a generous man; but ... nothing has been said to suggest that where the character trait can be predicated the action will invariably follow; it has not been supposed that a man who can truly be said to be generous never acts ungenerously even under given conditions.

This time, Foot's key word is 'invariably'. She seems to have been highlighting the difference between saying that an action was caused-in-the-sense-of-*explained* by something, such as one's character – and saying that the action was caused-by-*laws*, ones that made it inevitable, even given that character, for instance. If Foot was correct, there can be intentions, desires, etc., and there can be actions *resulting from* (and explained by) them – without *laws* overseeing this resulting-from.

Maybe, then, we can retain the word 'determined' by using it more loosely, hence without finding it worrying. Can we sometimes say that something has determined our action – without regarding the action as having been *forced* by the past and laws? It could feel reassuring to think that an action has arisen in an orderly explicable way, perhaps reflecting our will (our intentions, desires, etc.) – even if this explanation was not quite *law*-like.

1.6.4 Edna Ullmann-Margalit's big decisions

When asking whether we have a free will, we should also ask whether we would always *want* our wills to be free. Might it depend on *how* powerful a person's will can be? Here is a surprising question: is a personal will ever *too* powerful for a person's own good? And here is a way to make that surprising question even more so: is a personal will ever too powerful for remaining *who* one is – retaining literally one's identity?

In asking that question, I am thinking of the following sort of situation. I want to do X. But what if X is so significant that something major will change – maybe in the world around me, but definitely *in me*? Could this amount to *destroying* me – the me-overall-(including-in-the-future) who is currently functioning as me-now? Could I-now be creating someone-existing-tomorrow whom I-now expect will be an improved me? Yet might that person-tomorrow *not be me at all*?

To explain those questions, we can look to Edna Ullmann-Margalit (1946–2010), an Israeli philosopher. When a person makes a *big* decision about her life, might this be so transformative that a new person will literally be the result? As Ullmann-Margalit uses the word 'big' here, a big decision

> is transformative, or 'core affecting'; it is irrevocable; it is taken in full awareness; the choice not made casts a lingering shadow. ... [D]ecisions exhibiting these characteristics [are] cases of *opting*. Decisions such as whether to marry, to migrate, or to leave the corporate world in order to become an artist, might be examples. ... When facing an opting situation one stands at a critical juncture in one's life.

Imagine making that sort of decision. How could this affect, in a 'destructive' way, your existence as a particular person – not merely a particular kind of person, but an *individual* person? It is because these are

> cases in which the choice one makes is likely to change one's beliefs and desires ...; that is, to change one's cognitive and evaluative systems. Inasmuch as our beliefs and desires shape the core of what we are as rational decision makers, we may say that one emerges from an opting situation a different person.

Change the core; change the person – literally. A new me? Well, a new someone – *from* me.

And do I know that the resulting person would *thank* me-today – the person who made the decision that produced the new person – for creating them? Why must the new person (who I-now *hope* will be part of me-overall) appreciate my-now thinking that has led to her existing?

This reminds me of Parfit's puzzle (section 1.4.4) about teletransportation. In that puzzle, a new body is created (literally new bodily matter, looking just like the old matter) – but with the prior 'inner' psychology being maintained. In Ullmann-Margalit's case, it seems, the same body is maintained (depending on what the big decision is), with a new psychology being created. *Can* a person survive making this sort of big decision about herself, expecting that the resulting person will still be her, a continuation of her – her self?

I will think about this when next I face such a choice.

Readings for 1.6

For Aristotle, I use J. L. Ackrill's translation, in *Aristotle's* Categories *and* De Interpretatione: Translated with Notes and Glossary (Oxford: Clarendon Press, 1963); quotations from pp. 50, 51. For Alexander, see *De Fato* [On fate], 192.4–192.29, in *Alexander of Aphrodisias on Fate*, trans. R. W. Sharples (London: Duckworth, 1983); quotations from pp. 70–1. For Foot, see 'Free will as involving determinism', in *Free Will and Determinism*, ed. B. Berofsky (New York: Harper & Row, 1966), pp. 95–108; quotations from pp. 97–8. For Ullmann-Margalit, see 'Big decisions: opting, converting, drifting', *Royal Institute of Philosophy Supplements* 81 (2006): 157–72; quotations from pp. 158–9; repr. in her *Normal Rationality: Decisions and Social Order*, ed. A. Margalit and C. R. Sunstein (Oxford: Oxford University Press, 2017).

1.7 Personal significance

1.7.1 Lucretius living with death

We have been reflecting (in section 1.6) on the ancient-yet-still-with-us question of whether people, in being who they are, have free will. One motivation for that focus has often been the idea that having a free will adds *value* to being a person. Might it be part of the *worth* in being a person? (Recall section 1.2's also asking whether having a *soul* might be part of that worth, by making us something special.)

But, before that question appears, maybe we need to confront this logically prior one: might our lives fundamentally *lack* worth? Is human life pointless – objectively so? I am not asking about times when living *feels* personally pointless. Is it *actually* pointless, even when not feeling so? One reason why we might fear its being so confronts us with the reality of death. Does its inevitability drain meaning from living? This might depend on whether death is a *harm* to living. Is one already harmed because one will die?

In reflecting on this, we might savour some reasoning, in poetic form, from Lucretius (Titus Lucretius Carus, c. 99–55 BCE), in his *De Rerum Natura*. He was Roman, writing in Latin, influenced by the Athenian Epicurus (341–270 BCE). This was Lucretius' most distinctive argument for there being no harm in being dead.

> Look back upon the ages of times past
> Eternal, before we were born, and see
> That they have been nothing to us, nothing at all.
> This is the mirror nature holds for us
> To show the face of time to come, when we
> At last are dead. Is there in this for us
> Anything horrible? Is there anything sad?
> Is it not more free from care than any sleep?

This is an *argument by analogy* – discussing some X directly, which is itself taken to be similar enough to some Y, in order to learn indirectly about Y. We may describe Lucretius' reasoning strategy in this way.

> Reflect on the past, on years from long before you were born. Notice something striking about that distant past. Describe a strong analogy between that past and the future-beyond-your-death. Infer an analogous 'something striking' about that future-beyond-your-death.

At the heart of Lucretius' reasoning was a metaphor. Imagine *holding a mirror* to the past-before-your-birth, so that we can *see* something specific (and striking) revealed in it about that past. That result, by analogy, will be taken to apply also to the future-beyond-your-death. We hold the mirror to a past-before-you, in order then to infer something specific (and striking) about a future-after-you. (And the analogy that we see is not affected by the disanalogy of the past having occurred and the future's being yet to occur.)

That was Lucretius' general strategy, including its metaphor of the mirror. What are the details of putting the strategy into effect, as he did? What is the 'something striking' being noticed about the distant past?

We begin by asking whether your actual living is harmed or lessened by your not having been alive earlier, before you were actually born. The answer is clear: 'of course not!'

We then infer (by analogy) that the same is true of your not being alive later, after death. The past-before-you-were-born is analogous to the future-after-you-will-die, as regards your living. Each is an emptiness for you — empty of experiences. So, since *missing out* on the past-before-you-were-born does not harm your living, *missing out* on the future-after-you-will-die likewise does not harm your living. If the fact that (for so long) you *were not yet* born does not lessen whatever value there is in your living, then the fact that (for so long) you *will have been* dead does not lessen whatever value there is in your living.

This does not make all living meaningful. But does it allow me to set aside one possible reason — the fact that I will die — for *denying* that I am living meaningfully? Am I thereby being given at least that reason potentially to value my life?

1.7.2 St Anselm living with faith

Do I have further possible reasons (beyond section 1.7.1's Lucretian unconcern about death) for regarding my life as having some value? Would the existence of God, for example, add such value? What of a *belief*, at least, in God's existing? Seemingly, that belief can feel life-enriching, adding much apparent value to one's living. Could that be even more clearly so when the belief amounts to a *faith* in God's existing?

This might depend partly on whether God actually exists. I will not assume either that He does or that He does not. But, in case He does, I wish to improve my understanding of what forms a faith in His existing might take. In particular, could such faith ever be *deepened philosophically*, having philosophical value added to it?

Someone who might have thought so was St Anselm (1033–1109). Born in Aosta (in what is now north-west Italy), he became the Archbishop of Canterbury. Let us read from his *Proslogion* (from 1077–8).

> Well then, Lord, You who give understanding to faith, grant me that I may understand, as much as You see fit, that You exist as we believe You to exist, and that You are what we believe You to be.

Anselm thus set a tone. He was not questioning God's existence; nor was he asking for proof. He wrote as if speaking directly with God. He was about to present some reasoning as a *testament* to God's existence. He began with how he *thinks* of God.

> Now we believe that You are something than which nothing greater can be thought. ... [W]hat I am speaking about [is] 'something-than-which-nothing-greater-can-be-thought' ...

Personal significance

The core of Anselm's reasoning will be the phrase 'something-than-which-nothing-greater-can-be-thought'. What role did it play for him?

He introduced it as the *content of a thought* that he has. It is how, he said, he thinks of God, and in his view it is a powerful content. To explain its power, he started with a *general* thesis about thoughts and reality: 'it is one thing for an object to exist in the mind, and another thing to understand that an object really exists.' Anselm was distinguishing between, in general, a *thought* of 'an object' X and the *reality* of X.

Using that distinction, he then revisited his thought of God. Could this thought exist even while God does not? No, reasoned Anselm, given the thought's special content ('that-than-which-a-greater-cannot-be-thought'). Here is how he phrased that denial: 'that-than-which-a-greater-cannot-be-thought cannot exist in the mind alone.' And here, following immediately, was his reasoning in support of that denial.

> For if it exists solely in the mind even, it can be thought to exist in reality also, which is greater. If then that-than-which-a-greater-cannot-be-thought exists in the mind alone, this same that-than-which-a-greater-*cannot*-be-thought is that-than-which-a-greater-*can*-be-thought. But this is obviously impossible. Therefore ... something-than-which-a-greater-cannot-be-thought exists both in the mind and in reality.

That is complex reasoning. I will 'slow it down', formulating it more fully.

God is being conceived of as 'that-than-which-nothing-greater-can-be-thought' – as a *greatest possible* object of thought. But any *greatest possible* X must be an *actually existing* X. This is because greatness has grades (more vs less), and existing contributes to these: it *is* a component of greatness. X-in-reality is greater – it is more real, more really real – than is 'X'-just-in-mind.

A thought-of-a-frog is *less frog-reality* (to speak oddly) than a real-frog-*plus*-a-thought-of-a-frog. So, when 'X' = 'God' = 'that-than-which-a-greater-cannot-be-thought', we cannot settle for all of the God-reality being only a God-thought. For that would be less God-reality than is possible. Thus, there must be a real God *if* there is a God-thought at all. And manifestly there *is* a God-thought – Anselm's own, for a start. Hence, there is a real God.

Since the stakes are so high (God's existing!), I will stay a moment with Anselm's thinking. His God-thought was supposedly of something with as much reality as *anything* could be thought to have. So, his God-thought was of something with a reality beyond what could be *wholly contained within* that thought's own amount of reality, as it were. Hence, as long as the God-thought is coherent – even possibly accurate – God must have reality beyond that idea, by being the *possible reality being thought within* the thought of that-than-which-a-greater-cannot-be-thought. But God would therefore be the greatest possible object of thought. This must include God's actually being more than only an object of thought. God is *that* real. No thought claiming to be of God can be *all* there is to there being a God. God must be more than a God-thought.

That was not only complex reasoning by Anselm. It was also passionate reasoning. He *cared*. It was reason and passion. Religion was spurring philosophy, being enriched in return. Anselm was being religiously philosophical *and* philosophically religious. He was not seeking to discover God's existing, in the sense of finding new rational reasons for *deciding whether* to believe that God exists. As his opening words expressed, Anselm already believed – with faith. But could he better *understand, through reason*, his own words, including the word 'God'? Would his reasoning rationally enrich or strengthen his faith?

1.7.3 *Albert Camus living with absurdity*

That Anselmian thinking (section 1.7.2) offers a potentially optimistic view of life's potential value for us, it seems. But what if Anselm was mistaken? Might our lives fundamentally *lack* worth? Is human life pointless – objectively so? I am not asking about times when living feels personally pointless. Is it *actually* pointless, even when not feeling so?

Albert Camus (1913–60), a French existentialist philosopher, gave memorable voice to such questions when evoking the ancient Greek myth of Sisyphus: condemned by the gods, Sisyphus became 'the futile labourer of the underworld', whose 'whole being is exerted towards accomplishing nothing.' This was a myth. Can we learn from it, though? Camus would have encouraged us to do so: 'Myths are made for the imagination to breathe life into them.'

> The gods had condemned Sisyphus to ceaselessly rolling a rock to the top of a mountain, when the stone would fall back of its own weight. They had thought with some reason that there is no more dreadful punishment than futile and hopeless labour.

Thus Sisyphus became 'the absurd hero'.

> I see that man going back down [the hill, having reached it with the stone, before it rolls down yet again] with a heavy yet measured step towards the torment of which he will never know the end.

Does this bear on us? It does. 'The workman of to-day works every day in his life at the same tasks and this fate is no less absurd.' Think of how repetitive everyday living can be. Much of it is devoted to tasks required *merely to continue* living.

So, should we read Camus as having issued a warning? Need we feel it as a pronouncement of hopelessness?

Camus seemed not to feel like that. Yes, Sisyphus is fated always to do what he is doing. Must he feel despair? Maybe not. 'If the descent [by Sisyphus] is ... sometimes performed in sorrow, it can also take place in joy. ... [He] teaches the higher fidelity that negates the gods ...' Sisyphus teaches *us* 'the higher fidelity' – the deeper truth – that can limit how fully 'the gods' (or, more generally, whatever forces oversee the world) control us.

How does that occur? I assume that the 'joy' is not to arise randomly. Would it be *chosen*? Is this how, in Camus's view, a free will can make living valuable even when circumstances seem dire? 'He ... concludes that all is well. ... The struggle itself towards the heights is enough to fill a man's heart. One must imagine Sisyphus happy.' In spite of what Camus's final sentence suggests, we *need* not imagine Sisyphus being happy. Camus's point, I assume, was that Sisyphus has an 'inner' choice. Even if he sees his situation accurately, he is free to react with 'joy'. This is a form of personal power. Sisyphus' life of rock-rolling is absurd – lacking value – if he does nothing to change it. He cannot change the rock-rolling. But he can change how he regards it, how he feels about it.

In that way, Camus encourages us at least to *feel* optimism – happiness – even when noticing signs of Sisyphean rock-rolling in our lives. What if, perhaps more fortunately, you do not regard your life as including those signs? Then you might not feel that Sisyphus represents you. You might not feel that your life is repetitive, lacking fundamental variety, committed to the same-old-same-old. Yet what *if* you are mistaken? Would you *actually* be living absurdly, partly by overlooking your life's Sisyphean nature?

1.7.4 Susan Wolf living with meaning
I introduced Camus (section 1.7.3) by talking of worth, value, and pointlessness in living as a person. We might

also talk of *meaning* in living. We could interpret Camus as saying that Sisyphus can *give* meaning to his life even when living in a way that otherwise offers none. The meaning would be created by choosing a suitable attitude towards one's life. If we do this, are *our* lives automatically meaningful?

Perhaps not, if Susan Wolf (b. 1952), an American philosopher, is correct. Like Camus, Wolf considers (what she calls) objective *and* subjective aspects of living. But she seems to weight them differently to how he does. She outlines a 'conception of meaningfulness [on which] ... meaning arises from loving objects worthy of love and engaging with them in a positive way.' For Wolf, having an uplifting attitude, say, is not enough; something of objective value is also needed.

Thus, witness her phrase 'worthy of love': 'meaning arises when subjective attraction [to something] meets objective attractiveness [of that thing], and one is able to do something good or positive about it.' Being 'gripped, excited, interested, engaged' is the subjective aspect of Wolf's account. Both aspects are needed – the objective and the subjective. Meaning does not result 'if the objects or activities with which [a person] is occupied are [objectively] worthless.'

How do we apply Wolf's general idea? Which activities are objectively worthless? Her suggestions include these: 'smoking pot all day long, or doing endless crossword puzzles'. In any case, her point is that doing simply *what one wants to do* is not enough to be living meaningfully. It matters *what* one wants to do.

Wolf recommends 'that one get involved with something other than oneself – that is, with something whose value is independent of and has its source *outside of* oneself.' 'Find your passion' – but not simply because it is a passion. Find something that *deserves* to be an object of passion. Then actively care about it.

Wolf calls this 'the Fitting Fulfillment View'. It values being 'able to see one's life as valuable in a way that can be recognized from a point of view other than one's own.'

To some, it will seem as if Wolf is being needlessly elitist when telling us what to value if we are to live meaningfully. But that is not true of her *general* account. Like many philosophers, she is writing a general story – before offering *one possible* way to make it more specific. Her *philosophical* proposal is her general idea – which we could adopt without following her specific preferences.

Here is another way to convey that potential response to Wolf's idea. She outlines a *schema* – her general account. This is her official proposal; her views on smoking pot, etc., amount to just one instance of that proposal. The schema is her general idea about blending subjective and objective aspects, *whatever* in particular these might be. Her schema is like a mathematical formula containing 'x' and 'y'. Her key proposal is that we should blend two kinds of value – the objective and the subjective. Having accepted that broad outline, we can then assess specific life-descriptions (substituting these for 'x' and 'y') – asking which, if any, contribute real life-meaning within Wolf's general structure.

As an example here, we could revisit Anselm (section 1.7.2). Here is how we might apply Wolf's structure and terms to his thinking. What could have *more* objective value than an almighty Being – God? If the answer is 'nothing', and if He does exist, then *faith* in His existing would be a subjective valuing of something with objective value – indeed, maximal objective value. If the faith is suitably strong, too, it would be *fitting* (to use Wolf's term). One's life *would* thereby, on Wolf's schema, include this real meaning, thanks to God and one's fitting faith in His existing.

Readings for 1.7

For Lucretius, see *On the Nature of the Universe*, trans. R. Melville (Oxford: Oxford University Press, 1997), Book 3, lines 972–7; quotation from pp. 96–7. For Anselm, see *St. Anselm's* Proslogion, trans. M. J. Charlesworth (Oxford: Clarendon Press, 1965), ch. II; quotations from p. 117. For Camus, see *The Myth of Sisyphus*, trans. J. O'Brien (London: Hamish Hamilton, [1942] 1955), pp. 96–9. For Wolf, see 'Meaningfulness: a third dimension of the good life', *Foundations of Science* 21 (2016): 253–69; quotations from pp. 256, 257, 260, 261.

2

Philosophical Reading and Writing

2.1 Wondering what it is to be philosophical?

This book invites you to be philosophical – and offers hints and ideas about *how* to be so. Here is a first hint, via another example.

Imagine being asked to *act morally well* in various situations. You picture doing your best each time. You are then asked not simply to assume that those actions would have been morally good, but to explain why. What *made* them morally good? How do you *justify* classifying them as morally good?

Suppose that you think again about each situation and how you imagined acting in it. Probably you look for *patterns* – in the situations, in your actions. Maybe you hope to find *marks* or *indicators* of moral goodness in those actions that you thought were morally good.

Could reflecting like that give you knowledge about what *makes* actions morally good – your own actions, but also other people's? Would you come to understand, even a little, *what it is* to be acting morally well?

That depends. You will probably not have reached a full formulation, a decisive definition, a thorough theory. (Not every possible case could be imagined. Not every possible detail can be noted.) Still, might you have *an improved understanding* of what it is to act in a morally good way?

Now reflect on chapter 1 in that same careful spirit. You began the book by thinking philosophically about selves and your reality as a person. In diverse voices and styles, you were *being* philosophical about selves and persons. Already, therefore, in reading this book you have had experiences of being philosophical.

And what were those experiences like? What were *you* like, while having them? What did being philosophical *feel* like? Was it distinctive? People often say that philosophical thinking is different. Saying *how* it is different, though, could remain challenging.

I doubt, for example, that you already have in mind a full formulation, a decisive definition, or a thorough theory of what it is to be philosophical. You might have thought about what you were doing. Even so, this might not have entirely revealed philosophy's nature to you, if it even has one – what it is and what it can be.

Yet have you made some early moves towards *an improved understanding* of being philosophical – *what it is* to be philosophical? I hope so.

This chapter will move cautiously, in that same spirit – taking a few small steps, setting the stage for later chapters where bolder moves will be made. Right now, I am asking just two questions.

What might philosophy *look* like, on the page?
How might we approach *reading* philosophy?

Neither question has an immediately obvious answer. Each can assist us, however, to appreciate some ideas, *about* being philosophical, that helped to shape chapter 1. (Then chapter 3 will resume being 'directly' philosophical, in its case about knowing. After which, chapter 4 returns to this chapter's 'indirectly' philosophical challenge – being philosophical *about* being philosophical. We will be seeking further understanding of *what being philosophical is*.)

2.2 Reading

2.2.1 Selfless philosophy (and Āryadeva)
What, if anything, is distinctive about *reading* philosophy? I will not attempt an exhaustive answer. But we can usefully consider some options. Each reflects an idea about what we might *want* from being philosophical.

As it happens, chapter 1 opened with two readings from Buddhist philosophy. As it also happens, we may again begin with some Buddhist thoughts. This time, I look to Āryadeva (c. 180–250), a student of Nāgārjuna's (whom we will visit in section 3.2.3). Āryadeva helped to found the Madhyamaka tradition (section 1.4.1) and seems to have been born either in south India or off that coast. His major (partially) surviving work was the *Catuḥśaka* (Four Hundred Verses), originally in Sanskrit, translated into Chinese and Tibetan.

I want to quote from Āryadeva because he was writing about travelling a path to Buddhahood – being a *bodhisattva*. We are not doing that. But we are seeking to be philosophical, for a while. And what strikes me as helpful here is a way to adapt and apply some of Āryadeva's advice about how to hear and use the Buddhist *no-self* view (section 1.1.2). We might, or might not, agree with that view. But in either event we can discover within Āryadeva's words some advice (which was possibly in his mind, possibly not) about *a way in which we might approach reading any philosophy*.

Here are some of Āryadeva's remarks (ch. 12, verses 12–14).

> 12. For an unwise person [= in effect, one who is *not* on the path to Buddhahood], the apprehension [= the positing] of ego [= a self] is better than the theory of selflessness. ...
> 13. Selflessness is called 'the door to tranquillity of which there is no second', 'terrifying to those with wrong views', and 'the sphere of all the Buddhas'.
> 14. Even the name of this teaching terrifies unwise people.

Āryadeva, it seems, was contrasting those who always presume that there is a self with those who live with 'selflessness' in their thinking. Is it scary to relinquish the presumption that you have a self? Āryadeva clearly thinks that an 'unwise person' feels a need to cling to the presumption that they have a self. An alternative is available: one *can* live without fearing that idea.

How might that thought from Āryadeva apply to the challenge of reading philosophy? I see in his distinction, and his response to it, a spirit that we might wish to bring, retrospectively, to what we were doing with chapter 1. We can try to read philosophy *in a spirit of selflessness*. By this, I do not mean one's striving to be generous in a charitable way, helping others. I mean one's reading philosophy without feeling that one has a self that is being implicated, judged, or even threatened, say, by what one is reading. One would read *without ego* (ch. 12, verses 24–5), *putting the no-self thesis into practice*, in the spirit gestured at by Āryadeva.

> 24. All people love their own thesis, just as they love their own birthplace. Yet why should a reason that defeats it [= your own thesis] distress you?

25. An intelligent person who desires good fortune accepts things that are appropriate, even from opponents. Isn't the sun common to everyone on earth who has eyes?

When you begin reading philosophy, you might already have views on some of its topics. But a no-self strategy for reading, as I picture this, would set aside any pre-existing commitments *by your self* to those views: your aim would be to find truth, *no matter whose, if anyone's*, it is. The truth is the sun, on this Āryadeva-inspired picture. Everyone shares the sun. It does not shine just for me or just for you. It is not *my* sun or *your* sun. It is no *one's* – no self's. So, can we read philosophy as if we lack selves, never being *personally* invested in defending a specific view? Can we *share* truths, whatever and wherever these are?

2.2.2 Self-philosophy (and John Perry)
The Āryadeva-inspired picture (section 2.2.1) – of reading selflessly – is one possible way to be a philosophical reader. It is not the only way. We might place *our selves* front and centre, asking in effect how a piece of philosophy can apply to *one's self*. Can I become a better self, thanks to reading philosophy? How does reading philosophy assist me, *as* a self, as *this* self?

I call that approach *self-philosophy*, by analogy with the term 'self-help'. I might have called it 'selfish philosophy', by analogy with 'selfless philosophy' – except that this would have been uncharitably misleading. 'Self-philosophy' it is. But the point is not that reading philosophy in this spirit will assist you in personal relationships, your job, and so on. That might occur, or it might not. It is not the *point* of doing philosophy as self-philosophy, though. The immediate point involves learning about, and even improving, oneself *as a self* by reading philosophy.

We might even wonder whether this is how at least some philosophy *must* be done – always self-sensitive or -aware or -directed. Here I have in mind a story from John Perry (b. 1943), an American philosopher.

> I once followed a trail of sugar on a supermarket floor, pushing my cart down the aisle on one side of a tall counter and back the aisle on the other, seeking the shopper with the torn sack to tell him he was making a mess. With each trip around the counter, the trail became thicker. But I seemed unable to catch up. Finally it dawned on me. I was the shopper I was trying to catch.
>
> I believed at the outset that the shopper with a torn sack was making a mess. And I was right. But I didn't believe that I was making a mess. That seems to be something I came to believe. And when I came to believe that, I stopped following the trail around the counter, and rearranged the torn sack in my cart. My change in beliefs seems to explain my change in behavior.

Does this story suggest that we cannot do philosophy entirely selflessly? What if I cannot read philosophy productively *without* imagining its applying to me, its possibly helping me, in effect its being about me? It would not need to be about only me. Others could read it in the same way, gaining something helpful from it for themselves – as (on this picture) I would do for myself when reading it. But reading philosophy would be reading at least partly (even if implicitly) *about oneself* – how one is, how one might be, and so on.

When reading chapter 1's philosophers, say, was I implicitly applying some or all of their ideas to myself? Was I 'testing out' their ideas in that way? Was *that* motivating me? If it was not, was I like Perry's shopper *before* realising that what he was seeing (or, in my case, reading) was about himself (or, in my case, my self)?

For example, when thinking about causal determinism (section 1.6) might I have been feeling the issue's urgency only by implicitly applying it to myself? I could have been focused, even if silently, on whether *my* actions are controlled by the past. The philosophical writing might be presented as if it is about anyone – hence about no one in particular. But could this be read as an implicit invitation to 'put oneself in the place' of the writing's apparent subject – which, again, could be about 'any given person'? Sometimes, the potential for reading something in that imaginative way is clearer, such as when the writing is more literary or 'fanciful': think of de Pizan's allegorical tale (section 1.3.1).

In any event, the question – for me – behind this general approach is that of whether, in reading at least some philosophy, I must imagine how the issue applies to myself. Is this how philosophy *matters* to me – by raising issues that I can test on myself? And, if so, is that how philosophy would matter to anyone? Is all philosophy ultimately self-philosophy?

2.2.3 The Way of Truth (and Parmenides)
When one begins reading philosophy, we might portray this as one's setting foot upon a path of selfless philosophy (section 2.2.1) and/or self-philosophy (section 2.2.2). What else might we say, in advance, about this? What kind of journey stretches ahead of one?

Maybe – even today – we will be travelling an ancient path, sketched long long ago by Parmenides (b. c. 515 BCE) from Elea, a Greek colony in southern Italy. He is known mainly for one poem, thanks to fragmentary quotations by other scholars from that ancient world. What was the poem's title? *On Nature* is sometimes used. Often it is called 'Parmenides' Poem'. It endorses what has become known as *the Way of Truth*. Parmenides portrayed our being guided along that Way by no less than a goddess. Through her, he sought to impart a vital truth – a truth *about* truth, a truth about *finding* truth. So, should we walk that Way? Will this enrich our appreciation of chapter 1's readings?

Here are some of the goddess's words (fragment 2).

> Come now, I shall tell – and convey home the tale once you have heard –
> just which ways of inquiry alone there are for understanding:
> the one, that [it] is and that [it] is not not to be,
> is the path of conviction, for it attends upon true reality,
> but the other, that [it] is not and that [it] must not be,
> this, I tell you, is a path wholly without report:
> for neither could you apprehend what is not, for it is not to be accomplished,
> nor could you indicate it.

Here is more from the goddess (fragment 6).

> It is necessary to say and to think that What Is is; for it is to be,
> but nothing it is not. ....
> For [I shall begin] for you from this first way of inquiry,
> then yet again from that [= that way of inquiry] along which mortals who know nothing
> wander two-headed: for haplessness in their breasts directs wandering understanding. They are borne along
> deaf and blind at once, bedazzled, undiscriminating hordes,
> who have supposed that it is and is not the same
> and not the same; but the path of all these turns back on itself.

The goddess's poetic words are powerful. I will highlight a few of them (my citations list a fragment number, followed by the line number).

- The goddess's 'ways of inquiry' (2.4) are different paths along which we *might* wander in our thinking.
- *One* of them meets with her approval – the 'path of conviction' (2.4).
- What does that phrase mean? Does it denote only confidence?
- No, it denotes the path that 'attends upon true reality' (2.4).
- The goddess's *What Is* (6.1) equals what we call *truth* – real truth, not merely what seems true. Truth is what we *should* seek: it is 'necessary to say and to think' (6.1). Truth – 'nothing it is not' (6.2).
- Otherwise, we are travelling 'the other' path (2.5), 'a path wholly without report' (2.6) – a path leading to 'what is not' (2.7).
- To travel that path would be unfortunate. We would be among those 'mortals who know nothing' (6.4), who 'wander two-headed' (6.5) – not keeping eyes fixed on What Is. We would be 'deaf and blind at once', among 'bedazzled, undiscriminating hordes' (6.7).
- Who wants *that*?

Presumably none of chapter 1's philosophers would wish to be travelling that second path. So, what are *signs* or *marks* of a philosopher seeking truth – travelling the first path? Which signs should we embrace and welcome when reading philosophy? Which should we spurn?

Perhaps the most obvious sign of someone's trying to travel the goddess's first path appears when they *defend* or *propose* a claim as to What Is. How would they do this? The clearest sign is probably their offering an *argument* – some *reasoning*. This can take many forms, some subtly presented, some more overt. At times, a philosopher says 'Here is my argument – my support, ground, or reason – for my view.' She might then present her reasoning in a formally arrayed way, with supposedly supportive *premises* appearing in an organised way (they might be numbered, for easy citation), harmonising with each other so as to invite readers to accept her *conclusion* – the view that she was trying to defend or explain. This conclusion will thus be treated by her as *true*. (At any rate, it is, if she really was trying to defend it, and so long as she found no reason, when developing her reasoning, to change her mind about the conclusion's being true.)

Parmenides would presumably approve of that sort of guided journey towards a Truth, even though *he* was not presenting a formally arrayed argument. He used a poem. But philosophy takes different forms (as section 2.3 will emphasise). As we have experienced in chapter 1, it need not always appear as an organised argument with numbered premises. Even arguments – pieces of reasoning – can wear different clothes. Chapter 4 will convey a fuller sense of that potential variety. In the meantime, I will start preparing a path that we might travel towards all of that, by enlarging our shared sense of the many ways in which a philosopher may aim for truth.

As I indicated, she might be direct and clear by saying explicitly 'Here is what, I claim, is true: …. Here is my argument for its being true: ….' But that is not the only possible way to travel the Way of Truth. One could adopt any of the following approaches (or more).

- *Questions*. It might be true that *a specific question* arises – and that we can improve our understanding of an issue by appreciating the question's relevance. Maybe we have been thinking in needlessly limited ways, not even noticing this new question. But noticing new questions can reflect one's becoming more open-minded about the issue. New answers might arise for us only after we ask the new question. *Asking good questions*, including *new* ones, can improve our awareness of significant truths.

- *Interpretations*. It might be true that *a new way of interpreting* an issue is available to us once we are shown how it applies to data that we had assumed could be read – interpreted – only in other ways. *Finding new interpretations* might reveal significant truths. That can also be true of finding a new interpretation *of what some other philosopher has said or written* in her inquiries into the issue. The aim is always to find the *best* interpretation, or at least a *better* one, in one's quest for significant truths.
- *Implications*. It might be true that a thesis, such as some theory, has *implications* previously overlooked – and now being uncovered. Maybe they are true. Even when they are not, becoming aware of them can help: seeing how they flow from some thesis or theory could reveal that the thesis or theory is *itself not* true. This could be a significant truth itself, especially if people have been defending that thesis or theory. They might need to change their minds – such as by *doubting* that the thesis or theory is true, *given these newly noticed implications*.
- *Formulations*. It might be true that a thesis, even a theory, can be improved, such as by being *formulated* more precisely. More-precisely-described *truths* might then emerge, once we have in hand more precise formulations of our ideas. This could even help in practical ways if we use these *newly-able-to-be-described truths* in negotiating the world.

That list is not complete. But it can alert us to how our surroundings might look once we start travelling along the Way of Truth. After all, *all of the list's entries are truth-aims*, some directly, some indirectly.

The list also reflects many of chapter 1's readings. If I was setting 'Exercises for Readers', I would issue this invitation: 'Please revisit chapter 1, deciding which of its readings fit well with some or all of these truth-aims (and any others that might occur to you).' There are various potential outcomes for any instance of philosophical thinking. But, when being philosophical, *always*, in *some* way, *some* instance or kind of *truth* is being sought.

- The potential truth in question might be about *the wider world*. For example, *in fact do we* have selves, or non-physical minds, or free wills, etc.?
- Or the potential truth might be about *thinking about* the wider world. For example, *should we think* of ourselves as in fact having selves, or non-physical minds, or free wills, etc.?

It seems that always our aim when writing or reading philosophy is to discover or display *some* element within What Is – that is, Truth. That Parmenides-inspired theme spans a wide variety of possibilities. In broad terms, though, we can simplify the variety:

What Is can include any reality (= truths) *beyond* our thinking – but also *the reality of* (= truths about) our thinking.

Truths about our thinking can matter, even when seeking truths about a wider world beyond our thinking. This is because our thinking is *what we must use in seeking* those truths about that wider world. Our thinking therefore needs to be *good* – that is, *actually* good for discovering reality's details. It is important, then, not only to use our thinking, but to *evaluate* it.

Thus, our inquiries generally take one or both of these two forms.

- We may seek truths about the world *directly*. We pose and formulate questions, interpretations, implications, and so on – in ways that, we hope, lead us

to accurate (= truthful) views *about* personal identity, free will, etc. We aim to uncover such truths. We think about what, we hope, are truths 'out there', *beyond* our thinking.
- We might seek truths about the world *indirectly*. Again we pose and formulate questions, interpretations, implications, and so on – in ways that, we hope, lead us to accurate (= truthful) views *about* our attempts to seek specific truths about the world directly. We talk or write in ways that, we hope, are accurate (= truthful) *about how* to talk or write accurately (= truthfully) about personal identity, free will, etc. We aim to *uncover how to uncover* such truths. We *think about thinking about* what (we hope) are truths 'out there' *apart* from our thinking.

2.2.4 *Forms of Truth (and the* Mahābhārata*)*

Respecting a goddess's words sounds sage – wise beyond compare. So, is Parmenides' goddess-endorsed Way of Truth (section 2.2.3) the Way to Go?

Even if it is, that is not the full story. We need added guidance. *Being* on the Parmenidean path is different from *knowing* that one is on it.

- Being on the Way of Truth does not guarantee knowing that one is there. One might doubt oneself, even when actually gazing at What Is.
- Not being on the Way of Truth does not guarantee knowing that one is not there. One might mistakenly credit oneself with seeing What Is, even when actually being misled.

I suspect that we do not always know What Is. But what if we never do so?

Chapter 3 will engage with that question. We will try to understand *knowledge* – including how we attain it at times, even if at other times we fail to do so. Right now, we may begin preparing for that discussion with further reflection on truth. Parmenides might seem to have been strict in his thoughts on Truth. But can we add to his thinking, in an inviting way, with some thoughts from the *Mahābhārata* (c. 200 BCE – 100 CE), a famed Sanskrit epic? (I will quote from ch. 162 of the *Śānti-Parvan* – the Book of Peace.)

> Yudhishthira said, '... What are the indications, O king, of truth? How may it be acquired? What is gained by practising truth, and how? ...'
> Bhishma said, '... With those that are good, Truth is always a duty. Indeed, Truth is an eternal duty. ... Truth is duty; Truth is penance; Truth is *Yoga*; and Truth is the eternal *Brahma*. Truth has been said to be Sacrifice of a high order. Everything rests upon Truth.'

That still sounds strict in its portrayal of Truth. But Bhishma expands the picture, making it more varied and flexible. Truth will remain Truth; can it take different forms, though?

> Truth, ... as it exists in all the world, is of thirteen kinds. The forms that Truth assumes are impartiality, self control, forgiveness, modesty, endurance, goodness, renunciation, contemplation, dignity, fortitude, compassion, and abstention from injury.

For Bhishma, those are different forms that Truth can take *as it arises in our lives*. Even so, 'Truth is immutable, eternal, and unchangeable. It may be acquired through practices which do not militate against any of the other virtues.' Bhishma explains that general idea, specific form by specific form. Here is one example.

> When desire and aversion, as also lust and wrath, are destroyed, that attribute in consequence of which one is able to look upon one's self and one's foe, upon one's

good and one's evil, with an unchanging eye, is called impartiality.

Truth, even in one's sense of oneself or 'one's foe', is not guaranteed. One must not be *distracted*, such as by 'desire and aversion' and 'lust and wrath', when seeking truth about oneself or another. Even oneself-truth arrives only with *impartiality* in how one is viewing oneself.

Or is that a point about how we *find* Truth, not about what Truth *is*? Without impartiality, for instance, one might perpetually overlook some truths even about oneself. Still, maybe Bhishma is talking about Truth *as it is once* it is found. When impartiality does help to reveal personal truths, those truths, *now that they have been found in that way, will continue wearing marks* of the impartiality. They will *be* impartial truths, once found.

The same sort of point arises for all thirteen of Bhishma's forms. The general point is that truth is only ever present, for us, *in combination with* one or more of those qualities. Truth for us always has one or more of those thirteen forms. We might think of those forms as like clothing: for us, truth *is* always clothed in one of Bhishma's forms; Truth is never 'naked' or 'bare'. Truth functions for us by reflecting one or more of those admirable qualities. That is what truth is *like*.

What else can we learn from this *Mahābhārata*-picture? We might note Truth's underlying *unity*.

> These thirteen attributes, though apparently distinct from one another, have but one and the same form, *viz.*, Truth. All these ... support Truth and strengthen it. It is impossible ... to exhaust the merits of Truth.

And what of Truth's possibly supreme *value*? That image was implicit in Parmenides' advice – from a goddess, remember! – about walking the Way of Truth. But something is being added here – about Truth's possibly supreme value *within us*.

We can expand that idea. If Truth for us, on this *Mahābhārata*-picture, always has at least one of those thirteen forms, is it only ever present for us in a *personally rich* way – a way that enriches us *as* persons? When we attain Truth, maybe we are expressing not only our intellect but our wider character, even our moral character – again, as displayed in one or more of those thirteen 'forms of Truth'. For example, are we being encouraged by this *Mahābhārata*-picture to be a Truthful Person – that *kind* of person?

In such ways, adding this *Mahābhārata*-picture to Parmenides' poetic vision promises to enlarge our range of potentially rewarding ideas *even about ourselves*. Chapter 1 asked *what a person is*. Now we are adding to that earlier inquiry by asking what a person is *when travelling the Way of Truth*. Such a person gains Truth *along with* one or more of those personally valuable attributes from the *Mahābhārata*.

That suggests something further about selves – something inviting but also puzzling. *Travelling the Way of Truth* sounds as if it could amount to *Knowing*. Maybe our currently blending the *Mahābhārata* with Parmenides is leading us to this more complex question: *what is a person when she is gaining knowledge*?

The answer depends, of course, on *what knowing is*. Thinking philosophically about this will be our initial challenge in chapter 3.

Readings for 2.2

For Āryadeva, see *Āryadeva's Catuḥśaka: On the Boddhisattva's Cultivation of Merit and Knowledge*, trans. K. Lang (Copenhagen: Akademisk Forlag,

1986); quotations from pp. 115, 117. For Perry, see 'The problem of the essential indexical', *Noûs* 13 (1979): 3–21; quotation from p. 3. For Parmenides, see J. Palmer's translation in *Parmenides and Presocratic Philosophy* (Oxford: Oxford University Press, 2009); quotations from pp. 365, 367. For the *Mahābhārata*, see *The Mahābhārata of Krishna-Dwaipayana Vyasa*, Vol. VIII (*Santi Parva*, Part I), 5th edn, trans. K. M. Ganguli (New Delhi: Munshiram Manoharlal, [1970] 1991); quotations from pp. 352–3.

2.3 Writing

I will now comment, very briefly, on philosophical *styles* of writing (and thereby of thinking, naturally). No single style is, or should, be used by all philosophers. Chapter 1 made this apparent – literally so, by having various styles *appear*. Section 2.2.3 reinforced the point by gesturing at different aims (even if all have something to do with truth) that philosophers might have. What should we notice next, so early in this book? Here is one simple motivating idea: a *choice* of style might then await and even flow, since differing styles could suit differing philosophical *aims*.

We may reinforce that idea by recalling chapter 1's philosophers, along with those from a moment ago in section 2.2. I will not repeat their ideas. We need only note the range of their styles. Roughly described, and in no special order (and maybe not exhaustively), here is that range (including section numbers, with some repetition when more than one of these styles appeared).

- poetry and metaphor – Upaniṣads (1.1.1), Lucretius (1.7.1), Parmenides (2.2.3)
- dialogue (perhaps fictional, perhaps not) – King Milinda (1.1.2), Plato (1.2.1)

- introspection – Hume (1.1.3), Plato (1.2.1), Descartes (1.2.4), St Anselm (1.7.2)
- interpreting empirical data – Churchland (1.1.4), Wang Chong (1.2.2), Midgley (1.3.2), Ullmann-Margalit (1.6.4)
- interpreting linguistic data – Menkiti (1.1.5), Kneale (1.2.5), Foot (1.6.3)
- interpreting cultural data – Menkiti (1.1.5), de Pizan (1.3.1), Fanon (1.5.2)
- fictional thought experiment – Avicenna (1.2.3), Parfit (1.4.4)
- fictional allegory – de Pizan (1.3.1), Buddhist demons (1.4.1), Camus (1.7.3), maybe the *Mahābhārata* (2.2.4)
- personal experience (self-interpreted) – Fanon (1.5.2), St Anselm (1.7.2), Perry (2.2.2)
- applying (in defending) a definition or theory – Wang Chong (1.2.2), Descartes (1.2.4), Frankfurt (1.3.3), Locke (1.4.3), Marx (1.5.1), Haslanger (1.5.3), Ullmann-Margalit (1.6.4), Wolf (1.7.4), perhaps Āryadeva (2.2.1)
- applying (in opposing) a definition or theory – Vasubandhu (1.4.2), Aristotle (1.6.1), Alexander of Aphrodisias (1.6.2)

Those groupings can be debated. For example, some authors might be better allocated to a different category. But the general spirit remains correct enough, as does its immediate moral: if we are to be as philosophical as possible, we should welcome philosophy in *all* of its forms. It can adopt many of these. It has long done so. It will probably continue doing so. It might even find new ones, soon or in the distant future.

Nor need that potential variety be a matter merely of fluctuating intellectual fashions. Philosophical styles can be more substantial than clothing styles. A difference of philosophical style might *mean* something.

It could reflect a distinct way of being linked to Truth. Parmenides might insist that there is only one overall Way of Truth – one overall path along which Truth is ever met. Yet we also read, in the *Mahābhārata*, the idea of there being different forms that Truth can take, *even along that single Way*. Could those disparate forms be best conveyed in different ways – so that varying styles of language would be apt for describing and imparting those respective truths?

Might that be particularly true when those truths are philosophical – hence when those people are *being* philosophical? Given philosophy's having emerged, and then developed, within such strikingly disparate cultures over millennia, it enjoys many forms. Are these different forms that instances of philosophical Truth might display – even along a single overall Way of philosophical Truth? Are varying philosophical styles therefore not only fun to meet – but important to recognise and encourage?

And would Parmenides' goddess in particular welcome that expansive and liberating thought, if (as we might imagine in a flight of fancy) she had been chatting with the *Mahābhārata*'s Bhishma?

3

What Do You Know?

3.1 What is knowledge?

3.1.1 Plato's knowing beliefs
Chapter 1's focus was metaphysical, on *what we are*. What is a self? What is a person? Thanks to that chapter, do we now know the answers to those questions?

That depends: what is knowledge itself? Plato (we met him in section 1.2.1) investigated this in two dialogues, *Theaetetus* and *Meno*. Let us eavesdrop on Socrates' conversation with Meno (in the segment 97a–98a). 'A man [says Socrates] who knew the way to Larissa ... and went there and guided others would surely lead them well and correctly?' So, the idea of knowing is introduced, immediately being thought of as helpful: one travels successfully when using knowledge.

Yet is that enough to identify knowledge, marking it off from anything else? No. When asked *what knowledge is*, we need to say more than 'It is useful.' Otherwise, we could confuse it with something similar that is also useful.

To illustrate that danger, Socrates compared knowing with having a 'correct opinion' (what we would call a true, or accurate, belief).

> What if someone had had a correct opinion as to which was the way but had not gone there nor indeed had knowledge of it, would he not also lead correctly? ... So correct opinion is no less useful than knowledge?

That question, with its use of 'also', acknowledged a *similarity*. What *difference*, then, is being mentioned? Meno proposed that 'the man who has knowledge will always succeed, whereas he who has true opinion will only succeed at times.' Meno's key contrast was thus between 'always' and 'at times': even if both knowledge and true belief can help, knowledge does this more often – indeed, always.

Yet why would that be so? As Socrates allowed (97c), holding fast to an accurate belief will always succeed, and one can lose knowledge. So, Meno was right to 'wonder ... why knowledge is prized far more highly than right opinion, and why they are different' (97c–d).

In response, Socrates described what he took to be an extra element within knowing (97d–98a), an element beyond 'correct opinion'. He did this by introducing an analogy (an approach used also by Lucretius: section 1.7.1). It was between 'correct opinions' and 'the statues of Daedalus', which were reputed to be so marvellous that 'they too run away and escape if one does not tie them down but remain in place if tied down':

> true opinions, as long as they remain, are a fine thing and all they do is good, but they are not willing to remain long, and they escape from a man's mind, so that they are not worth much until one ties them down by (giving) an account of the reason why. ... After they are tied down, in the first place they become knowledge, and then they remain in place. That is why knowledge

is prized higher than correct opinion, and knowledge differs from correct opinion in being tied down.

That is complex. I will highlight details.

First, 'tied down', when describing knowledge, is a *metaphor*. It was being used *literally* in Socrates' comment on the statues. What was to be read literally in his account of knowing was his phrase '(giving) an account of the reason why' (*'aitias logismos'*). Socrates meant something like 'giving good evidence that states why, or how, the belief is correct'. When this evidence is present (he was suggesting), the belief is true or accurate *in a way that amounts to knowledge*. We might paraphrase this (in today's terms) as 'Knowledge = a belief that is true *and well supported by good evidence*' – a *logos*.

Was that a useful definition? Maybe, if it shows us how to distinguish knowledge from a lucky guess, say, or from wishful-yet-accurate thinking. Are those states *not rational enough* to be knowledge – because they do not involve enough good evidence?

3.1.2 Nyāya's knowing episodes
The *Meno*'s proposal (section 3.1.1) for *what knowledge is* was among philosophy's first steps within *epistemology*. This word comes from two ancient Greek words, *'epistēmē'* and *'logos'* – 'knowledge' and 'account'. 'Epistemology' is philosophy's usual term for attempts to understand knowledge's nature and whatever flows from that nature. We are now, in this book's chapter, 'doing' epistemology.

Western epistemology began, perhaps, with Plato. But classical India, too, produced early epistemology, notably in its Nyāya tradition. That Vedic tradition began around 150 CE, and was written in Sanskrit. Its name can be translated as 'right reasoning'. Hence, it has much to say about knowing. It tells us that knowing is *what should result from* good reasoning.

Let us meet some indicative passages from the tradition's initial text – the *Nyāya-sūtra* (528 sūtras, from Gautama Akṣapāda; 'sūtra' means 'thread') – and from a classical commentator (Vātsyāyana, c. 450 CE, writing on sūtra 1.1.1).

> When an object is comprehended through a knowledge source (*pramāṇa*), it becomes possible to engage in successful goal-directed activity. Thus, a knowledge source is useful (*arthavat*). Without a knowledge source, ... there would be no successful action.

We are being alerted to the idea of a knowledge *source* – a *means* of knowing. Not just any awareness-episode that seems true is knowledge; it must have *arisen properly*.

We also gain a Nyāya sense of why knowing *matters*: it leads to, and is needed for, 'successful action'. Knowing enables a knower to act, to *do* things (such as to travel, with Socrates, to Larissa?). Vātsyāyana added this: 'veridical cognition produced in the right way is *knowledge*.'

What are real knowledge sources? Sūtra 1.1.3 says that they 'are perception, inference, analogy, and testimony.' Vātsyāyana explained this (I add bold text for clarity):

> **perception** is the functioning of each sense *faculty* upon its *own proper* object. ... **inference** is the *source* that works *after*. Inference normally occurs after perception, giving knowledge about something that possesses an inferential mark by means of knowing the mark. ... [**A**]**nalogy** is the *source* that shows *proximity*, nearness, as in 'A buffalo is like a cow.' Proximity should be understood here as a connection with universals, shared properties. ... [**T**]**estimony** is that by which something is asserted, *is heard* – so it is spoken of, that is, made known.

Knowing is always an *event* or *episode* that has arisen in any of those stable ways.

That is different from how Socrates in the *Meno* (section 3.1.1) described knowledge: he required it to be held stably *in place*. This meant a belief's being 'tied down', held in position. For Socrates, knowledge is a belief 'tethered' (like a statue) by a *logos* – good evidence for why it is true and hence should be retained. Now we see the Nyāya emphasis on knowledge's *arising* stably. The Nyāya picture was of knowledge as *appearing* – 'Now I know!' – even if it does not stably *persist*. It is knowledge, so long as it has *arisen* stably.

This reflects a further disparity, in conceptions of knowing, between Plato's *Meno* and the Nyāya school. (Even fine philosophers can disagree.) The *Meno* classified knowledge as *a kind of belief*. A belief can be present, 'sitting quietly', overlooked long after it arrives. One might learn something and then retain the belief without remaining conscious of it. This could be how knowledge persists when one is asleep, for example. But that way of knowing is not what the Nyāya thinking highlighted: when asleep, one is not having knowledge episodes. One is not *gaining* knowledge, in a knowledge *event*. The Nyāya focus was on these active episodes – cognitive events amounting to moments (or longer) of knowing by *gaining* knowledge. The Nyāya conception might reflect the idea that active episodes of knowing are what we use in our active lives – putting knowledge into action.

3.1.3 Bertrand Russell's stopped clock

Both the *Meno* (section 3.1.1) and the Nyāya tradition (section 3.1.2) say that knowing is more than being correct. The *Meno* says 'A true belief needs to be supported by a *logos*' – good evidence. The Nyāya tradition says 'An accurate cognitive episode must arise in a proper way' – stably (via perception, etc.). But might knowing need even more?

We might consider *the (imagined) case of the stopped clock*. It is from Bertrand Russell (1872–1970), an English philosopher who won the Nobel Prize for Literature (1950).

Russell wrote with the *Meno*'s picture of knowledge in mind:

> knowledge is a sub-class of true beliefs: every case of knowledge is a case of true belief, but not vice versa. It is very easy to give examples of true beliefs that are not knowledge.

He then gave examples. Before we meet one of them, though, we might make it even more significant for us.

Specifically, we might adapt his case, making it about both knowledge-as-belief (the *Meno*'s conception) *and* knowledge-as-cognitive-episode (the Nyāya conception). Russell aimed his case at knowledge-as-belief. We could make it more general by replacing its talk of 'belief' with the term 'belief *or* believing'. (The latter would be active – a cognitive episode.) Here is Russell's version.

> [Imagine a] man who looks at a clock which is not going, though he thinks it is, and who happens to look at it at the moment when it is right; this man acquires a true belief as to the time of day, but cannot be said to have knowledge.

Russell was inferring (with his 'but cannot be said') that it is possible to have a true belief that falls short of being knowledge – presumably due to the lack of good evidence for its being true. (Russell did not *say* that good evidence was present.)

May we infer an even stronger moral than Russell's? We can, if the case may be interpreted as one where the person lacks knowledge – but where his true belief

What is knowledge?

is supported in ways that would satisfy both the *Meno* and the Nyāya tradition. For then we could interpret the case as showing that *even those approaches* fail to do justice to what knowing involves.

Let us test that idea. Here are two ways to expand the case (using terms speaking, respectively, to those suggestions from the *Meno* and the Nyāya school).

1. The man might be thinking like this: 'Clocks are very reliable. Hence, this one probably is correct. It says that the time is 10:22. So, I believe that it is 10:22.' He has this *belief*.
2. Clocks are very reliable. Hence, this one probably is correct. It says that the time is 10:22. The man sees this. So, he infers – actively *believing* – that 'It is 10:22.'

And here is how we may interpret those expanded versions of Russell's case.

In version 1, the man consciously uses good evidence. Everything in the evidence is true, and it provides good rational support for his true belief. Does this satisfy the *Meno*'s picture? It seems to do so. Yet it also seems that knowledge is absent. Hence, the *Meno*'s picture is an inadequate portrayal of how to have knowledge.

In version 2, there is an accurate cognitive episode of believing, formed by perception (looking at the clock) and inference (reasoning from what one sees). Does this satisfy the Nyāya picture? It seems to do so. Yet it also seems that knowledge is absent. Hence, the Nyāya picture is an inadequate portrayal of how to have knowledge.

What emerges from those interpretations of those two versions? The apparent moral is this: maybe neither Plato *nor* the Nyāya tradition drew a complete picture of knowledge. Still, did those classical accounts provide a *good enough* picture, allowing us to understand ourselves *well enough* as knowers? Do we know *at least approximately* what knowing is?

Readings for 3.1

For the *Meno*, the translation used is G. M. A. Grube's, in *Plato: Five Dialogues* (Indianapolis: Hackett, 1981); quotations from pp. 85–6. For the Nyāya tradition, see *The Nyāya-sūtra: Selections with Early Commentaries*, trans. M. Dasti and S. Phillips (Indianapolis: Hackett, 2017); quotations from pp. 14, 17–18. For Russell, see *Human Knowledge: Its Scope and Limits* (London: Allen & Unwin, 1948), pp. 170–1.

3.2 Doubts

3.2.1 The Zhuangzi's *puzzling questions*
Both Socrates (section 3.1.1) and the Nyāya tradition (section 3.1.2) linked *having* knowledge to *using* it. I will now focus on one way to use knowledge – namely, *in answering questions*. Can we do this definitively enough to remove rational doubt and uncertainty?

I am unsure. Some questions are puzzling in philosophical ways, even raising philosophical doubts. The Daoist *Zhuangzi* (fourth century BCE) has plenty of these. That book might, or might not, have been mainly written by Zhuang Zhou ('Zhuangzi'), from inland eastern China. It questions much, in a teasing way, building on simple stories.

> Nie Que asked Wang Ni, 'Do you know what all things agree in considering right?'
> ... 'How could I know that?'
> ... 'Do you know that you don't know?'
> ... 'How could I know that?'

> ... 'Then are all beings devoid of knowledge?'
> ... 'How could I know that? ... How could I know that what I call "knowing" is not really "not-knowing"? How could I know that what I call "not-knowing" is not really "knowing"?' (ch. 2: 38)

Nie Que is asking about knowledge – not knowledge of everything, but of what is called 'right'. His questions exemplify a pattern of thinking that could apply more widely. The questions prompt Wang Ni to consider several cases. He compares people with various animals, noting how something that harms a person can be perfect for another animal (such as sleeping somewhere damp, or living in a tree):

> humans regard Mao Qiang and Lady Li as great beauties – but when fish see them they [the fish] dart into the depths, when birds see them they [the birds] soar into the skies ... Which of these ... 'knows' what is rightly alluring? (ch. 2: 38)

Different perspectives, different reactions: which – if either – perspective *knows*? No answer emerges. But questions can have a point even when unanswerable. They might make us receptive to new possibilities.

> Zhuangzi and Huizi were strolling along the bridge over the Hao River. Zhuangzi said, 'The minnows swim about so freely ... Such is the happiness of fish.'
> Huizi said, 'You are not a fish, so whence do you know the happiness of fish?'

Indeed, I would not claim to know whether a fish that I see in the water is happy. Still, is happiness even a possibility for fish? Zhuangzi continues: 'You are not I, so whence [= how, or from where] do you know I don't know the happiness of fish?' This time, the question concerns Zhuangzi, not the fish. How does Huizi know another's mind – including whether the other person (Zhuangzi) has something inside their mind that is knowledge? Huizi seems to acknowledge this limitation, before saying,

> I am not you, … so I don't know what it is to be you. But by the same token, since you are certainly not a fish, my point about your inability to know the happiness of fish stands intact.

So, Huizi insists that, even if he does not know what is inside Zhuangzi's mind, he knows that it *cannot* be knowledge of what is inside the fish's mind. This is seemingly a comment again on the fish, more so than on Zhuangzi. But Zhuangzi does not hear it in that way:

> You said, '*Whence* do you know the happiness of fish?' Since your question was premised on your knowing that I know it, I must have known it from here, up above the Hao River. (ch. 17)

Is Zhuangzi being fair? Huizi might have meant only to be asking 'Whence do you know the happiness of fish *if* you do?' This would have lengthened the interplay of perspectives. Is there no decisive way to resolve this back and forth?

That depends on whether we can find a manageable list of *ways* to know. Recall the Nyāya tradition's trying to do that (section 3.1.2). Could any of their favoured ways be a means of knowing the happiness of a fish? One of their ways was the use of *analogy*. Could it help Zhuangzi? We will soon (section 3.4) discuss knowing another's mind, and the idea of knowing it through analogy will reappear there.

In the meantime, I notice that, in spite of these questions-plus-puzzlement, the *Zhuangzi* is not obviously advocating a *sceptical* frown – concluding that neither person has knowledge. After all, Zhuangzi claims knowledge. Still, it appears that we are being encouraged to tread carefully – and playfully? – when either denying *or* claiming knowledge.

3.2.2 Sextus Empiricus' competing appearances

I used the term 'sceptical' just now (section 3.2.1). It is from ancient Greek philosophy. Their first 'official' sceptic was Pyrrho of Elis, in the Peloponnese (c. 360–275 BCE), although his endorsing those sceptical ideas might have been added to the 'record' by his student Timon of Phlius (c. 325–235 BCE). Our best source for Pyrrhonist sceptical thought is Sextus Empiricus (c. 160–210). A doctor and philosopher, Sextus spent time in Alexandria, in Egypt. His books convey how to think like a Pyrrhonist.

Pyrrhonism is a way of inquiring. It is a technique and a spirit. It aims to be non-dogmatic and open-minded. It delves into competing viewpoints. It asks where, within those viewpoints, definite truth is found – before apparently finding none and choosing to live quietly with that apparent result.

> Scepticism is an ability, or mental attitude, which opposes [= compares] appearances to judgements in any way whatsoever, with the result that, owing to the equipollence [= apparently equal probability] of the objects and reasons thus opposed, we are brought firstly to a state of mental suspense [= we suspend judgement on either 'side' being correct-because-more-probable] and next to a state of 'unperturbedness' or quietude [= 'an untroubled and tranquil condition of soul']. (Bk I, ch. IV)

That reasoning moves quickly. I now 'slow it down'.

Its talk of a sceptical attitude does not mean being cynical, critical, or destructive, aiming just to win arguments. Its technique is to compare 'appearances to judgements', being receptive to differences of opinion. We can always, it seems, find these: time and again, any view is apparently counterbalanced by a competing one. Sextus compared different kinds of animal, different groups of people, different individuals, different senses for an individual, different conditions in which to use senses, different times of doing so, different social and moral customs, etc.

How do Pyrrhonists then reason?

First, they *suspend* judgement, neither believing nor disbelieving, time after time. This is not the same as saying, resignedly, 'The truth is somewhere between.' That would be a claim, albeit a vague one, as to where truth is. No Pyrrhonist would make it. Second, Pyrrhonists *do not worry* about abstaining like that. They live without beliefs as to what is really true. They live with how things *appear*. This seems to work well enough.

I can imagine living like that. I would still think about what to do, wondering how things are. But I would not presume that always there is a definite answer: 'the Sceptic's End [= the reason why the sceptic inquires] is quietude [= calm] in respect of matters of opinion and moderate feeling [= being moved naturally] in respect of things unavoidable [= how things appear]' (Bk I, ch. XII).

> Men of talent, who were perturbed by the contradictions in things and in doubt as to which of the alternatives they ought to accept, were led on to inquire what is true in things and what is false, hoping by the settlement of this question to attain quietude. (Bk I, ch. VI)

If I never inquire, I am never 'perturbed'. But I will also make little, if any, progress in my thinking. Alternatively, if I do inquire, I might meet competing views. Is that a problem? No, it seemed to Sextus.

I say 'seemed' because he did not present even his own thinking as definitely true. (Otherwise, he would have been contradicting himself!) He said that 'we simply record each fact, like a chronicler, as it appears to us at the moment' (Bk 1, ch. I).

> The phrase 'I suspend judgement' we adopt in place of 'I am unable to say which of the objects presented I ought to believe, and which I ought to disbelieve', indicating that the objects appear to us equal as regards credibility and incredibility. As to whether they are equal we make no positive assertion; but what we state is what appears to us ... at the time of observation. (Bk 1, ch. XXII)

A Pyrrhonian sceptic opens her mind, in an inquiring way, to all views. She treats them at least as expressions of how-things-appear-in-some-respect-to-some-perspective-at-some-time – but as nothing further. If something seems true to you, this might be because it fits with what you already believed. Why would *that* make it probably true? Sextus said that 'the Sceptic refrains from dogmatizing [= insisting on the truth of what she believes] ...; for the Pyrrhonean philosopher assents to nothing that is non-evident [= nothing that goes beyond appearances]' (Bk 1, ch. VII). Appearances, yes; anything further, no.

That is unworrying: I do not need opinions on everything, let alone confident ones, in order to live well – or even to be philosophical, it seems.

3.2.3 Nāgārjuna's empty words

Sextus envisaged sceptics attaining tranquillity, no longer scratching an itch to find truth-beyond-appearance (section 3.2.2). Around that same time, in India, the Buddhist Nāgārjuna (c. 150–200) developed similar thoughts. He seems to have founded the Madhyamaka school (we met a 'demon story' from it: section 1.4.1). Like Sextus, but possibly unlike Zhuangzi (section 3.2.1), Nāgārjuna developed a sceptical view of what we achieve when inquiring. In his *Vigrahavyāvartanī* (The Dispeller of Objections), he was, it seems, responding to Nyāya ideas (section 3.1.2) about how people know. (The *Nyāya-sūtra* were seemingly from around the same time as Nāgārjuna.)

As we saw, *Nyāya-sūtra* 1.1.3 cited perception, inference, analogy (similarity), and testimony as knowledge sources. Why those four? How do we *establish* their worth (asked Nāgārjuna)?

> If according to you [= an imagined objector, defending Nyāya thinking] objects of some kind are established [= as known] by [= by using] the epistemic instruments [= those Nyāya-approved supposed-knowledge-sources], you have to indicate how ... the epistemic instruments are established [= as known to be ways of producing knowledge] in turn. (Verse 31)

I should explain the word 'epistemic'. Like 'epistemology', it comes from the Greek *'epistēmē'*. Epistemic instruments are ways to seek and, hopefully, to gain something 'epistemic' – such as 'knowledge'. Nāgārjuna asked how we can show that perception, etc., are successful epistemic instruments – ones that produce real knowledge, not merely what feels like knowledge.

Nāgārjuna then argued that no one *can* show that those Nyāya four are successful. He began with a general point:

> if the [Nyāya] epistemic instruments were established [= as known to be ways of producing knowledge] by something that was not an epistemic instrument, the thesis that 'the objects [= any objects] are established [= as known] through the epistemic instruments' is refuted. (Verse 31)

Nyāya thinkers would agree that the worth of their favoured epistemic instruments (perception, etc.) could be known only through some epistemic instrument. But Nāgārjuna then says that such Nyāya thinking must call on *further* epistemic instruments (a fifth, a sixth, etc.) – a sequence whose existence implies the following problem for Nyāya thinking: 'If the epistemic instruments were established by other epistemic instruments, there would be an infinite regress' (verse 32a).

What did Nāgārjuna mean by that? What was his underlying reasoning? Here is my attempt to convey it.

- If we must cite further ways to gain knowledge – in order to explain how perception, etc. (the Nyāya 'favoured four'), are ways to gain knowledge – then those four were not *enough* for explaining how all knowledge arises.
- Still, could citing a further epistemic instrument succeed anyway? Could it explain why those four produce knowledge?
- No, because we would have begun an endless task. We would need to find a *further further* epistemic instrument, for showing that the *first* further one succeeds in *its* task (directed at the initial four); after which, *even further* further further ones are needed; and so on.
- That is what Nāgārjuna meant by 'an infinite regress'. The citing of *ever more* epistemic instruments would stretch endlessly, *ad infinitum* – to infinity.
- In practice, we stop citing, and so the process is not in fact endless: we become tired; we have other things to do. But that is beside the point. We do many things that, *ideally*, we would not do. In this case, ideally, we *would* continue, citing ever further epistemic instruments. (I say 'ideally' because Nāgārjuna was being a philosopher, not a man of everyday casualness. His point was that, once we cease citing further epistemic

instruments, we are *leaving unfinished the job* of establishing that *even the initial Nyāya four* provide knowledge.)
- In which case, to insist that those Nyāya four provide knowledge is more a matter of wishful thinking than of real – accomplished – understanding.

We might ask whether that Nāgārjuna-reasoning could have been sidestepped by Nyāya-thinking. In that same spirit of imagined debate, Nāgārjuna offered this potential objection to his argument. 'As fire illuminates itself as well as others, so the epistemic instruments prove themselves and others' (verse 33). This analogy (offered on behalf of the Nyāya account) was intended to *avoid* needing to continually find further epistemic instruments in support of the Nyāya four. Can each of those four *stand alone* (like a fire providing illumination) – providing you with knowledge of, for example, both a pot in the room *and* your gaining that knowledge of the pot? Nāgārjuna denied so (verse 34): 'fire does not illuminate itself.' How can we compare a fire's illuminating a 'pot in the dark' with its illuminating itself ... in the dark? This makes no sense (continued Nāgārjuna): no fire is *in* the dark; the fire *removes* the darkness. The claimed analogy thus fails to help the Nyāya account.

Nāgārjuna combined that argument against the fire analogy with his argument about infinite regress. His result was an *argument by dilemma*, taking this form:

Either X or not-X. If X, then Y. If not-X, then Y.
Hence, either way, Y.

The idea in such reasoning is that, since X and not-X exhaust the possible options, and each leads to Y, Y is established. In the present case (of Nāgārjuna's reasoning), we had the following instance of that form of reasoning. Either (1) the Nyāya four need to be established by a *further* epistemic instrument, or (2) they can be established *without* the help of a further epistemic instrument. If (1), then (because of the infinite regress) *none of them can be established*. If (2), then (because the fire analogy fails) *none of them can be established*. Hence, either way, *none of them can be established*.

That is indeed a sceptical conclusion, given how tempting its target – the Nyāya thinking – might have seemed. Should we end our inquiry there?

Not yet; what of Nāgārjuna's own thinking? Was *he* claiming knowledge when denying it to others?

Every sceptic must confront that sort of question – the danger of being self-contradictory. We saw Sextus (section 3.2.2) avoiding claims about what is *real*, staying with claims of what *appears*: it appeared to him, upon experiencing apparently conflicting appearances of what is true, that there is no truth-beyond-appearance. Similarly, Nāgārjuna talked of an *emptiness* in reality – its being empty of intrinsic natures. Was that itself a view of reality's intrinsic nature? It should not be. Consider Nāgārjuna's sceptical reasoning. Was it itself a view of intrinsic nature – our own, our being intrinsically empty of knowledge? It should not be. So, does that questioning imply Nāgārjuna's needing to have retracted his sceptical conclusion – since he could not consistently have regarded it as revealing how we *really* are?

Here is his own version of how that 'inconsistency objection' would be made against him (as part of his imagined debate with a Nyāya thinker).

> If the substance of all things is not to be found anywhere [= Nāgārjuna's idea of *universal emptiness*], your [= Nāgārjuna's] assertion which is [therefore] devoid of substance is not able to refute substance [= not able to establish a sceptical result]. (Verse 1)

In reply to which, Nāgārjuna said (verse 29), 'I do not have any thesis' – not one with 'substance'. Really? He *seemed* to have a thesis, ending his reasoning with it – his anti-Nyāya conclusion. Did he not *really* have a sceptical anti-Nyāya result?

I have a suggestion, on Nāgārjuna's behalf, that might help him to remain sceptical (but not self-contradictory). Could he have viewed his words as *tools*, employed temporarily? Was he engaging with the Nyāya account by using *its* terms to reach a result undermining it? Was he then, in a move that the Nyāya account itself would have to approve, 'throwing away' both that account and those words directed against it? He said this (verse 22):

> In this context, the dependent existence of things is emptiness [= the opposite of substance]. ...
>
> For instance a chariot, pot, cloth, and so forth, which are empty of substance because they are dependently originated, perform in their respective ways by removing wood, grass, earth, by containing honey, water, or milk, and by bringing forth protection against cold, wind, or heat. Similarly my speech [= my uses of words in these discussions], which is also without substance because it is dependently arisen [= in responding to the Nyāya account], plays a part in establishing the lack of substance of things.

So, perhaps Nāgārjuna was treating his words purely as tools – like a hammer, say. Even as intellectual tools, they have practical uses; otherwise, they lack meaning 'in themselves'. A hammer is meaningless apart from potential uses. Nāgārjuna's words were being used, initially, in presenting the Nyāya non-sceptical ideas, before shaping those ideas into a failure (by Nyāya thinkers) to evade a sceptical result. Once this failure has been given form and shape (like a sculpture) in his reasoning, all of those words – the Nyāya ones, along with Nāgārjuna's – are discarded, not denoting a lingering sceptical reality. Emptiness remains. The words fade away, their job done. An appearance has been reached. That is all.

3.2.4 Abū Ḥāmid Muḥammad ibn Muḥammad al-Ghazālī's dreams

Centuries passed; sceptical worries persisted. Here is one from Abū Ḥāmid Muḥammad ibn Muḥammad al-Ghazālī (1058–1111), a Persian theologian, jurist, and mystic, born in Tus (within modern-day Iran) and notable for questioning philosophy's coherence. This sceptical argument is from *The Rescuer from Error*. It begins optimistically.

> The thirst for apprehending things as they really are has been my preoccupation and principle from a very early age. It is part of my God-given instinct and nature, a matter of temperament not of choice or invention.

Al-Ghazālī wanted knowledge of 'things as they really are'. Could he gain it?

> [E]very knowledge that is insecure is not certain knowledge.
> Then I searched the sum of my knowledge and found myself devoid of knowledge characterized by this attribute, apart from sensory beliefs and necessary beliefs.

Ah! So there *is* some 'certain knowledge' – indicated by the phrase 'apart from'? Do the senses provide some? Does reason provide some (of what is 'necessary')?

Alas! For al-Ghazālī, even those beliefs succumbed: 'After a lengthy process of doubt, my mind did not allow me to maintain my trust in' any of these beliefs.

Why? What was the argument behind that 'process of doubt'? Al-Ghazālī started by locating the source of our 'confidence [especially] in sensory beliefs'. Vision is the 'strongest sense'. Yet it cannot bear the weight even of our sensory beliefs – *or* our judgements of reason. Al-Ghazālī imagined 'sense perception ... saying' this to him.

> Do you not believe things in dreams and imagine situations that you believe to be permanent and stable, never doubting them while you are in that state? And do you not then wake up and come to know that all your imaginings and beliefs were baseless and futile?

But al-Ghazālī worried even about those reassuring moments. He considered this question (still posed for him by 'sense perception'): 'Why are you so sure that everything that you believe in your waking state on the basis of the senses or reason is true in relation to your current state?' Even if al-Ghazālī felt sure, what did that prove? He imagined sense perception's proposing a different way for him to respond.

> A state may arise that bears the same relation to your waking state as your waking state does to your dream state. By comparison to that state your waking state would be like sleep. If such a state were to occur, you would become certain that all the things conjured up by your reason were inconsequential imaginings.

So, could al-Ghazālī look beyond the two everyday states, of dreaming and being awake, in a particular way? Specifically, might there be a state that regards being awake as a lesser guide to reality, much as being awake regards just dreaming as a lesser guide to reality? This further state would be more accurate and insightful than being awake is. It might regard *both* dreaming and being awake as inadequate guides to reality. If we compare dreaming with being awake, the latter seems like an excellent guide. But if there is a further possible state, more reliable than those two, then even being awake should not be regarded as a state producing real knowledge.

Did al-Ghazālī have ideas of what the further possible state – a state *beyond* being awake, as being awake is beyond dreaming – could be? Two were mentioned.

> Perhaps that state is what the mystics hold to be their state, for they claim to have a vision in their states when they are immersed in themselves and lose awareness of their senses, which does not agree with these rational beliefs.

Here is the second.

> Or perhaps that state is death, for the Prophet of God (blessings be upon him) said: 'People are asleep, and when they die they wake up.' Thus, perhaps the temporal life is slumber by comparison with the afterlife, and when you die things will appear differently to you from the way they do now. At that point, you will be told: 'We have removed your veil, and your vision is now acute.' [Qur'ān 50: 22]

Al-Ghazālī was describing a possibly enticing vision, arising in response to his sceptical reasoning. As to the sceptical argument itself, he sought a rational response to it – but failed. No matter, though: 'Eventually, God cured me of this disease [= this scepticism] and my mind was restored to health and balance. ... This [came] about ... by a light that God Almighty cast into my breast, which is the key to the greater part of cognizance.'

I cannot set aside al-Ghazālī's supposed escape route from his sceptical argument: if God really did assist him in that way, so be it. Until similarly aided by God, I must remain alone, puzzling over this sceptical argument (and others that we have encountered).

3.2.5 Francisco Sanches's unknowing words

When reading sceptical arguments for no one's knowing anything, we should notice precisely what is being denied: what would knowledge be, *if* we were to have it? Earlier (section 3.1), we asked 'What is knowledge?' The *Nyāya-sūtra* offered a possible answer (section 3.1.2); in reply to which, Nāgārjuna pounced (section 3.2.3). Suppose, more generally, that someone says 'knowing = X'; whereupon some sceptic pounces: 'Because X is impossible for us, so is knowledge!' This will be surprising if we had thought that X *is* possible for us.

Sceptical pouncing is especially surprising if X has been championed by a great philosopher, influential for centuries. Let us meet Francisco Sanches (1551–1623), a Portuguese doctor and philosopher in France. His 1581 book *Quod nihil scitur* (That Nothing Is Known) argued against Aristotle's account of knowing. Sanches's message was that, if *this* (Aristotle's account of it) is what knowledge would need to be like, there is none.

How did Sanches write? Boldly. Even brashly. But memorably. Here are some of his ideas (presented in terms that look beyond Aristotle's account).

If we can know the world, we do it by knowing '*natures* of things'. How, though? We must reach for names of things, our best words for describing reality: 'the entire investigation is about naming.' But always these are arbitrarily chosen. Even when we use more of them, seeking an instructive definition, how can this help? Is it *only* more words, never reflecting reality directly?

We might reply that definitions can succeed if the right words are chosen: 'You will say that what you define by the terms "animal, rational, mortal" [= as an example] is a thing (namely Man), not a verbal concept.'

But Sanches had 'further doubts about the word "animal", the word "rational", etc.' These are substantive words, each denoting something real and possibly complex. What is involved in defining *them*?

> You will further define these concepts by higher genera [= the plural of 'genus'] and differentiae [= the plural of 'differentia', which is 'difference'] ... until you arrive at the thing's 'Being'. [But] I will ask the same question about each of these names in turn.

Defining seeks categories ('genera') within which to place something – but (said Sanches) this is *always just more* words. This forces us to find even more words, now for defining those previously offered ones.

How would that process end? Or will it continue indefinitely? We might think that it could end with one special word – 'Being' – that denotes the largest category of all. Is 'Being' *beyond being defined* by other words, because it *underlies all* other words?

> Finally, I will ask it [= my same question] concerning the last of them, namely Being; for you do not know what this term signifies. You will say that you will not define this Being, for it has no higher genus to which it belongs.

Yet even that would not be the same as this special word's being *understood*.

> This I do not understand; nor do you. *You* do not know what Being is; much less do I. Yet you will say that we must eventually make an end of questioning. This does not resolve my doubt ...

How could it? Just because, in practice, we must end our questioning somewhere, sometime, this does not amount to insight being reached. It is no better than 'I'm tired now. I must stop!' As Sanches said, '*You* are obliged to reveal your ignorance ...; so also am *I*.'

We might not *feel* ignorant. We can feel as if we make progress when constructing definitions, reasoning from these, constructing complexity. But we do not gain knowledge if we do not base our thinking on knowledge of *natures*. And we do not if we are merely debating meanings of *words*. Words are not facts. Words are not the world. Words are tools. We *can* misuse them, mistaking them for a further reality – one that we hope they name.

> True knowledge, ..., if it existed, would ... proceed from a free intellect; and if such an intellect does not by itself perceive a fact, then no 'demonstrations' will make it perceive. Accordingly, 'demonstration' constrains only the ignorant, for whom belief alone is sufficient.

Sanches did offer (in capitals!) a conception of knowing.

KNOWLEDGE IS PERFECT UNDERSTANDING OF A THING.

Then he continued arguing that we never really have this. It is what our knowledge *would* be. Sanches said, 'I do not know what "understanding" is; define it for me.' But why bother? For 'definitions cannot be *proved*, but have to be *believed* ... [Even] first principles will be things assumed, not things known. ... In order to know, we have to be ignorant!'

Nor can we evade these problems by asking other people. Think (recalling Sextus: section 3.2.2) of variability in opinions and experiences. What of our powers of perception? Here we confront our imperfections. Isn't reality too large for us to know? For a start, 'who has complete understanding of God?' Moreover, 'in order to understand any one thing perfectly we must understand everything; and who is capable of this?'

Sanches's book ended bluntly, with a single-word question: *QUOD?* (*WHAT?*)
Indeed.

3.2.6 René Descartes's demon
Did 'big' philosophical doubts end with Sanches (section 3.2.5)? Far from it. The early 1600s were greeted by a sceptical argument whose aura pervades present philosophy. It is from Descartes. Earlier (section 1.2.4), we met his dualism – a person's being a combination of non-physical mind and physical body. That was from Descartes's 'Meditation VI'. However, he had begun those *Meditations*, in 'Meditation I', by challenging himself to overcome some striking sceptical arguments. I will mention two of them.

He started optimistically, citing instances of what (it seemed to him) he could never be mistaken in believing: 'two and three added together are five, and a square has no more than four sides. It seems impossible that transparent truths should incur any suspicion of being false.'

Yet *is* that impossible? Descartes reminded himself of his 'long-standing opinion that there is an omnipotent [= all-powerful] God who made me the kind of creature that I am.' He then raised these questions.

> How do I know that he [= God] has not brought it about that there is no earth, no sky, ... no place, while ... ensuring that all these things appear to me to exist just as they do now? ... how do I know that God has not brought it about that I too go wrong every time I add two and three or count the sides of a square ...?

An all-powerful God could do such things, yes? And if He was doing it, then Descartes's evidence (how 'all these things appear to me') would be misleading.

But Descartes's idea of God also includes His being 'supremely good', which suggests that He would never

– let alone always – permit such deceptions. However (continues Descartes), even

> if it were inconsistent with his [= God's] goodness to have created me such that I am deceived all the time, it would seem equally foreign to his goodness to allow me to be deceived even occasionally; yet this last assertion cannot be made.

That 'last assertion cannot be made' because Descartes does at times make mistakes in his beliefs, and so is misled by trusting his evidence, at least 'occasionally'. Why does God allow even that? And why not always so, if even occasionally?

Descartes then reinforced that worry. He supposed (for the sake of argument) that no God perfectly oversees how he forms his beliefs. How would that affect his argument? If there was no God, would this make Descartes's beliefs more secure, less likely to be mistaken? No, it would render the sceptical possibility more likely to be correct. For if God was not overseeing Descartes and his beliefs, then

> I [would] have arrived at my present state by fate or chance or a continuous chain of events, or by some other means [= all of these being some means other than God]; yet since deception and error seem to be imperfections, the less powerful they [= anyone proposing one of those alternatives to God's role in my forming beliefs] make my original cause [= one of those alternatives], the more likely it is that I am so imperfect as to be deceived all the time [in my beliefs].

The reasoning is clear: if not God, then something less powerful (and perhaps less good) created Descartes-the-person-with-beliefs; in which case, it is even more likely that the process resulted in Descartes's having mistaken beliefs. (Weakening how he gains beliefs increases imperfections in the process, making false beliefs more likely to arise.)

> I have no answer to these arguments, but am finally compelled to admit that there is not one of my former beliefs about which a doubt may not properly be raised; and this is not a flippant or ill-considered conclusion ... So in future I must withhold my assent from these former beliefs just as carefully as I would from obvious falsehoods, if I want to discover any certainty.

That completes one of Descartes's sceptical arguments. He might have ended 'Meditation I' with it – but he did not. He added another sceptical argument, helping him 'to remember' the first. We may think of the second one as a *memory aid* – needed because 'My habitual opinions keep coming back.' We have habits of belief, while forgetting that many – maybe all – of our beliefs could be false even when feeling true. What did Descartes do to avoid being trapped in such habits? He *deliberately overcompensated* for that potential weakness.

> I think it will be a good plan to turn my will in completely the opposite direction and deceive myself, by pretending for a time that these former opinions are utterly false and imaginary.

This was Descartes's deciding to pretend, to himself, that even what seems true is not really true. What else did he need to pretend as part of that story?

> I will suppose therefore that not God, who is supremely good and the source of truth, but rather some malicious demon of the utmost power and cunning has employed all his energies in order to deceive me.

That was dramatic, especially in seventeenth-century France. Descartes was supposing, in effect, that this 'demon' – *not* God – was overseeing his beliefs. This would have made the demon a threat – a force for deception.

But Descartes was not conceding defeat. He adopted what could be seen as a defence, while continuing to develop his *Meditations*. He said that 'the deceiver … will be unable to impose on me in the slightest degree' – because Descartes would make himself invisible, in a sense: he would *suspend* all belief. How would this evade the demon? Simple: if Descartes had no beliefs, he also had no false ones, hence none that were misleading him.

Or was that conceding too much to the threat of the demon? No, said Descartes, 'because the task [of suspending all belief] … does not involve action but merely the acquisition of knowledge.' Descartes could still *do* things. He would just not be claiming to be a *knower*. We saw Sextus (section 3.2.2) suggesting that one can live without beliefs about reality. We now find Descartes suggesting, to himself, that he could live without knowledge.

This second sceptical worry is often called *the evil demon argument*. Can you know that no evil demon – no spirit as powerful as God, but evil, in wanting you always to be making mistakes – controls your cognitive life? You believe that it is not happening. This belief is comforting and habitual. Is that *all* it is, though?

Readings for 3.2

For the *Zhuangzi*, see *Zhuangzi: The Essential Writings*, trans. B. Ziporyn (Indianapolis: Hackett, 2009); quotations from pp. 17, 18, 76. For Sextus, see *Sextus Empiricus: Outlines of Pyrrhonism*, trans. R. G. Bury (Cambridge, MA: Harvard University Press, 1933); quotations from pp. 5, 7, 9–11, 19, 115. For

Nāgārjuna, see *The Dispeller of Disputes: Nāgārjuna's Vigrahavyāvartanī*, trans. and commentary J. Westerhoff (New York: Oxford University Press, 2010); quotations from pp. 19, 27, 29, 30. For al-Ghazālī, see *Medieval Islamic Philosophical Writings*, ed. M. A. Khalidi (Cambridge: Cambridge University Press, 2005); quotations from pp. 60, 61–3. For Sanches, see *That Nothing Is Known*, ed. E. Limbrick and D. F. S. Thomson (Cambridge: Cambridge University Press, 1988); quotations from pp. 174, 175, 177, 178, 188, 200, 201, 206–7. For Descartes, see 'Meditation I', in *Descartes: Meditations on First Philosophy*, ed. and trans. J. Cottingham (rev. edn, Cambridge: Cambridge University Press, 1996); quotations from pp. 14–15.

3.3 Knowing a physical world?

3.3.1 René Descartes's dreams

Section 3.2 engaged with dramatic sceptical arguments for *no one's knowing anything*. But some scepticisms have smaller targets. How does it feel, for example, to be told that you know nothing of the physical world? What if a good argument could be given for that sceptical pronouncement?

We met al-Ghazālī's dreaming argument earlier (section 3.2.4), with its doubting our capacity for knowing through either our senses *or* our intellect. I will now examine how Descartes, a few centuries later, talked about dreaming in relation *just* to our senses. His *dreaming argument* appeared immediately before his *evil demon argument* (section 3.2.6).

He began with this reflection upon some incidents in his life.

> How often, asleep at night, am I [= have I been] convinced of ... familiar events – that I am here in my

dressing-room, sitting by the fire – when in fact I am
[= when I was actually] lying undressed in bed!

Descartes was reminding himself that his life has 'often' included misleading dreams. They felt like real experiences of the world; they were not, though.

But that was then; this – the moment when Descartes was doing his philosophical thinking – is a now. He assured himself that he was not being misled in that way *when* writing and thinking the following thoughts:

> my eyes are certainly wide awake when I look at this piece of paper; I shake my head and it is not asleep; as I stretch out and feel my hand I do so deliberately, and I know what I am doing. All this would not happen with such distinctness to someone asleep.

Yet how good is that reasoning (asked the philosophically careful Descartes)? To repeat: one generally feels wide awake. However (continued Descartes), what of the following doubt? 'As if I did not remember other occasions when I have been tricked by exactly similar thoughts while asleep!' From which realisation, Descartes worriedly inferred this.

> I see plainly that there are never any sure signs by means of which being awake can be distinguished from being asleep. The result is that I begin to feel dazed, and this very feeling only reinforces the notion that I may be asleep.

That was Descartes then. What of oneself now? (You can apply this thinking to yourself. I will try it on myself.) Might I be asleep? I am confident that I am not. But can I be certain that I am not? *Only* if I can find 'sure signs' – ones I can use at the time to distinguish my 'being awake ... from being asleep'. Descartes was conceding that *he* could not find such signs when writing and thinking about this. (Dreaming can include feelings of writing and thinking.)

That is this sceptical argument's first step. It seems to be saying that no one can know that they are awake. It feels as if I am awake. But I do not really know it (according to this argument): I do not know that I am not dreaming.

And from that step (possibly already worrying), does a worse one follow? If I do not know that I am not dreaming, how can I know anything now about my *surroundings*? I would be relying on current experiences that seem to be about the world around me. Again, though, these might be merely part of my currently dreaming. Hence, my experiences now are not providing me with *good enough evidence* supporting my beliefs about the world. It seems to me that I am sitting in a chair. Yet might I be dreaming this? I seem to be seeing a hand – mine. Might I be dreaming this, too? And so on. Do I not know *anything* of my own body, let alone anyone else's, let alone of a wider physical world?

3.3.2 George Berkeley's ideas

Descartes's dreaming argument (section 3.3.1) denies us knowledge of the physical world. It issues a challenge – and denies that this can be met. Can you find a secure route, of good reasoning, from your known 'inner' ideas (so that you know what you are apparently seeing) – to a known 'outer' reality (so that you know what, if anything, you are really seeing)? Not if Descartes's *external world scepticism* is correct. It claims that we have no knowledge of anything about a world external to, or beyond, our 'inner' evidence.

But what if the physical ('external') world that we claim to experience with our ideas *just is* our ideas – our 'inner' evidence? The 'outer' world would not be quite so outer. It would be real, albeit in a different way from what we might have expected. Would this be a way to evade Descartes's dreaming argument?

Meet George Berkeley (1685–1753), an Irish philosopher and bishop. Whether we can know the physical world depends partly on *what kind of thing it is* – not just its day-to-day physical intricacies but its *underlying nature as physical at all*. Berkeley's view was clear: physical matter is mental matter. What could that mean?

Here are details from his *Treatise Concerning the Principles of Human Knowledge* (1710).

> It is indeed an opinion strangely prevailing amongst men, that houses, mountains, rivers, and in a word all sensible [= able to be sensed or perceived] objects, have an existence natural or real, distinct from their being perceived by the understanding. (Sec. 4)

That is what people generally assume about the physical world – namely, that it can exist even when not being perceived. But their assumption is mistaken, claimed Berkeley. He began by asking 'what is meant by the term "exist" when applied to sensible things' (sec. 3). Here is his answer.

> The table I write on, I say, exists, that is, I see and feel it; and if I were out of my study I should say it existed, meaning thereby that if I was in my study I might perceive it, or that some other spirit [= mind] actually does perceive it. ... This is all that I can understand by these and the like [= similar] expressions. For as to what is said of the absolute existence of unthinking things without any relation to their being perceived, that seems perfectly unintelligible. (Sec. 3)

The key step in that reasoning is 'The table I write on ... exists, that is, I see and feel it.' The key element in that key step is the 'that is'. Because it amounts to 'equals', it gives Berkeley's sentence the form 'X = Y'.

I am puzzled. *Does* a table's existing equal – genuinely equal (being neither-more-nor-less-than) – its being seen and felt? Berkeley continued, inferring the following (from what he said a moment ago).

> Their *esse* is *percipi* [= their being or existence is nothing more or less than their being perceived], nor is it possible that they should have existence, out of [= away from] the minds or thinking things which perceive them. (Sec. 3)

That is Berkeley's *idealism* about reality (as in 'idea-(l) ism', not 'ideal-ism'). It is a *metaphysical account* of the physical world. It posits ideas-in-minds and thinkers-with-minds. It finds 'perfectly unintelligible' any counter-claim that something exists without being a mind or an idea-in-mind. Even a physical world is nothing beyond a kind of mental world.

I will explain that picture with Berkeley's example. Think about a table's details. I accept that colours, as we describe them ('It is brown'), reflect our eyes reacting to what is 'out there': the table is brown in that sense, reflecting how our eyes process light waves reaching them from the table. Are light waves colours? The same sort of question arises for sounds. If a tree falls in the forest, with no one around, does it make a sound? Everyone has heard that question, as a philosophy joke. (What if no one hears the joke? Does it exist anyway?) Yet it captures a serious point. The tree would not make a sound *of the kind* that we experience. Does it make no sound in any *other* sense? Are sound waves not really sounds – because they are not 'completed' sounds?

I mentioned that Berkeley was a bishop. Here he offered a philosophically clever argument for God's existing. For if (as Berkeley claimed) everything physical is mental – an idea, or a group of ideas, in *some* mind

– and if no *person's* mind hears the tree falling, then some other kind-of-being's mind does so. Let that be God's mind, encompassing everything! Thus, the physical world ultimately owes its existence to God's mind – 'the mind of some eternal spirit' (sec. 6). Even when we are not observing some thing, it can exist – thanks to God's awareness of it. (And this sounds like something that a bishop *should* say.)

Before we accept that idealist picture, however, what of the table's other qualities? Even if we agree that colour-as-we-experience-it is created only when something in the object is perceived by us, what of that further 'something in the object'? For example, do the table's particles exist 'in themselves', without needing to be observed (ideas in a mind)? In Berkeley's terms, this amounts to the question of whether *matter*, in the sense of 'unthinking substance' (sec. 7), exists beyond our sensing of something. Even if we agree with Berkeley that a table's being brown depends on its being sensed, what of the table's shape or size? These could seem to be qualities that *can* be present in the table without ever being sensed, by us or anything else. 'It is said extension [= occupying space] is a mode or accident [= a feature, property, or quality] of matter, and that matter is the *substratum* that supports it' (sec. 16). That word '*substratum*' is suggestive. The idea (on this suggestion – 'it is said' – being considered by Berkeley) would be that the table has a core – some underlying 'matter', an unthinking substance. To this core would be *attached* the table's various properties – shape, size, colour, etc.

However, Berkeley dismissed that suggestion as relying on an empty metaphor. 'It is evident "support" cannot here be taken in its usual or literal sense, as when we say that pillars support a building. In what sense therefore must it be taken?' (sec. 16). He found no good answer:

when I consider the ... signification of the words 'material substance', I am convinced there is no distinct meaning annexed to them [= no meaning other than what he has described]. (Sec. 17)

So, as a whole, the world is always in God's mind. But at times parts of it are also in your mind. Is this welcome news? Do you feel more powerful – or even less so?

Readings for 3.3

For Descartes, see 'Meditation I', in *Descartes: Meditations on First Philosophy*, ed. and trans. J. Cottingham (rev. edn, Cambridge: Cambridge University Press, 1996); quotations from p. 13. For Berkeley, see *Berkeley: Philosophical Writings*, ed. D. M. Clarke (Cambridge: Cambridge University Press, 2008); quotations from pp. 84, 85, 88, 89.

3.4 Knowing other minds?

3.4.1 Dharmakīrti's idealist reasonings

Berkeley regarded reality (section 3.3.2) as containing only minds and ideas. But how does anyone know that there are minds at all – 'minds' plural? It seems that one's own mind is real. What of anyone else's? Do I, while writing this, know that you, reading this, have a mind? That question may sound bizarre. Please stay with it for a moment, though. It is posing the sceptical problem of *other minds* – another's thoughts, feelings, intentions, etc. This is the philosophical challenge of explaining how one ever knows that these exist. Can one know that someone *else* has an active mind, with an 'inner' life?

That *is* a socially unsettling question. I am not encouraging its being taken seriously *except* in a philosophical spirit. So, in that spirit, I ask myself: when was the last time that I directly experienced another's pain? Never! How, then, can I know that there is pain inside someone else, even when blood seeps from a wound? How can I know that she feels pain when saying 'I'm in pain'? If I never directly sense her feelings, her thoughts, do I never know that they exist?

Here is a suggestion, a step towards trying to answer that question. Maybe direct experience of another's pain is not the only way to know it. Can it be known indirectly? I usually assume that this is what *words* provide, such as when someone says 'I'm in pain.' Yet maybe those are merely words.

Let us see what Dharmakīrti (c. 550–610), a Buddhist logician, wrote about this. From South India, he moved to Nālandā, a centre of Buddhist training (in effect, a monastic university) in what is now the state of Bihar. Like Berkeley, Dharmakīrti was an idealist (endorsing the Yogācāra doctrine of *cittamātra* – 'mind-only'). Unlike Berkeley, he did not posit a God. For Dharmakīrti, there were only ideas and minds – without one of those minds being God's. How did the idealist Dharmakīrti argue that there are other (human) minds?

In his *Santānāntara-siddhi* (Proof of Other Mental Continua; originally Sanskrit, extant in Tibetan translation, one of his series of 'seven works on epistemology and logic', as they were called in Tibetan annals), Dharmakīrti presented an imagined dialogue with a realist opponent.

> Dharmakīrti: Even if bodily actions and speech *were* real entities apart from mental representations [= of them, by an onlooker], how would that help you [= the realist] to cognize the existence of another mind?

Knowing other minds?

That is a strategic question. As an idealist, Dharmakīrti did not *believe* that 'bodily actions and speech' are 'real entities apart from mental representations' – ideas – of them. But he *supposed*, for argument's sake, that they are. Would their being so make it more likely that other people have inner mental lives? The realist replies that it would. Why?

> Realist: Because the real bodily actions and speech of another person are the effects of the movement of the other person's mind.

The realist is interpreting what we observe – another's 'bodily actions and speech' – as being *caused* by the other's inner mental life. This is how the realist infers the other person's *having* an inner mental life.

Dharmakīrti replied by questioning whether we *need* to talk of those 'bodily actions and speech' rather than our ideas of them.

> Dharmakīrti: How is your case different [= in its style of reasoning] from ours [= the idealist's case]? For we believe [= like you] that the *representations* [= ideas] of another person's body and speech are the effects of another person's mind. It is just that we do not believe that there are 'real' bodily actions and speech, or external objects, which exist apart from the representations [= ideas] of them. So, why not take the simpler course, as we do, and simply say that other minds are inferred directly on the basis of our own immediate *impressions* [= our ideas] of the actions and speech of others?

I added emphasis to 'impressions'. Dharmakīrti was pointing to what Descartes and Berkeley, centuries later, also highlighted (section 3.3). He noted our being restricted, when inferring something's existence in the 'outer' world, to what appears to us – whatever representations (ideas) we have. These are needed. Is anything else needed? What else must we infer as existing? Nothing?

> Dharmakīrti: ... if representations are *necessary* for cognizing another person's mind, why not say, as we do, that they are also sufficient?

This seems like a rhetorical question, affirming our not needing to posit 'external actions' *in addition to* our ideas of them (since the ideas might be 'sufficient' for explanatory purposes).

Still, some of those ideas apparently about others' thoughts and feelings seem not to come *from* ourselves – from our own minds. This is evidence for their coming from other minds. To say even this, however, is not to concede our positing something beyond ideas. We are recognising that our own minds do not *create* whatever they seem to be about or denoting. This reinforces the impression that some ideas are about, and prompted by, *other* minds.

> Dharmakīrti: ... we cognize the existence of other minds by means of the representations themselves [= the ones that we have], which are caused directly by those other minds. Those impressions [= ours] which are caused by a movement of one's own mind are experienced as our own, while the impressions [= ours] caused by other persons are experienced as external things.

It is all ideas. It is all seemings. That is enough, on an idealist's world-view. In that way, there can be 'those other minds'.

3.4.2 John Stuart Mill's realist analogies
How might a *realist* about the wider world try to solve the sceptical problem of other minds? We heard from the *idealist* Dharmakīrti (section 3.4.1). Now we meet

an argument from the English philosopher John Stuart Mill (1806–73). When wondering about other people's minds, Dharmakīrti claimed that idealist evidence was as good as any realist evidence. What might such realist evidence look like?

Mill began by focusing on himself: 'I am aware, by experience, of … my body, … which my experience shows to be an universal condition of every part of my thread of consciousness.' So, Mill was aware of his own body and 'consciousness', including the fact, given to him 'by experience', that his body is always a 'condition' of his consciousness.

By this stage of the book, we realise that there may be sceptical doubts even about whether Mill could know his own body. For the moment, though, I set aside those doubts by supposing that a person can know her own mind and body, along with another's body. Can she also know about the other's mind? Mill claimed (just now) that he 'is aware' of a link between his body and his consciousness. Could this help him to know of another's consciousness?

Here is how Mill introduced other bodies into his account.

> I am also aware of a great number of other [bodies], resembling [mine], but which have no connexion [= connection], such as that has [= such as my own body has], with the remainder of my thread of consciousness.

If I am to 'live' these words from Mill, I will say the following: I observe other bodies, similar to mine, but I lack awareness of their being *linked to my* thoughts and feelings. What did Mill then say? 'This disposes me to draw an inductive inference, that those [other bodies] are connected with other threads of consciousness, as mine is with my own.' 'Inductive' is a technical term. Inductive inferences are extrapolations (I call them 'spreading' movements-of-mind) in one's thinking, *from* some observations *to* something beyond them. Mill was aware of his own body–consciousness link. He observed other bodies. He inferred, inductively, their being likewise embedded within body–consciousness links. Hence, Mill infers, there are other consciousnesses.

But that was not the end of his argument. How *strong* was that inference (he asked himself)? 'If the evidence stopped there, the inference would be but an hypothesis; reaching only to the inferior degree of inductive evidence called Analogy.' Do I want to settle for the 'hypothesis' that other people have thoughts and feelings? No. It seems also as if Mill was not enthusiastic about relying on 'Analogy'.

Yet philosophers usually call Mill's argument an *argument by analogy*. And in fact he apparently thought that in this case a *very strong* analogy is available.

> The evidence, however, does not stop here [= with our bodies looking similar]; for, – having made the supposition that real feelings, though not experienced by myself [= hence, others' feelings], lie behind those phaenomena of my own consciousness [= those ideas I have], which, from their resemblance to my body, I call other human bodies [= hence, those ideas I have that appear to be *of* other bodies, with 'their resemblance to my own body'], – I find that my subsequent consciousness [= my mind a little later] presents those very sensations [= further ideas], of speech heard, of movements and other outward demeanour seen, and so forth [= hence, further ideas apparently of other bodies' states and actions], which, being the effects ... of actual feelings in my own case [= hence, states and actions that in my case are caused by my feelings], I should expect to follow upon [= to follow] those other hypothetical feelings [= those feelings that I have hypothesised as linked with those other bodies] if they [= those others' hypothesised feelings] really exist; and

thus the hypothesis is verified [= the hypothesis that those other feelings, linked with those other bodies, *do* exist].

I will explain the core of that reasoning.

Mill's main point was that an inductive hypothesis can also *explain* what has been observed – hence making clear why those particular observations arose. Some explanations are especially strong. One mark of this strength is when an explanation helps with *predictions*, such as of further possible observations. Mill seems to have offered his 'supposition' (of there being other minds) in that spirit. Positing an inner life for someone else can be part of *explaining* and *predicting* her bodily actions. The hypothesis is thus 'verified' (as Mill said, above) by what one *continues* observing and predicting as to how other bodies act. One sees and hears them acting like one's own. One also observes similar actions – some of one's own – being linked to one's own thoughts and feelings. So, Mill was reinforced in his supposition that thoughts and feelings are likewise 'behind' those other bodies and their actions.

> It is thus proved inductively that there is a sphere beyond my consciousness: i.e., that there are other consciousnesses beyond it ... And it is proved inductively, that ... the laws which obtain in my consciousness also obtain in the sphere beyond it; that those other threads of consciousness are beings similar to myself.

Should I share Mill's confidence? Feeling pain is one thing, and many predictable bodily movements are apparently associated with it. But I am unsure that there is an outwardly observable, internally felt way in which I have been acting while reading this book, say – thinking, feeling unsure, then clearer, puzzled again, etc. This is an inner life. Yet no one else could see signs of it in my behaviour. I can appear to them just the same as I appear when *not* thinking.

Mill might have replied that his argument shows how we establish a *basis* – a first step – for showing that *something* 'inner' exists within others. Would that move us at least past the main challenge posed in other minds scepticism? After all, such scepticism claims that, as a matter of principle, no one knows another's thinking or feeling *even something*.

3.4.3 Edith Stein's empathy

Could we disprove the sceptical stance about other minds by describing, as a realistic possibility, how one might *empathise* with another person? Not sympathise; empathise – somehow 'putting oneself into' another's consciousness. When we speak of empathising, might we be literally correct?

Edith Stein (1891–1942) was an early contributor to philosophy's phenomenological tradition, concentrating on the nature of consciousness. Born a Jew in Breslau (now Wrocław, Poland), she became a Catholic nun. Her doctoral dissertation, on empathy, had apparent implications for the sceptical problem of other minds.

Empathy is 'the experience of foreign consciousness' ('foreign' meaning 'another'). It is 'how human beings comprehend the psychic life of their fellows'. Although this comprehension is 'a kind of act of perceiving', it is not simply perceiving.

> I have no outer perception [= 'normal' perception] of the pain [of another]. Outer perception is a term for acts in which spatio-temporal concrete being [= objects] and occurring [= events] come to me in embodied givenness [= appear to me as physical]. ... The pain [= of another] is not a thing and is not given to me as a thing, even when I am aware of it 'in' the pained countenance [= even when someone looks in pain].

So, how is empathy *like* perception?

> [I]n progressive perception [= such as looking, in sequence, at an object's different sides] I can always [choose to] bring new sides of the thing to primordial givenness [= to experiencing something with a direct 'active' immediacy]. ... [For example,] I can consider the expression of pain, more accurately, the change of face I empathically grasp as an expression of pain, from as many sides as I desire. Yet, in principle, I can never get an 'orientation' where the pain itself is primordially given.

Thus, no matter how closely I perceive someone, there are no literal *angles* from which I can experience – observe – their pain: 'Perception has its object before it in embodied givenness; empathy does not.' In empathy, 'we are dealing with an act which is primordial as present experience though non-primordial in content.' Stein seemed to be saying that, although empathising is immediate and active, it is about something not happening to the empathiser. Stein continued:

> when I ... try to bring another's mood to clear givenness to myself ... the content, having pulled me into it, is no longer really an object. I am now no longer turned to [= attending to] the content but [instead I am attending] to the object of it, am at [= am now functioning as] the subject of the content in the original subject's place.

That is, if I empathise with someone feeling pain, I am not thinking *about* her pain; I am 'at one with' it (my term, not Stein's). Would I thereby experience it just as she does? No. Consider another example:

> while I am living in the other's joy, I do not feel primordial joy. It does not issue live from my 'I'. Neither does it have the character of once having [been]

lived like remembered joy. ... In my non-primordial experience I feel, as it were, led by a primordial one not experienced by me but still there, manifesting itself in my non-primordial experience.

Does empathy thereby give one knowledge of another's 'inner' life? Stein did not regard empathy in that way. She distinguished such knowing from empathising.

> Knowledge reaches its object but does not 'have' it. It stands before its object but does not see it. Knowledge is blind, empty, and restless, always pointing back to some kind of experienced, seen act. And the experience back to which knowledge of foreign experience points is called empathy. I know of another's grief, i.e., either I have comprehended this grief empathically but am longer in the 'intuiting' act, [being] content with empty knowledge, or I know of this grief on the basis of a communication. Then the grief is not given to me intuitively, though surely to the communicator. ... And from his experience I once more have an experience, i.e., I comprehend the grief empathically.

Has Stein shown exactly what empathy is, in relation to such knowing? She did not claim quite that: 'It is enough that we have reciprocally limited them.' In other words, it is enough that we have *sharpened* our understanding, *of each in terms of the other*. Here is part of the story of where X ends – and where Y begins. It can be helpful to chart partial boundaries before, if ever, we know full ones. That could be at least *some* real understanding.

Readings for 3.4

For Dharmakīrti, see T. E. Wood, *Mind Only: A Philosophical and Doctrinal Analysis of the Vijñānavāda*

(Delhi: Motilal Barnasidass, [1991] 1994), Appendix II (trans. Wood); quotations from pp. 211–12. For Mill, see *An Examination of Sir William Hamilton's Philosophy* (4th edn, London: Longmans, Green, Reader & Dyer, 1872); quotations from pp. 259–60. For Stein, see *On the Problem of Empathy*, 3rd edn, trans. W. Stein (Washington, DC: ICS, 1989); quotations from pp. 6–7, 10, 11, 19–20.

3.5 Knowing in action

3.5.1 Wang Yangming's knowledge-action unity
In the past few sections, we have engaged with some forms of knowledge-scepticism. Why, exactly, might we find them confronting? Why does it *matter* whether we have knowledge?

One possibility is that knowing matters because it helps us to *do* things – moving, lifting, choosing, thinking, etc. Generally, we do not collide with things or drop them. Generally, we think in ways that seem to work well enough. Is such success due to our knowing much – and our using this knowledge well? (Remember Socrates, in the *Meno*, immediately calling knowledge useful: section 3.1.1.)

We met a version of that question earlier. Recall Descartes's distinguishing between knowledge and action (section 3.2.6), when he imagined suspending his beliefs while battling sceptical self-challenges. He seemed to feel relief at the thought that he *could* suspend belief without losing agency. Even when formulating sceptical worries, in casting aside his claims to knowledge, he was assuming that he could still do things – hence that he could live normally even while thinking sceptically.

Not all philosophers, however, have been willing to separate action from knowledge. Wang Yangming

(1472–1529), from Zhejiang Province, did not. (He was the 'Wang' in the title of the 'Lu-Wang school' of Neo-Confucianism.) One of his ideas was that there is an inherent *unity* of knowledge and action:

> knowing is the intent of acting and ... acting is the work of knowing and ... knowing is the beginning of acting and acting is the completion of knowing. ... [I]f one only talks about knowing, [the idea of] acting is already present, or if one only talks about acting, [the idea of] knowing is already present.

That picture is a response to this comment (by Wang's student Xu Ai).

> The ancients talked about knowing and acting as two things, ... because they wanted people to distinguish them clearly. On the one hand, one was to work at knowing; on the other hand, one was to work at acting. In this way, one would have a place to begin one's spiritual training.

So, must we gain knowledge *before* doing things? Not if Wang is correct. Knowing and acting arrive, and grow, *as one*, on his view. One acts *in* knowing. One knows *in* acting. These cannot be separated in the way that Descartes imagined when confronting his sceptical argument.

Yet does that make sceptical arguments even more worrying? If I do not know anything, am I also not really doing anything? Yes, things happen, even involving this body. But are none of those bodily movements really *actions*? Are none of them *personal* actions – being done by *me*? I think that I am a person doing things, not an automaton making movements. But do sceptical arguments show that, actually and without realising it, I am an automaton – thanks to lacking knowledge?

3.5.2 Gilbert Ryle's knowledge-how

Can we evade section 3.5.1's parting Wang-inspired worry by restricting the reach of sceptical worries about lacking knowledge? Here is an idea. Maybe those sceptical worries concern only one kind of knowledge. Could we perform actions, *with* personal agency (unlike the possibility that arose at the end of section 3.5.1), by using another kind of knowledge?

I will discuss an argument from Gilbert Ryle (1900–76), an English philosopher. It concerned knowing-that and knowing-how. Knowing-that has been this chapter's topic – knowledge of truths, facts, how things are: I think I know that I am typing. Knowing-how is knowing how *to do* something: apparently, I know how to type. This seems to be an ability or skill – a way to manifest personal agency, such as by doing things deliberately. In principle, do we have and use *both* kinds of knowledge?

Ryle thought so. To show so, however, he had to disarm the 'intellectualist legend', about what he called *intelligent* actions. These are bodily movements that *express* or *manifest* knowing-how (such as one's typing, expressing or manifesting one's knowing how to type). How do these actions arise? Do they depend on applying some knowledge-*that*? The intellectualist legend says 'yes'. Ryle argued for 'no'.

He began by explaining the thinking behind that 'legend'. (This is welcome. Before deciding whether a thesis is true, one should try to understand why it might seem true.)

> [On the intellectualist legend,] the agent is thinking what he is doing while he is doing it, and ... he would not do the action so well if he were not thinking what he is doing. ... Champions of this legend are apt to try to reassimilate knowing *how* to knowing *that* by arguing that intelligent performance involves the observance of

> rules, or the application of criteria. ... [So, this] is ... always to do two things; namely, to consider certain appropriate propositions, or prescriptions, and to put into practice what these propositions or prescriptions enjoin.

Picture a baseball player or cricketer hitting a ball that has reached her very quickly. Is she applying knowledge-that of angles and movements – even unconsciously? Intellectualism says 'yes'. How did Ryle argue against intellectualism?

> The crucial objection ... is this. The consideration of propositions [= one's intellect telling one what to do] is itself an operation [= an action,] the execution [= the doing] of which can be more or less intelligent, less or more stupid. But if, for any operation to be intelligently executed [= intelligently done], a prior theoretical operation [= one's intellect consulting in advance some 'inner' rule or criterion] had first to be performed and performed intelligently, it would be a logical impossibility for anyone ever to break into the circle.

That is abstract. I will apply it to an example.

Imagine trying to explain how a batter is moving well in hitting a ball. It looks skilful. It looks as if she is manifesting knowledge-how to hit a fast-moving ball. Intellectualism says that she is applying instructions (even if instantaneously and unconsciously): she is using knowledge-that, even in manifesting knowing-how.

But Ryle would reply that the *applying*-of-those-instructions must itself be an intelligent action. Otherwise, the batter is not using those instructions to *guide* her body properly so that she hits the ball well. So, in moving well, she has some knowledge-that – those instructions – which she is *actively applying*. Thus, she must *know how to* apply the knowledge-that – the instructions.

And this remains so, no matter how extensive (and potentially complete) those instructions are. Hence, Ryle concluded, there are two distinct kinds of knowledge: knowing-a-truth (such as instructions for an action) is not *all* of the knowing within knowing-how-to-do-something; further knowing-how is also involved. It might be expressed *in* the action.

Do those two forms of knowledge have different strengths and weaknesses? Our sceptical worries have concerned whether people can know truths (knowing-that). Have we now found that we can link people, as knowers, with actions (knowing-how)? Can we do what Descartes (section 3.2.6) presumed that he could do – namely, continue doing things, *with* personal agency – *before* (if ever) resolving his sceptical worries? Even *if* we lack personal knowledge of truths, can we express personal agency by using knowledge-how?

3.5.3 Elizabeth Anscombe's practical knowledge
It might be important to understand more fully the nature of knowledge-how. G. E. M. [Elizabeth] Anscombe (1919–2001), an English philosopher, sought to do so, focusing on what she called 'practical knowledge' and 'speculative knowledge'. Anscombe directed us to the Italian theologian and philosopher St Thomas Aquinas (1225–74):

> the account given by Aquinas [in his posthumous *Summa Theologica*] of the nature of practical knowledge holds: Practical knowledge is 'the cause of what it understands', unlike 'speculative' knowledge, which 'is derived from the objects known' … [W]ithout [practical knowledge] what happens [is not an] execution of intentions …

We can illustrate this by imagining two people making the same movements, such as placing groceries in a shopping trolley. Imagine that only one of the two is acting on an *intention* to do this. In a sense, only she knows what she is doing: 'I know that I am shopping, because it is what I intended doing.' Perhaps the other person cannot think that. Is he acting as an automaton, since he is not acting on an intention? He might observe his body's movements, as if 'from outside', just like anyone else could observe them. Without the 'inner' sense of acting on an intention, though, how can he realise that *he* is making the movements? (Here I revisit Perry's example of the un-self-aware shopper: section 2.2.2.) This person would not know *from within* that 'it is me' – himself – making those movements.

Maybe, at best, the observing gives him knowledge-that he – or 'this body' – is making those movements. Again, this would be akin to an *observer's* knowledge of this fact about him. Anscombe called this *speculative* knowledge. I doubt that this is a perfect name, since one is not taking conscious risks (speculating) in one's thinking. But Anscombe's idea is recognisable. The person has knowledge of something (about himself) that is *independently* available to be known *from 'the world outside'*. In Anscombe's terms, this knowledge is 'derived from' what is being known, *reflecting* the fact being known. One knows that it is Sunday by deriving this knowledge *from* the fact of its being Sunday. One knows that a person is placing groceries in a trolley by deriving the knowledge *from* that observed fact.

And what of *practical* knowledge, the other half of Anscombe's distinction? How similar is it to Rylean knowledge-*how* (section 3.5.2)? Anscombe saw these as related but not identical, it seems.

> A man has practical knowledge who knows how to do things; but that is an insufficient description, for he *might* be said to know how to do things if he could give a lecture on it, though he was helpless when confronted with the task of doing them.

Anscombe was alerting us to a kind of self-knowledge – knowing what one is doing, but not as anyone *else* could know it. As indicated by her citing of Aquinas, she highlighted the role of *intention* within practical knowledge:

> we really can speak of two knowledges – the account that one could give of what one was doing, without adverting to observation; and the account of exactly what is happening at a given moment (say) to the material one is working on. The one is practical, the other is speculative [= using evidence provided by observation of what one is doing]. ... 'Intentional action' always presupposes what might be called 'knowing one's way about' the matters described in the description under which one's action can be called intentional, and this knowledge is exercised in the action and is practical knowledge.

Anscombe was suggesting that practical knowledge reflects not only skill but intention. It is manifested as a skilled (knowing-how) action, yet also as intentional. Hence, you can know what you are doing without *waiting to observe afterwards* what your body did. (Waiting to observe would give you at most *speculative* – an observer's – knowledge of what you were doing.) You know what you are doing by knowing (from within) that you are acting on your intention. You know that you are cooking, and you know this *from inside* the action (as we might say), in effect an action expressing your knowing how to cook. You are not knowing (speculatively) from *outside* yourself, so to speak, that you are cooking. For your knowing is 'the cause of what it understands' (to apply Anscombe's phrase from above). In this sense, practical knowing is *creative*: it is creating *what* it knows, *in that very act of knowing* what it is knowing. I have never thought of cooking in quite that way. Should I begin doing so?

3.5.4 *American Indian questioning-knowledge-how*

We might even be tempted to accord an idea of knowledge-how (sections 3.5.2, 3.5.3) a *leading* role within our reflections on knowledge. It seems to have received such respect from some American Indian [= Native American = indigenous people of North America] thinking, as Brian Yazzie Burkhart, a contemporary Cherokee philosopher, explains.

> Coyote is described as a philosopher in many American Indian stories. ... [H]e wonders about things, about how they really work. Often in doing so, however, he forgets his place in the world; he does not remember how he is related.

So, how does one find – or remember – one's place in the world? One can ask questions, which is an exercise of skill – knowledge-how.

> Coyote also shows us that the questions we choose to ask are more important than any truths we might hope to discover in asking such questions, since how we act impacts the way the world is, the way in which a question will get answered.

Are those questions more important? Important, yes, but more so? Why would questions not be important mainly when they might guide us towards facts that matter – with its being just as important to know those facts, those truths? No, we are told:

> American Indian philosophy has a very different relationship to questions and question-formation than does its Western counterparts. It is generally thought by Native philosophers that questions are most often a sign of confusion and misunderstanding.

Questions can be asked in order to remove confusion in 'larger' thinking. That will happen only if the questions themselves are not confused. The idea here seems to be that to ask the right question is to have done the *most* important thing in knowing.

> The answer to a question often lies in the question itself rather than in some solution outside of the question. The problem a question addresses is typically one that is raised by the very question itself rather than some actual state of affairs.

Maybe the idea is this: good questions arise when they *need* to arise, not at random or trivially. This need is not determined merely by facts 'out there', 'waiting' to be asked about and to be known. Any real need to know the facts is created by the questions, in their being asked – not by the facts themselves.

I do not know how a fact on its own could do that, anyway. There is an unlimited array of facts 'out there'. If *they* somehow generate questions (how? by 'demanding' to be known?), then questions can arise endlessly – and pointlessly, by being disconnected from our gaining ever more knowledge of those facts. Burkhart sees 'Western epistemology' as asking 'How can less knowledge be better?' – the implication (he says) being that, if facts are 'sitting there', and if this already creates our need to know, then our mission as knowers is automatically to know more, not fewer, of these facts! But we are not under that obligation merely because facts are 'out there'. Knowing is something that we *do*. We can *choose not* to do it, when this is better – as at times it is. In realising this, we confront 'Western epistemology's incapacity to grasp the idea that certain things *should* not be known ... From the American Indian perspective, our knowledge is not limited [= less than it should be] since we have as much as we should.'

Yet (we might wonder) how could that be so? Are we so powerful as inquirers? Not exactly; our power is not the point. Rather, knowledge's nature is the key. For example, if all knowledge is 'speculative' (to use Anscombe's word: section 3.5.3) – thus, merely a way of absorbing facts – then in principle this could extend indefinitely.

> For American Indians, [however,] knowledge is knowledge in experience, or if knowledge does not simply amount to this, it is at least the most important knowledge. ... This knowledge is embodied knowledge. We might do best to call this knowledge 'lived knowledge'.

This 'is a know-how'.

> Knowledge is what we put to use. Knowledge can never be divorced from human action and experience. Thus, just because we can imagine something that we would like to know, or can formulate a question regarding, this does not mean that there is, in fact, something to know or that we have formulated an actual question.

Again, real questions arise because they need to arise, in living our lives. In this practical and lived sense, questions are real. What is more,

> American Indian philosophy is concerned with the right road for humans to walk in relation to all that is around them. ... [And] what is right is true and what is true is right: the universe is moral.

I will hold that in mind, when (in section 5.4) meeting questions about how we should act towards 'the universe'. And might we blend this American Indian thinking with Parmenides' Way of Truth (section 2.2.3)? Would we be striving to walk at once both the Way of Truth *and* of What Is Moral – what we could call *the Way of Moral Truth*? Is *that* our ultimate goal as inquirers, as potential knowers? Yet what would that Way look like? Might Moral Truth admit of different forms – maybe in line with what we read from the *Mahābhārata* (section 2.2.4)? Important questions along these lines will be the heart of chapter 5.

Readings for 3.5

For Wang, see 'A record for practice', in *Readings from the Lu-Wang School of Neo-Confucianism*, trans. P. J. Ivanhoe (Indianapolis: Hackett, 2009); quotations from pp. 141–2. For Ryle, see *The Concept of Mind* (London: Hutchinson, 1949); quotations from pp. 29, 30. For Anscombe, see *Intention* (Oxford: Blackwell, 1957); quotations from pp. 87–9. On Native American epistemology, see B. Y. Burkhart, 'What Coyote and Thales can teach us: an outline of American Indian epistemology', in *American Indian Thought*, ed. A. Waters (Malden, MA: Blackwell, 2004), pp. 15–26; quotations from pp. 15, 16, 17–18, 20, 21, 23.

3.6 Knowing's rights and wrongs

3.6.1 Maria Montessori's methods

We have noticed (section 3.5) possible links between knowing and agency. Those links include actions manifesting knowledge-how. How do such links arise in practice? *How* does someone form abilities and skills to enrich her life as a knower?

Here we may consider some ideas from Maria Montessori (1870–1952), an Italian doctor turned educator who established what remains a distinctive method of schooling ('Montessori schools') in many countries. Her methods for encouraging and refining children's intellectual powers overlapped with various philosophical ideas about knowing: 'A science should establish *by means of experiments* what is necessary to the primordial psychical requirements of the child ...' This does not mean a child's being subjected to insensitive laboratory testing! Montessori was adopting a scientific spirit, seeking carefully observed data on which to build theories. She continued:

> and then we shall witness the development of complex vital phenomena, in which the intelligence, the will and the character develop together, just as the brain, the stomach and the muscles of the rationally nourished child develop together.

So, Montessori was expecting data to reflect aspects of the child as a physical whole, especially his cognitive capacities:

> the first coordinated cognitions will be fixed in the child's mind, and the *known* will begin to exist in him, providing the first germs of an intellectual interest, supplementing his instinctive interest.

From cognition to knowledge: thus it begins in childhood, when embarking on a lifetime of knowing – so long as care is taken and interest fostered. The *interested* mind is an *attending* mind (Montessori was saying). Then it can learn. Then it can know. Attention must be given to how a child is guided and encouraged initially, with structured sensory exercises. These 'make it possible for the child to *distinguish* and to *classify*.' The intelligent mind takes shape, partly by gaining capacities to give shape to experiences, finding order in them.

> When [the child] discovers with so much emotion that the sky is blue, that his hand is smooth, that the window is rectangular, he does not in reality discover

the sky, nor the hand, nor the window, but he discovers their position in the order of his mind by arrangement of his ideas.

With those comments on 'ideas', was Montessori espousing an idealism, such as Berkeley's (section 3.3.2), about the physical world? Her point seemed to be more about how a child forms a conception of the world, using ideas of it as sensory data. A notable feature of those data is the 'order' – the ordering, the orderliness – that they display to the child. That is notable also by affecting the child's character:

> this ['arrangement of his ideas', coming to him in his sensing the world] determines a stable equilibrium in the internal personality, which produces calm, strength, and the possibility of fresh conquests ...

It is good for the child's 'internal personality' to sense the world, experiencing its order. This order in the world *outside* the child becomes order *inside* him. Not only that, but understanding can emerge within him. It begins with attention.

> The phenomenon to be expected from the little child, when he is placed in an environment favourable to his spiritual growth, is this: that suddenly the child will fix his attention upon an object, will use it for the purpose for which it was constructed, and will *continue* to repeat the same exercise indefinitely. ... This [is] the basis of all psychical construction, and the sole secret of education. ... [T]he child really acquires by these means definite knowledge ....

And that generates understanding.

> Between 'understanding' because another person seeks to impress upon us the explanation of a thing by speech,

and 'understanding' the thing of ourselves, there is an immeasurable distance ... Perhaps no emotion is more fruitful for man than the intellectual emotion.

That welcome capacity, for real understanding, can and must be deliberately strengthened. Childhood seems to be the best time to start.

Montessori was not merely asking whether children might develop in those ways. She saw her account as strongly supported by attentive observation and useful in practice. It is *empirical* in tone – meaning that it stands or falls with whether it reflects and fits observations of what actually happens. I do not know whether her account was right, even in broad outline. But she seems to have offered potentially useful hypotheses based on – and testable by – observations, which could be useful also to philosophical theorising about how we gain knowledge.

3.6.2 Linda Zagzebski's intellectual virtues
Montessori's proposed methods (section 3.6.1) were intended to improve us as cognitive beings – as thinkers, as knowers. May we read this as advice for practising intellectual *virtues* and avoiding intellectual *vices*? Is that how knowing occurs?

Montessori also distinguished knowing from understanding. But may we lessen the distance between those two by regarding knowing as a *kind* of understanding? If so, might it then involve personal virtues of an intellectual kind, ones that are clearly involved in understanding? Linda Zagzebski (b. 1946), an American philosopher, has argued so in her *virtue epistemology*.

Here are some instances of what Zagzebski deems to be intellectual *vices*:

> intellectual pride, negligence, idleness, cowardice, conformity, carelessness, rigidity, prejudice, wishful

thinking, closed-mindedness, insensitivity to detail, obtuseness, and lack of thoroughness. ... probably also ... giving up too soon ... [and] some forms of self-deception ...

Zagzebski's idea is not that these are moral vices. Rather, they are *very like* moral vices. We might call them ways to waste or misdirect our abilities to perform, instead, acts of intellectual goodness. In contrast, here are some intellectual *virtues*:

intellectual carefulness, perseverance, humility, vigor, flexibility, courage, and thoroughness, as well as open-mindedness, fairmindedness, insightfulness, and the virtues opposed to wishful thinking, obtuseness, and conformity. One of the most important virtues ... is intellectual integrity.

How are these (and others, including maybe imagination) related to knowing?

For Zagzebski, knowing has a virtuous component. It includes having been *motivated to know* – and this motivation is itself an intellectual virtue. It is what a 'real inquirer' (as we might say) would have. It is also a virtue manifested *through* other intellectual virtues. These are three examples (I have added emphases):

the aim of *open-mindedness* is to be receptive to new ideas and arguments even when they conflict with one's own in order to ultimately get knowledge. The aim of *intellectual thoroughness* is to exhaustively investigate the evidence pertaining to a particular belief or set of questions in order to ultimately get knowledge. The aim of *intellectual courage* is to defend one's belief or a line of inquiry when one has good reason to believe that it is on the right track, and to fearlessly answer objections from others in order to ultimately get knowledge.

Here is how Zagzebski uses those examples to gain her general picture.

- Any intellectual virtue (being a virtue at all) has a distinctive *point* or *aim*. In particular, each is a way of using one's *intellect* in pursuit of that aim (such as by being 'receptive to new ideas').
- That pursuit involves *intellectual actions* (such as receiving new ideas in an open-minded way).
- Those intellectual virtues also share a *further*, or *underlying*, point or aim – which is to 'get knowledge'.
- So, when intellectual actions like that are performed well (concludes Zagzebski), knowledge should flow in either of two ways: 'Getting knowledge can be a matter either of reaching more truths or of gaining understanding of truths already believed.'
- But this happens only if those truths, or that understanding of them, have been reached in intellectually *virtuous* ways.

With this condition in mind, then, we can again ask (as we did in section 3.1): 'What *is* knowledge?' For Zagzebski, it is 'a state of cognitive contact [which can include 'true belief' and 'understanding and certainty'] with reality arising out of acts of intellectual virtue'. Knowing arises from actions expressing or manifesting any of those intellectual virtues, expressing or manifesting also the *underlying* aim of gaining knowledge. Open-mindedness, for instance, does not produce knowledge when one is not genuinely seeking it. Merely hearing others is not enough. One might not do it in a genuinely open-minded way, *really* seeking knowledge.

3.6.3 *Helen Longino's feminist sensibility*
Can we enrich virtue epistemology (section 3.6.2) with some feminist epistemology? Yes, if Helen Longino

(b. 1944), an American philosopher of science, is correct. She encourages us to 'think not about a feminist science, but about doing science as a feminist' (and science, we may hope, is a way to gain knowledge). What might Longino mean by that distinction?

She is advocating, it seems, for science at least not to ignore feminist ideas, partly because the science can be *improved* by not doing so. Ignoring them would be closed-minded – an intellectual vice (section 3.6.2). We need to be

> approaching the many activities that constitute science practice with a feminist sensibility [= being alert for feminist ideas and their potential applicability within science practice]. ... This is a recommendation I would like to extend to epistemology as well.

That recommendation is energised by some social-historical realities.

> To do epistemology as a feminist is to engage the questions of epistemology with an awareness of the ways in which participation in socially-sanctioned knowledge production has been circumscribed [= many groups of people, including women, have often been excluded from society's main ways of discovering knowledge, such as universities and research bodies], of the ways in which epistemological concepts like rationality and objectivity have been defined using notions of masculinity (and vice-versa), of the ways in which women have been derided as knowers [= ways in which their claims to *be* knowers have been dismissed], and of the need for alternative theoretical approaches to satisfy feminist cognitive goals.

How might we extend epistemology in feminist-sensitive ways? Longino highlights several intellectual virtues. One is 'ontological heterogeneity' – namely, not ignoring variety in what one is examining. Here is a famous example.

> Feminists writing about biology have urged that we take account of individual difference among the individuals and samples that constitute the objects of study. ... [1983 Nobel Laureate in Physiology or Medicine] Barbara McClintock's attention to the individual kernels of a cob of corn (which helped her to recognize an underlying pattern of mutability) has been taken as a paradigm of what a feminist attitude to nature ought to be.

Why is that feminist? The key is

> the rejection of theories of inferiority ... [which] are supported in part by an intolerance of heterogeneity [= difference]. Difference must [on any such theory] be ordered, one type chosen as the standard, and all others seen as failed or incomplete versions.

A feminist sensibility could be especially attuned to that general idea by noticing this instance of it.

> Theories of inferiority which take the white middle class male (or the free male citizen) as the standard [= for measuring or evaluating] grant ontological [= a basic form of reality] priority to that type [= in how those theories claim to interpret reality]. Difference is then treated as a departure from, a failure fully to meet, the standard, rather than simply difference.

We might say that difference is being judged evaluatively, not simply being noticed – with the judging applying a socially biased standard. Clearly, that can be bad for people (such as women) who are judged as falling short of a standard imposed, even implicitly, by allowing white middle-class males to be what, ideally, everyone would be. Longino highlights a better way of reading reality: 'Ontological heterogeneity permits equal standing for different types, and mandates investigation of the details of such difference. Difference is resource, not failure.' The term 'ontological heterogeneity' is ungainly. But the idea is simple: 'a community characterized by diversity is more epistemically reliable.' Listen to more people; do not ignore varying data; you will uncover more truths that do and should matter to more people.

And feminist sensitivity to gender's social history can help. Being open to variety in one's evidence is not exclusively feminist. But being feminist should make one more aware of what can all too easily occur when diversity is ignored.

> Feminists are as concerned as anyone with the distinction between knowledge and opinion and differences between well- and poorly-grounded beliefs [e.g. ones that are, and ones that are not, well supported by evidence]. To reflect philosophically on these matters in critical awareness of women's historical cognitive disenfranchisement and with a view to feminist cognitive objectives is to do epistemology as a feminist.

Longino advocates that 'we [should] understand feminist epistemology as practice rather than content.' In other words, she is not prejudging what *contents* will result (as objects of our thoughts) from adopting a sensibility of openness to difference, say. She welcomes *whatever* results will transpire once we approach inquiry with inquiring minds open to more, not fewer, truths emerging – including historical ones about when, where, and how women's voices have been silenced and ignored. What matters most is that we listen well, ideally to everyone.

3.6.4 Miranda Fricker on epistemic injustice

Making such changes as Longino advocates (section 3.6.3) might not always feel needed. But that could be because sometimes we *mistakenly* think that we are already being intellectually virtuous. Can we actually be thinking or talking unfairly at those times without realising this about ourselves? Miranda Fricker (b. 1966), an English philosopher, thinks so. She describes two socially important ways for this to occur.

Each is a form of epistemic injustice, closely tied in practice to social injustice. Remember (from section 3.1.2) that the word 'epistemology' stems from the Greek *'epistēmē'*, for 'knowledge'. Epistemic injustice treats people unfairly *in their capacity as* potential knowers. In seeking to understand this, Fricker reaches for guidance from both virtue epistemology (section 3.6.2) and feminist epistemology (section 3.6.3). Here is one form of epistemic injustice described by Fricker (I add the emphasis).

> *Testimonial injustice* occurs when prejudice causes a hearer to give a deflated level of credibility [= believability, as being true] to a speaker's word ... An example ... might be that the police do not believe you because you are black ...

Sadly, that example is realistic. It involves *'identity prejudice'* – 'prejudices against people *qua* social type'. That means treating someone *purely as* (this is what *'qua'* means here) an instance of a socially noticed type, maybe by noticing and reacting to only her racial aspects. (Earlier, we read Fanon's powerful account of how this can feel: section 1.5.2.)

Imagine asking how women are faring in an important social setting – before consulting only men for answers. That is socially *and epistemically* unfair, by according less weight to evidence that would be offered by women. It is also epistemically unwise – seemingly an intellectual vice (section 3.6.2). For a good source of evidence – women's experiences and views – is being ignored.

A second kind of epistemic injustice identified by Fricker is *hermeneutical injustice*.

> [It] occurs at a prior stage [= prior to testimonial injustice's occurring], when a gap in collective interpretive resources puts someone at an unfair disadvantage when it comes to making sense of their social experiences. ... [A]n example ... might be that you suffer sexual harassment in a culture that still lacks that critical concept.

'Hermeneutics' studies *interpretation's* nature and significance. Hermeneutical injustice is interpretive injustice. It is present when there is an interpretive failing, perhaps reflecting larger social injustice. If a concept of sexual harassment is absent from society, for instance, people will not hear with – literally – understanding when someone tells them what has happened in that respect. They will lack a concept needed for doing interpretive justice to what they are being told. Their powers of understanding will *fail* that person. Their thinking, no matter how sincere they feel they are being, will not do justice to *how it is for her*.

Such injustice falls most often and most heavily upon some groups, not others. Concepts used especially by socially dominant groups dominate 'official' discourse. Those concepts might feel adequate within those groups, with members not spurring each other to learn alternative concepts, notably those that are distinctive of socially disadvantaged groups. Hence,

> members of the group that is most disadvantaged by the gap ['in collective hermeneutical resources' = in significant differences between *their* shared concepts

and *other* groups' shared concepts] are, in some degree, *hermeneutically marginalized* – that is, they participate unequally in the practices through which social meanings are generated.

Fricker's idea of hermeneutical injustice could be thought of as reflecting a more general one – namely, the importance of finding epistemically good concepts – truthful ones, insightful ones, rationally supported ones – with which to describe the world at all. This is what science (section 3.6.3) may be viewed as doing. But that general idea stretches throughout our lives. When using words to describe the world, we are interpreting it, using some words, not others. We literally choose words; they do not literally choose us – hovering in the air like mosquitoes until they find suitable hosts. We hope to be using good ones.

If we do choose good ones, maybe we could think of this as being *epistemically fairer to the world* – in the way that (as Fricker is emphasising) some words are epistemically fairer to other people. Is the world enough like a person – one with whom we interact, genuinely trying to understand it? Maybe we could learn (from Fricker's approach) the aim of *listening fairly to the world*, not ignoring what it is 'saying'. If we are to *know* the world, we might seek concepts and words with which to be interpretively fair to it. But should we also do this in order to *act* fairly towards the world, much as we should act fairly towards people? (Those ideas and questions depend on an analogy between other people and the world. Is it a good analogy? At the very least, it paints a picture that might be morally significant, as section 5.4 will discuss.)

3.6.5 Charles Mills on white ignorance

The concept of epistemic injustice (section 3.6.4) seems widely applicable. One instance was described by Charles

Mills (1951–2021), a Jamaican-British-American philosopher, with his concept of *white ignorance*.

Ignorance is an epistemic lack. It can also be an epistemic vice (section 3.6.2). Imagine its arising in some cases from deliberate or easily avoidable ignoring of evidence, including of social injustice experienced by various social groupings. Mills argued that Western societies have included *much* systemic ignoring of socially significant claims by non-white people.

What did he mean by 'white'? Mills was denoting a politically and historically defined group, saying that we

> need to distinguish ... white ignorance from general patterns of ignorance prevalent among people who are white [= e.g. in appearance] but in whose doxastic [= belief – from the ancient Greek word 'doxa'] states race has played no determining role.

Nor is white ignorance 'confined *to* white people. ... Provided that the causal route is appropriate, blacks can manifest white ignorance also.' That causal route need not even have involved individually racist motivations:

> the racialized causality I am invoking ... [can] include both straightforward racist motivation and more impersonal social-cultural causation, which may be operative even if the cognizer in question is not racist. ... [W]hite ignorance need not always be based on bad faith.

Mills also extended the reach of his basic idea. The socially developed, and reinforced, ignorance need not be of *racially* delineated groups:

> white ignorance is not the only kind of privileged, group-based ignorance. Male ignorance could be analyzed similarly and clearly has a far more ancient history and arguably a more deep-rooted ancestry in human inter-relations, insofar as it goes back thousands of years.

Still, Mills focused on the racial case, for white-dominated populations: '*white ignorance* as a cognitive phenomenon has to be clearly historicized.' He had at least two reasons for that focus. First, there are striking historical facts – about how various racial groups have been treated – that seem relevant. Second, we have a philosophical thesis – a *social constructivism* about race's nature – that explains their relevance. Mills took

> for granted the truth of some variant of social constructivism, which denies that race is biological. So the causality in the mechanisms for generating and sustaining white ignorance on the macro level is social-structural rather than physico-biological, though it will of course operate through the physico-biological.

Some or all of those social-structural facts might be traceable to intellectual (even moral) vices practised by individuals who openly endorsed racist claims. But whether that occurred was not essential to Mills's main point, which concerned 'the epistemic principle of what has come to be called "white normativity", the centering of the Euro and later Euro-American reference group as constitutive norm.' Mills's critical emphasis was thus on a way of speaking and thinking that favours one epistemic standard – one 'norm' – over others, often with prejudicial results. Longino (section 3.6.3) described something similar, talking about 'theories of inferiority'. It is a recurring danger. Mills tells us that,

> with Europe's gradual rise to global domination, the European variant [of that form of ethnocentrism] becomes entrenched as an overarching, virtually unassailable framework, a conviction of exceptionalism and superiority that seems vindicated by the facts, and thenceforth, circularly, shaping perception of the facts. We rule the world because we are superior; we are superior because we rule the world.

Maybe it never *had* to be that white people, when exercising physical and political power over black people, say, would be epistemically self-serving – disrespectful towards what was being thought and known by those people being controlled. Still, this *has* often occurred. Mills's point was that the failing was not only socio-political (as is obvious); it was also epistemic. Everyone is a source of evidence. Anyone might be correct. Everyone should remember this – always – and act accordingly, in speech and thought.

3.6.6 Vrinda Dalmiya's relational humility
How can we evade the intellectual failing highlighted by Mills (section 3.6.5)? The idea of *relational humility* might help. This is an intellectual (and moral) virtue described by Vrinda Dalmiya (b. 1954), an Indian philosopher teaching in the USA.

Dalmiya calls particularly upon passages from the *Mahābhārata* (section 2.2.4). Her proposal contributes to the projects of Zagzebski (section 3.6.2), Fricker (section 3.6.4), and one that we will discuss later (from Nel Noddings, in section 5.2.5). The *Mahābhārata* is not mainly about knowing. But philosophers should remain alert for sources of understanding, wherever it might be found. And it seems to me that Dalmiya does find new insight, from the *Mahābhārata*, into how knowing can arise in intellectually – and ethically – virtuous ways.

This is Dalmiya's main idea:

> the key virtue underlying epistemic excellence in the [*Mahābhārata*] is a form of humility that is intrinsically relational. Relational humility is analysed as a disposition to acknowledge our own ignorance *while* acknowledging the knowledge of others.

And here is a structural aspect of that feature.

[Relational humility] thus decentres [= shifts explanatory focus away from merely] the self [= the person with the knowledge] in order to incorporate [= as valuable] other epistemic voices, making the pursuit of truth a social enterprise [= being conducted by the person who is knowing *plus* others involved in her knowing].

Dalmiya's structural moral is this: when relational humility is present, one knows *by including also* how others (at least one, maybe more) view the world in the relevant respect. One is not knowing wholly on one's own terms. One is not relying only on how things appear to oneself. This is already a curb on arrogance as to one's knowing more than others do. One is knowing partly by seeing the world *as others do*. (So, is this an intellectual form of *empathy* – which we discussed, thanks to Stein, in section 3.4.3?)

Nor should the humility end there:

knowing is shown to become the conscious pursuit [= following, the taking-seriously] of ignorance – of finding out the limits of what one knows. [Thus] ignorance itself emerges not merely as a lack antithetical to knowing, but as a positive intentional [= mental, cognitive] state that makes us aware of (and enables a grasp of) an object *as unknown*.

One knows partly by having accepted that one does not – and might never – know! Even once one does know, one accepts one's lacking further knowledge. One might be accepting that *others* have this 'further knowledge'. There is humility in having, and acting on, these kinds of awareness of those *relational* aspects of oneself.

Dalmiya is alerted to that idea through some *comparative* philosophy, learning from diverse traditions. She tells us about Kauśika (in the *Mahābhārata*'s *Vana Pavan*, 206–16). He was a Brahmin 'sage ... famed for his knowledge' 'who is *made to learn* from two figures positioned clearly at the margins of society ... an ordinary woman and a lowly butcher'. Kauśika 'comes to recognize their cognitive excellence'. He undergoes 'a deep characteriological transformation brought on by his acquiring an intellectual virtue' – *relational humility*. Dalmiya guides us through Kauśika's 'struggle to come to terms with and assess the *limits* of his knowledge'. He acts badly, 'angrily killing' a bird, after which the shame that he feels 'shocks [him] into realizing that he ... does not even "truly" *know*'. This leads him to 'search ... for teachers (for community) who have and can impart to him the knowledge that he does not have.' As it happens, these teachers are socially 'marginalized' – 'the housewife ... given the public-private dichotomy, and the butcher ... by caste hierarchy'. Each of them has knowledge that is not clearly scholarly. Is that a problem? No.

> Kauśika accepts more than the mere fact that the housewife and the butcher are also 'knowers' in their own right. He also recognizes that they actually know what he does not but [what he also] needs to know. He learns from them, thus marking them as epistemically superior to himself.

That is relational humility *in action* – albeit fictional action. But real action might await, too, for anyone reading Dalmiya's proposal. Can I become more relationally humble in my attempts to know the world, even my attempts to know myself? At least I am now aware of this *as* an aspiration.

Readings for 3.6

For Montessori, see *The Advanced Montessori Method I* [formerly: *Spontaneous Activity in Education*] (Oxford:

Clio Press, [1918] 1991); quotations from pp. 119–20, 125–6, 157, 158–9, 162, 166. For Zagzebski, see *Virtues of the Mind: An Inquiry into the Nature of Virtue and the Ethical Foundations of Knowledge* (Cambridge: Cambridge University Press, 1996); quotations from pp. 152, 155, 269, 270. For Longino, see 'In search of a feminist epistemology', *The Monist* 77 (1994): 472–85; quotations from pp. 475, 477, 480, 483. For Fricker, see *Epistemic Injustice: Power and the Ethics of Knowing* (Oxford: Oxford University Press, 2007); quotations from pp. 1, 6. For Mills, see 'White ignorance', in *Race and Epistemologies of Ignorance*, ed. S. Sullivan and N. Tuana (Albany: State University of New York Press, 2007); quotations from pp. 20, 21, 22, 25. For Dalmiya, see *Caring to Know: Comparative Care Ethics, Feminist Epistemology, and the Mahābhārata* (New Delhi: Oxford University Press, 2016); quotations from pp. 32–3, 108, 112–14.

4

Philosophical Reasoning

4.1 Elements

Philosophical thinking, as we have seen, takes *many* forms. Yet it is always built around *reasoning* in some more or less obvious way. The reasoning can take differing forms, but always, somehow, it comprises what we may call 'reasoning elements' being used in 'reasoning ways', playing 'reasoning roles'. This chapter describes several of those elements and ways. (Then chapter 6 will focus on potential aims and results of such reasoning.)

I begin with some *elements*, including the following ones, that may appear within instances of philosophical thinking.

> Ideas. Concepts. Phenomena. Data. Interpretations. Theses. Reasons. Questions. Puzzles. Conclusions.

I might be forgetting some. This is a good start, though, with some or all of these being present in any instance of philosophy, it seems.

This list also links well with Parmenides' Way of Truth (section 2.2.3) – his goddess-endorsed path. For *what* is true would be a thesis. And various elements can play distinctive *roles* in any search – along Parmenides' path – for a true thesis. Here is a brief sense of those possible roles.

> A thesis includes ideas and concepts.
> A thesis can be about some phenomenon/phenomena.
> A thesis can be about some datum/data.
> A thesis can be an interpretation.
> A thesis can be an answer to a question.
> A thesis can be a prelude to a question.
> A thesis can be a reason.
> A thesis can be an attempted solution to a puzzle (a reason for considering the puzzle to be solved).
> A thesis can be a prelude to a puzzle (a reason for thinking that there is a puzzle yet to be solved).
> A thesis can be a statement of a puzzle.
> A thesis can be a statement of a conclusion.

4.2 Uses

What will a piece of philosophical writing or thinking *do* with elements such as those (section 4.1)? What 'reasoning moves' are made with them, as the writing or thinking gets under way, unfolding, developing?

Here are some possibilities. These are not exclusively philosophical. They can be used *whenever* something is being discussed or examined. (Philosophers are far from the only people who think hard about difficult ideas.) But you should expect to be making one or more of these moves whenever you are being philosophical.

> Suggest. Hint. Hypothesise. Uncover. Wonder.
> Affirm. Deny. Doubt. Compare. Combine.

Analyse. Find complexity. Find distinctions. Clarify. Explain. Infer. Imply. Test. Apply. Show. Repeat some or all of those, as needed.
Do any of this either explicitly (by stating directly what you are doing) or implicitly (such as by showing or demonstrating, without stating directly, what you are doing).

That list might not be exhaustive; I have probably overlooked further possible uses of 'reasoning elements'. Nor have I offered detailed descriptions of those that I mentioned, let alone of how they might be combined in complex ways (such as when immersed in detailed and sustained philosophical thinking). But hopefully the list conveys a flavour, a sense, an aura.

Can we then *understand* the list better by pointing to something uniting those possible uses – a common core around which they cluster or a shared thread to which they attach? Maybe – a little. To some extent and in some way, it seems, each is contributing to philosophical *reasoning*. Philosophical thinking is always philosophical reasoning. At times, this is made apparent by one or more of those 'reasoning moves' being obviously present; at other times less obviously, more subtly, so. In any instance of philosophical thinking, however, *somehow* there is *some* presence of *some* such use(s) of *some* 'reasoning element(s)'.

For example, when trying to understand a particular philosopher's writing, one might need to make explicit what she did not: what she left unsaid could be vital to understanding what she was thinking. Or imagine a piece of philosophy being written conversationally without saying explicitly what thesis it is supporting. Even then, I encourage you to 'keep digging': you should be able to find – by inferring from what *is* being said and *how* it is being said – *some* thesis as being at stake.

As general advice, whenever a philosopher is not making it immediately apparent in her writing what thesis is at stake, I suggest your not walking away from the interpretive challenge of *uncovering* that thesis. This can be rewarding. At times, great ideas 'hide' inside writing that could be clearer. At times, writing can obscure an idea. But until one has *tried* looking within the writing, searching for ideas that might be there, one should not simply dismiss the writing. So, ask yourself why a philosopher has written what she has written, why she did not write more (perhaps clarifying what she did write) – and what she seems to have *wanted* readers to take from what she has written. You will be practising what is often called *interpretive charity*: you will be seeking to interpret someone with an eye on how they *could* be correct, and how they would have been more *clearly* correct if they had also written ... well, that is where you can offer your suggestions, trying to understand – charitably – what the writer had in mind.

We may think of philosophical writing as like a philosophical conversation. Often, when chatting, we *say* less than in fact we want the other person to hear. The same can be true in philosophical conversation. And whenever we read philosophy we are, in effect, having a conversation with the author. In her favoured way, she is guiding readers towards awareness of a thesis. She might do this explicitly *or* implicitly, like a person using his hands and face to reinforce or to complicate what his words say. She might do it precisely *or* suggestively, too, with this choice depending on the kind of thesis being discussed. Even then, there are further options. A philosophical author might be trying *in any of many ways* to guide readers towards a view of a thesis, perhaps as true, perhaps as false – but also perhaps as puzzling, perhaps as needing further investigation, perhaps .... Are the possibilities endless? Is this ever part of the challenge – and potentially the thrill

– in being philosophical? (Chapter 6 will revisit these questions.)

4.3 Examples

I will illustrate those general descriptions from sections 4.1 and 4.2 by revisiting four readings from chapter 3. I will apply, in **bold** text, some of the terms highlighted in section 4.2 denoting possible 'reasoning moves'.

4.3.1 Revisiting Plato's Meno
Section 3.1.1 eavesdropped on Socrates and Meno, thanks to Plato in his *Meno*. Here (in my own words) is a taste of their conversation's structure, as a case of collaborative reasoning.

> **Phenomenon.** Knowledge.
> **Question.** What is knowledge?
> **Hypothesis.** Knowledge = true belief.
> **Question.** Is true belief as useful as knowledge?
> **Implication.** *If* true belief is not as useful as knowledge, they are not identical.
> **Denial.** True belief is not as useful as knowledge. (**Reason, for denial.** True belief does not remain stably in place, as knowledge does. **Explanation, of reason for denial.** True belief is like Daedalus' amazing walking statues when they are untethered; knowledge is like them when they are tethered.)
> **Inferences.** Therefore, knowledge and true belief are not identical.
> **Implication.** If knowledge and true belief are not identical, the **hypothesis** above is false.
> **New hypothesis.** Knowledge = true belief + *logos*.
> **Explanation.** *Logos* = a kind of good evidence. (This is how a contemporary philosopher might translate Plato's term 'logos'.)

Implication. If so, then knowledge = true belief + a kind of good evidence. (This adds **analytical** detail to the **new hypothesis**.)
Conclusion. Knowledge = true belief + a kind of good evidence.

This does not report everything that gave energy and form to Socrates' and Meno's conversation. But it does provide guidance as to how we might track their reasoning, which weaves in and out, from here to there, travelling towards the thesis that is its conclusion, ideally a shared one. I encourage you to attempt this sort of structured revisiting of other readings from chapter 3. What I have provided here is not the only possible way of structuring the reasoning portrayed by Plato. It is not unusual for there to be debate over how best to represent some particular philosophical reasoning: there could be *different* ways, all good, to convey the reasoning's structure.

Before leaving you alone with that challenge, though, I offer another three examples. (Some of chapter 3's presentations, by the way, included hints as to possible renderings of the reasoning. The rest of this chapter will not revisit those readings.)

4.3.2 Revisiting the Zhuangzi
In section 3.2, we met six ways to raise considered doubts about whether people ever have knowledge. I will now reconstruct the example possibly least like that from a moment ago (Socrates meets Meno: section 4.3.1) – namely, the *Zhuangzi*'s puzzling questions (section 3.2.1). Those questions might look less like *reasoning*. Yet they are: they exemplify a reasoned-questioning pattern, not a mere-questioning sequence. (Questions are met with questions. I will quote some, adapting others, omitting some. I revisit only the start of the interchange, since it rapidly becomes complicated.)

Question. What do you know (about 'all things' knowing what is 'right')?
Question. How could I know that? (**Implication.** I know *what* is known, only if I know *how* I would know it. **Hypothesis.** I do not know how I would know it. **Inference.** So, I do not know what is known. **Doubt.** The question that was being asked cannot be answered by me.)
Question. Do you know that you don't know? (**Reason for question.** Your hypothesis is not known. **Doubt.** Your doubt is not based on a good reason.)
Question. How could I know that? (**Reason for question.** To know that I do not know is still knowledge. I have *this* knowledge, only if I know how I *would* know it, if I could. **Hypothesis.** I do not know how I would know it. **Inference.** So, I do not know that I do not know. **Doubt.** The question that was being asked cannot be answered by me.)
Question. Is there no knowledge at all? (**Implication.** If there is no knowledge even of not knowing – for the very same reason as there would be all of that not-knowing – then there is no knowledge. **Inference.** So, there is no knowledge. **Doubt.** That sounds like a position not to be accepted without further questioning.)
Showing, by raising reasoned questions. Any claims either of knowing, or of not knowing, need to be reasoned.

And so it begins. The interaction then continues, in that reasoned-questioning spirit. But already it is complex. My aim is simply to sketch a possible uncovering of some subtleties in those duelling questions. For they *are* duelling – in a reasoned way, each wondering what could possibly be known, each giving voice to inner reasoning, inner reasons, inner doubts, inner questions. What should we infer from this? Many lessons are possible. One of them is clear, though: philosophical reasoning need not be overt, laid out in easily noticed steps; it can be implicit and hidden, even questioning, *yet still powerful and motivating*.

4.3.3 Revisiting Longino's feminist sensibility

I revisited both the *Meno* (section 4.3.1) and the *Zhuangzi* (section 4.3.2) because they illustrate different styles of philosophy. Socrates and Meno were proposing a thesis, then testing it by mentioning a phenomenon that seemed to reveal an explanatory inadequacy within it, before replacing it with a new thesis, an alternative hypothesis about knowledge's nature. The *Zhuangzi* did not take that approach. Its theses were implicit, not explicit. It examined them, however, by explicit questioning, counter-questioning, and so on.

There is much variety of philosophical styles throughout this book's readings. Almost at random, I add another illustration, from Helen Longino (section 3.6.3).

> **Phenomenon.** Epistemology!
> **Hypothesis.** Epistemology would be improved in practice (all else being equal) if done with a feminist sensibility.
> **Question.** Can we explain what that would involve?
> **Hypothesis.** A feminist sensibility within epistemology could be like a feminist sensibility within science.
> **Proposal.** We could examine actual examples of doing science with a feminist sensibility.
> **Datum.** Barbara McClintock's important scientific research.
> **Question.** How does that research fit a feminist sensibility?
> **Hypothesis.** It involved a way of thinking that would fit well with a specific feminist intellectual virtue.

Question. What was that virtue?
Hypothesis. It was the virtue of ontological heterogeneity.
Question. Why is that a feminist intellectual virtue?
Reason for its being an intellectual virtue. It respects different kinds of evidence-sources.
Reason for its being feminist. It does not ignore evidence-sources that differ in their gendered or social histories or profiles.
Inference. When we combine those two reasons, we infer that ontological heterogeneity is a feminist intellectual virtue.
Conclusion. Our initial hypothesis has received support. We can improve the practice of epistemology (all else being equal) by doing it with a feminist sensibility.

Longino's reasoning blends historical data about scientific research with feminist interpretation, aiming to improve epistemological practice. That is immediately relevant, too. Since chapter 3 was guiding us through ways in which people have practised epistemology, Longino's reasoning can be seen as a way to reflect on chapter 3 *itself*. Throughout that chapter, we met philosophers from a range of intellectual, cultural, and historical backgrounds. Did we favour any of them, seeing some *but not others* as potentially providing good evidence for how we might seek to understand knowledge, say? *I hope not.* Part of my aim has been to be putting ontological heterogeneity *into philosophical practice*.

What we can also now appreciate, even more clearly (thanks to this section), is the *reasoning* underlying a proposal such as Longino's. We may readily welcome her *conclusion*, with its encouraging us to embrace a diversity of viewpoints – potential sources of a wider range of evidence, after all. But not only conclusions matter in being philosophical. We must never overlook *how* a conclusion has been reached – in this case, how Longino has *reasoned* her way to her welcome conclusion. This helps us to understand more fully her thinking as a whole, including its conclusion.

4.3.4 Revisiting al-Ghazālī's dreams

At times we may wish to display the structure of some reasoning more starkly and fully than in the previous three examples (the *Meno*, the *Zhuangzi*, and Longino). I will illustrate this with al-Ghazālī's dreaming argument (section 3.2.4). My aim is not to include every detail of his argument. But wherever, in the previous three examples, I said 'Inference', we might seek at least further detail: we may wish to appreciate the reasoning's *finer-grained* details. That sort of analysis is what I now present. (It is not the *only* possible way to represent al-Ghazālī's reasoning. Feel free to suggest a better one.)

I begin by listing a few of the key theses in al-Ghazālī's reasoning (using some of my own phrasing in trying to capture the spirit of his argument). They are key, thanks to how they appear and reappear within the reasoning.

A = One knows how things really are.
B = One is using evidence from one's senses.
C = One is awake.

Initially, al-Ghazālī's reasoning was as follows (where the '→' means 'if ... then ...', so that one is reasoning *from* what appears in front of '→', *to* what appears after '→'):

C. And C → B. So, B. And B → A. So, A.

At this initial stage of his reasoning, al-Ghazālī was not wondering whether he was awake. He was allowing himself C. From which (we would typically agree) it is easy to reason from C to A, via B. Thus, we would conclude that we know things as they really are. It could seem that al-Ghazālī had explained, by way of B, how it is true that C → A. (He began with C and ended with A, as you see.)

But his reasoning did not end there, with what I presented just now. *He continued sceptically.* He questioned whether being awake really is a definitive path to such knowledge. *Is* it true that C → A? In asking that question, al-Ghazālī introduced a new consideration into his reasoning.

We approach this new consideration by thinking about (i) being awake, seeming to sense the world, compared with (ii) dreaming, while seeming to sense the world. Each experience feels real. Each feels as though it reveals how things really are. But only one of those experiences could actually be doing so: dreaming *falls short* of sensing, in that respect.

That is a standard comparison upon which we rely when asking how we know reality. Dreaming falls short of being awake in that respect. But al-Ghazālī then added this question into his reasoning: what if being awake falls short – of a *further* state? Imagine a hierarchy reflected in the following theses. (I introduce the term 'Truly Awake' to capture al-Ghazālī's imagined higher state – 'standing above' *normal* waking states. C referred to being awake in a normal way.)

> D = One seems, to oneself, to be using evidence from one's senses.
> E = One is dreaming.
> F = One is Truly Awake.
> G = Dreaming does not provide knowledge of how things really are, compared to being awake.
> H = Being awake does not provide knowledge of how things really are, compared to being Truly Awake.

Al-Ghazālī's 'extended' reasoning then takes something like the following form.

> D → (E or C or F). [That is, if D, then at least one of E, C, and F.]
> (E & G) → not-A. [Equally, if E *but* G, then not-A.]
> (C & H) → not-A. [Equally, if C *but* H, then not-A.]
> So, (D & A) → F. [Equally, in case this is clearer: D → (A → F).]

What does that conclusion say? It is al-Ghazālī's advice, or warning, that being Truly Awake (=F) is *needed* for gaining knowledge (=A) when relying on what seems, to oneself, to be evidence from one's senses (=D). (Literally, the first version of the conclusion above is this: *if* one seems, to oneself, to be using evidence from one's senses [=D] *and* one is knowing how things really are [=A], *then* one is Truly Awake [=F].) Whenever we claim to be using our senses, we are relying on at least what *seems*, to us, to be coming from our senses. And what seems to come from one's senses provides (we take it) knowledge of how things really are – but only (we must concede, says al-Ghazālī) if one is also Truly Awake. (I should add that, in this reasoning, one would be using the evidence, *and* knowing, *and* being Truly Awake, all at once – at a *single* time.)

Yet *are* we ever Truly Awake – enabling us to gain what we might, in the spirit of al-Ghazālī's reasoning, call True Knowing? This is something that we could wish to know – Truly Know – about ourselves. Laying bare the bones of al-Ghazālī's reasoning might assist us.

Using the letters 'A', 'B', etc., to denote whole sentences, by the way, was useful in displaying those 'bones'. This makes clearer the reasoning's more detailed structure, like seeing an X-ray of a skeleton supporting – by providing an underlying structure for – a body's observed exterior. Strictly, this shorthand technique of using those letters was not needed. But it can help us to juggle several thoughts at once when evaluating the reasoning: it can be easier to hold in mind single letters, not whole sentences, while thinking about their interactions inside the reasoning.

4.4 Philosophical reasoning as rhythmic gymnastics?

I am no expert on rhythmic gymnastics. But I am wondering whether it is revealingly similar to philosophical reasoning. Can we add to our understanding – and appreciation – of such reasoning through an analogy with such gymnastics? (By the way, there are probably many other helpful analogies, too, including ones that you might prefer to this one. I offer it as just one possible way to 'picture' philosophical reasoning from a different angle, maybe an unusual one.)

So, imagine this: someone is gliding through the air, tossing a pink plastic ball – it looks like a child's party toy – far above her; she is twisting and turning, somersaulting, twisting again, and again, and again, before – with impeccable timing – gracefully allowing the ball to alight and remain upon the back of her hand, as she finishes gliding, in that same movement kneeling, head bowed, hand outstretched, ball at rest upon it. Seemingly effortless. A flowing whole. Mesmerisingly skilled. Astoundingly coordinated. Also *surprising*: notice, again, that pink plastic ball.

I am picturing a very good rhythmic gymnast. Equally, though, we have been reading examples of very good philosophical thinking in this book. If the comparison is apt, it might reveal something of what – *at least ideally, when done very well* – philosophical thinking is like.

So, is the comparison apt? Here, briefly, is why it might be.

Focus on how the rhythmic gymnast moves around her allocated space. Observe her performance's distinctive elements. Her movements are precise, poised, delicately powerful. And compare all of that with philosophical thinking, as *it* moves distinctively around its chosen topic, also with precision, poise, delicate power.

I used the word 'distinctively' because philosophical thinking is *somehow* distinctive, not simply 'everyday' in its style, in how it moves. It twists. It turns. And within it is *something* distinctive – something that we would not expect of non-philosophical thinking. Might that 'something' be akin to the rhythmic gymnast's pink plastic ball – surely not an 'everyday' part of being athletic? The ball helps to distinguish the rhythmic gymnast even from a 'traditional' gymnast. The rhythmic gymnast has many traditional gymnastic skills (those twists and turns), but she adds a kind of dancing – *and* an apparatus, such as the pink ball. (There are a few kinds of permitted apparatus. I select the ball for no special reason.) The apparatus, and the skill with which it is used, constitutes the performance's most distinctive element. So much so, that maybe we can view rhythmic gymnastics as standing to traditional gymnastics roughly as philosophical thinking stands to much other thinking.

- In rhythmic gymnastics, *as if from nowhere, once some comparatively 'normal' (traditional) gymnastics is under way, an odd apparatus appears, becoming central to the subsequent performance.* A ball is now at the heart of the gymnast's challenge. (Or maybe a long ribbon. Or a hoop. Or clubs. Or rope. In principle, the range of implements could be extended.)
  - The apparatus adds an *aesthetic* aspect, possibly making the performance more elegant.
  - The apparatus makes the performance *more*

Philosophical reasoning as rhythmic gymnastics? 177

  difficult – more challenging to perform and to complete successfully.
- In a sense, something *odd* is on display, thanks to the addition of the apparatus. Traditional gymnastics meets a party toy?
- Do analogous comments apply to philosophical thinking? When looking back through this book's readings, it seems that, within each, *as if from nowhere, once some comparatively 'normal' (everyday) thinking is under way, an odd thinking-move is made, becoming central to the subsequent reasoning.* The added – philosophically distinctive – thinking-move would be like a rhythmic gymnast's apparatus, added to a performance that might already have been skilful but that now involves new skills, perhaps becoming even more striking as a result.
  - The philosophical thinking-move might be seen as adding an *aesthetic* aspect, possibly making the performance more elegant.
  - Perhaps the philosophical thinking-move makes the overall thinking *more difficult* – more challenging to perform and to complete successfully.
  - In a sense, something *odd* is on display, thanks to the addition of the philosophical thinking-move. Normal thinking meets a surprising philosophical question, or idea, etc.?

I am not suggesting that the analogy between rhythmic gymnastics and philosophical thinking is perfect. But even partial analogies can help when we wish to understand something potentially complex and unusual, such as philosophical thinking.

In being philosophical, we are thinking-*plus*. We might initially be thinking in an everyday way, or even a technical or professional way (such as when immersed in scientific research) – before, suddenly, a philosophical question, idea, challenge, or the like may appear; whereupon the nature of the moment changes. The thinking ceases being everyday, or even 'everyday' in a technical or professional way. Now it is philosophical, at least partly. The pink plastic ball is hovering, needing to be controlled, thrown, caught, and so on – even while it is accompanying comparatively traditional movements, be these bodily or be they mental. Are those movements analogous to comparatively technical 'everyday' thinking?

Actually, I *want* the analogy not to be perfect. Is a piece of philosophical writing or thinking *merely* a performance – a chance simply to display mental dexterity, even elegance? I hope not.

So, I am reassured by another analogy, our earlier linking (section 2.2.3) of philosophical thinking with Parmenides' Way of Truth. Somehow, on that linking, philosophical thinking is answerable not only to *being done skilfully* (and maybe elegantly) but also to truth. A skilful, even elegant, philosophical performance is not an end in itself. What also matters is its *leading or guiding us towards* some aspect of What Is – whatever awaits a traveller along the Way of Truth. And that form of directedness is not present in a performance of rhythmic gymnastics (or many other kinds of performance). In that performance setting, the end – the aim – is merely to be performing skilfully, maybe elegantly.

Still, even if philosophical reasoning is not meant to be merely skilful, it can be judged *at least* on its skilfulness. This judging involves attentiveness to details. That can be helped by this chapter's earlier sections. You open a philosophy book. You read. You ponder. You ask yourself, 'How can I evaluate this?' You reply, still to yourself, 'First I must *identify* the reasoning. Where and how does it start, then continue, then end?'

What is your next move? You could consult this chapter, as an initial step.

Philosophical reasoning as rhythmic gymnastics? 179

- You might identify the reasoning's main *elements* (such as were mentioned in section 4.1).
- Then you can notice the *uses* being made of those elements (section 4.2). What *moves* are being made, taking the author in question from here (= one element) to here (= another element) within her 'philosophy performance space'?
- Finally, you could 'reconstruct' how the author has *organised* those uses of those elements so as to 'construct' her performance. You do this as part of seeking an understanding of how she is thinking – how she has combined those elements and those uses of them. (Those examples in section 4.3 offer some guidance for practising this. I say 'practising' because analysis and 'reconstruction' of a philosophy performance is not always easy.)

How should you then *evaluate* what you have uncovered – the reasoning that you have identified and described, element by element, move by move? Judges of rhythmic gymnastics competitions reach verdicts on the quality of the performances that they are watching. How may we do this for philosophy 'performances' that we read or hear? Some guidance awaits us in chapter 6.

Before then, however, I will mention another reason why the analogy between philosophical thinking and rhythmic gymnastics is partial, not complete.

At present, only a limited range of implements (apparatus) is officially available within rhythmic gymnastics. Maybe, one of these days, that range will be enlarged, possibly in imaginative ways. But philosophy places no limits upon the range of possible ideas, new styles of reasoning, that may be used once they occur to our imagination. (Consider the variety of readings already present in this book.) So, we might think of the oddity of using those implements within rhythmic gymnastics as a *limited* analogue of what, already, we do and can meet within philosophical reasoning.

Philosophy, as I said (but it is worth repeating), places no restrictions upon ideas and ways of thinking that may be used when introducing, shaping, or testing it. Some of these might be discarded if we do not find them philosophically helpful. In the meantime, however, they significantly enrich our philosophical experiences. They even expand our sense of how we may *be* philosophical – what is even *possible* as part of being philosophical.

It is not always simple, though, to decide what makes a move philosophically helpful. Chapter 6 considers this. Before then, still travelling along our shared philosophical path, we will encounter further examples of philosophical reasoning, courtesy of chapter 5. We will thus have *even more* philosophical data in hand upon reaching chapter 6.

5

How Should You Act?

5.1 Towards yourself

5.1.1 Confucius' Way

Chapters 1 and 3 were about reality and knowledge. Philosophically considered, what am I? (Am I a self *at all*? If I am, *how* am I one?) Philosophically considered, what do I know? (Do I know *at all*? If I do, *how* do I do it?) Philosophical questioning does not end there, though. I also think about values, especially about moral ones. At times, I wonder whether I *have* moral value and whether I *live* morally well. I regard those questions as genuine. I do not want to *assume* – arrogantly? – that I have moral value and that I act in morally good ways.

So, here I begin with some thoughts from Confucius (551–479 BCE – this is his Western name; his Chinese title and name were 'Kongzi' ['Master Kong']). Born in what is now Shandong Province, his worldwide influence has been enormous. That influence is centred upon his *Analects*, compiled by his students (disciples) after his death. It encompasses memories of his sayings and actions, his responses to questions. It portrays a *way* to live – indeed, *the* Way, the Confucian *dao*. It is a picture of how one should strive to be *as* a person – how to develop well as a person.

This Way – this Confucian *dao* – is long, in distance and in time. It is a *path* to be travelled. It is also the *travelling*. In either case, it calls for care and attention, which is shaped by practice: 'The Master [Confucius] said, "It is the person who is able to broaden the way, not the way that broadens the person"' (15.29). Yet if the person can be changed, what sort of person emerges? One might begin one's pursuit of the Way, one's travelling, as a *shi* – a scholar-apprentice. One might, with dedication, become a *junzi* – an exemplary person. In principle one might, with continued dedication, become a *sage* – a *sheng*, or *shengren*. Confucius did not claim to have attained that state. I will convey a brief sense of his advice, though, for following this path.

> The Master on entering the Grand Ancestral Hall asked questions about everything. Someone remarked: 'Who said this son of a man from the Zou village knows about observing ritual propriety (= *li*)? ...' When Confucius heard of this, he said 'To [ask such questions] is itself observing ritual propriety.' (3.15)

Is that because one is showing respect, wanting to know details – deferring aptly in a sacred setting, asking to be instructed? Recall the point of section 3.5.4 (some American Indian epistemology) about questions arising when they should, not simply because they can. Good questions can lead to knowledge, which could make one a *junzi*. That is valuable in itself, even when not in material riches.

> The Master said, 'The authoritative person alone has the wherewithal to properly discriminate the good person from the bad.' (4.3)

The Master said, 'If indeed one's purposes are set on authoritative conduct, one could do no wrong.' (4.4)

The Master said, 'Wealth and honor are what people want, but if they are the consequences of deviating from the way (*dao*), I would have no part in them. Poverty and disgrace are what people deplore, but if they are the consequence of staying on the way, I would not avoid them. ... Exemplary persons do not take leave of their authoritative conduct even for the space of a meal. When they are troubled, they certainly turn to it, as they do in facing difficulties.' (4.5)

The Master said, 'Zeng, my friend! My way (*dao*) is bound together with one continuous strand.' ... Master Zeng said [later, to disciples], 'The way of the Master is doing one's utmost and putting oneself in the other's place, nothing more.' (4.15)

Yan Hui said, 'Could I ask what becoming authoritative entails?' The Master replied, 'Do not look at anything that violates the observance of ritual propriety (= *li*); do not listen to anything that violates the observance of ritual propriety; do not speak about anything that violates the observance of ritual propriety; do not do anything that violates the observance of ritual propriety.' (12.1)

The Master said, 'Having a sense of appropriate conduct as one's basic disposition, developing it in observing ritual propriety (*li*), expressing it with modesty, and consummating it in making good on one's word: this then is an exemplary person (*junzi*).' (15.18)

The Master said, 'Exemplary persons make demands on themselves, while petty persons [= another Confucian category of person] make demands on others.' (15.21)

I offer that lengthy sequence of quotations without accompanying explanations because they 'flow' smoothly. They put me in mind of a growing coral reef, a living whole actively comprising a vast number of gems – of colour, of shape – best appreciated as parts of that emerging whole.

Still, I will highlight what seems like excellent advice for anyone currently a scholar-apprentice, hoping to travel further along the Way. When Confucius was asked what would be his 'first priority' if 'the Lord of Wey [were] to turn the administration of his state over to you', his answer was 'Without question it would be to insure that names are used properly.'

> When names are not used properly, language will not be used effectively; [hence] matters will not be taken care of; [hence] the observance of ritual propriety (*li*) and the playing of music will not flourish; [hence] the application of laws and punishment will not be on the mark; [hence] the people will not know what to do with themselves. Thus, when the exemplary person puts a name to something, it can certainly be spoken, and when spoken it can certainly be acted upon. There is nothing careless in the attitude of the exemplary person toward what is said. (13.3)

Those are inspiring words for anyone reading philosophy with an eye for accuracy. For example, was Fricker (section 3.6.4) describing ways in which people are treated unjustly when proper words are overlooked? Confucius' words also remind me of the *neo*-Confucian Wang Yangming's knowledge-action unity (section 3.5.1): using correct words matters for knowing, and thereby for acting correctly. Confucius proposed what we might treat as significant *details* for linking knowledge with action.

5.1.2 Aristotle's substantial happiness
Confucius' advice (section 5.1.1) concerned being a particularly fine person. For what should one strive as

a person, leaving aside riches and the like? Aristotle (whom we met in section 1.6.1) also had advice in his *Nicomachean Ethics*. What should we seek? For Aristotle, it was *eudaimonia*. This is often translated as 'flourishing', often as 'happiness'. What did that mean?

For Aristotle, it did not mean merely 'feeling happy'. He sought nothing less than to 'grasp the characteristic activity of a human being' (1097b24):

> just as the good – the doing well – of a flute-player, a sculptor or any practitioner of a skill, or generally whatever has some characteristic activity or action, is thought to lie [= reside] in its characteristic activity [= e.g. a flute-player does well *as* a flute-player purely as a matter *of* her flute-playing], so the same would seem to be true of a human being, if indeed he [= *any* human being, considered simply *as* a human being] has a characteristic activity. (1097b25–8)

I will slow down that thinking by Aristotle, to understand it better.

- There are kinds of being. And some activities are characteristic, in revealing ways, for each such kind.
- A particular being does well, in its role as an instance of such a kind, by performing well instances of whatever activities are characteristic for that kind.
- Each of us is an instance of the kind *human being*.
- So, that general picture – of kinds, characteristic activities, and 'doing well' – 'would seem to be true of' us, simply as humans *per se*.

How, though? Here is how Aristotle poses that question (1097b28–1098a1).

> Well, do the carpenter and the tanner [= a tanner of animal hides] have characteristic activities and

actions, and a human being none? Has nature left him [= considered purely as a human being per se] without a characteristic activity to perform? Or, as there seem to be characteristic activities of the eye, the hand, the foot, and generally of each part of the body, should one assume that a human being has some characteristic activity over and above all these? What sort of thing might it be, then? For living is obviously shared even by plants, while what we are looking for is something special to a human being.

Does something distinctive, then, amount to a human's 'doing well'?

Aristotle believed so. He looked to the human 'soul' and what seem to be various virtues. These also seem to be distinctive excellences in how a human soul can be used:

> the human good turns out to be activity of the soul in accordance with virtue, and if there are several virtues, [then it is an activity] in accordance with the best and most complete ... [all of this] over a complete life. For one swallow does not make a summer, nor one day. Neither does one day or a short time make someone blessed and happy. (1098a17–19)

Aristotle is talking about something beyond a passing feeling of contentment or pleasure, say. We must be acting 'in accordance with virtue'.

What does that involve? Some human virtues involve intellectual activity with theoretical – not merely practical – content (1178a6–8). When acting well, we do this partly by using our intellects:

> for a human being, therefore, the life in accordance with intellect is best and pleasantest, since this, more than anything else, constitutes humanity. So this life will also be the happiest.

And some human virtues are moral in nature (1178a11–15).

> For we do just actions, courageous actions, and the other actions in accordance with the virtues, in relation to each other, observing what is proper to each in contracts, services and actions of all kinds, and in feelings as well; and all of these are manifestly human.

What follows? 'Happiness, therefore, will be some form of contemplation' (1178b33). Is this a purely intellectual-moral vision? Yes, and no: 'human nature is not self-sufficient for contemplation, but the body must be healthy and provided with food and other care' (1178b34–5). These bodily aspects are needed in supportive ways for happiness. We take our cue from 'the gods':

> if the gods feel any concern for human affairs, as they seem to, it would be reasonable for them to find enjoyment in what is best and most closely related to them – namely, intellect – and to reward those who like and honour this most, on the assumption that these people care for what is loved by the gods, and act rightly and nobly. (1179a25–9)

Where does that lead?

> And it is quite clear that all of these qualities belong most of all to the wise person; he, therefore, is dearest to the gods. And it is likely that this same person is also the happiest; so in this way too the wise person will be more happy than anyone else. (1179a29–32)

Some people might be tempted by Aristotle's account without accepting there literally being gods. Can we regard various capacities – some intellectual; some moral – as deeply and distinctively human even if there are no gods? Can we think that these should be *developed* if one is to be fully and distinctively human? To that extent, might we seek to be god-*like*, at least metaphorically?

5.1.3 Yaḥyā ibn 'Adī's complete man

This morning, I heard – yet again – someone talking of being 'the best version' of themselves. What might this involve? Being physically fit? (A gym near me proclaims this to be 'your full potential'.) A welcome aim, although hardly the pinnacle of possible human achievement.

We might consult *The Reformation of Morals*, from Yaḥyā ibn 'Adī. (The book's title has also been translated as *The Refinement of Character*.) Ibn 'Adī (893–974) was born in Takrit, in Iraq, into a Christian (Syrian Orthodox) family. His career was in Baghdad, as a philosopher, logician, and translator – especially of Greek philosophy from Syriac into Arabic. (He was a member of the Baghdad Peripatetics 'school'.) I mention him especially for his concept of *the complete man*.

He began (part 1, para. 2) with an aspirational statement.

> The worthiest thing a man chooses for himself is his own fulfillment and perfection; he will not stop short of attaining the highest degree of it, nor will he be content with any failure to achieve its final reach. Part of a man's fulfillment and perfection is to be well trained in honorable and good moral qualities, to refrain from evil and wrong ones ...

How is this to be done? Ibn 'Adī developed a list of moral qualities, both good and bad, with proposals for how these can be embraced or spurned. A metaphysics underlies this (part 1, para. 5).

> A moral quality is a state proper to the soul, in which a man performs his actions without deliberation or study. A moral quality may come to be in some people as a natural impulse or disposition and in others only by way of practice and effort.

When ibn 'Adī wrote of 'the soul', he meant it literally (part 2, para. 1).

> The soul has three faculties, and they are also named souls: the appetitive soul, the irascible soul, and the rational soul. All of the moral qualities emanate from these faculties. Some moral qualities are specific to a particular faculty; in some, two faculties participate; and, in some of them, the three faculties participate. Some faculties belong to man and to the other animals, and some are specific to man alone.

The rational soul is pivotal in forming a complete man, an achievement described in part 5 (titled 'Man's attainment of perfection').

> The complete man is the one whom virtue does not bypass, whom vice does not disfigure. A man seldom ends up at this point. But, when a man does ..., it is the angels he resembles more than he resembles men. (Part 5, para. 2)

Can we be more specific? Ibn 'Adī listed (part 5, para. 3) 'the attributes of the complete man', including these:

> the complete man ... will be someone watchful over all his moral qualities, attentive to all his faults, and wary of the intrusion of any defect. He will be ready to put every virtue into action, assiduous to reach the goal, passionate for the image of perfection. He will be disposed to find pleasure in good moral actions. ... He will be disinclined to overestimate the virtues he

will have acquired but inclined to regard the least of the vices as grave. He will be disposed to regard high rank as of small value and ... will consider fulfillment beneath his station and perfection the least of his attributes.

In order to be like that, the complete man must

> direct his attention to the study of the 'exact sciences'. ... [He must] make it his goal to grasp the quiddities [= the inner natures] of existing things, to disclose their causes and occasions [= in what circumstances those causes operate], and to search out their final ends and purposes. (Part 5, para. 4)

That list continues. Personal completeness is demanding, relying on one's rational soul. It involves reading 'books on morals, ... of biographies and of policies'. One must 'always frequent [= attend] the sessions [= gatherings] of scholars and sages and continually associate with modest and abstinent people – this if [one] is an ordinary citizen.' (Slightly different advice pertains if one is 'a king or a leader'.)

Are there complications? Here are a few of the many (part 5, paras 5, 6).

> The complete man ... will strive for balance. He will avoid dissipation and excess. ... [H]e will take charge of his soul, hold it back from craving any abhorrent pleasure or excessive appetite. ... Whoever seeks fulfillment must know that there is no way for him to reach his goal as long as pleasure seems good to him and appetite desirable.

That might sound extreme. But is it, when seeking personal completeness? It seems more like a warning against letting the appetitive soul, for instance, overpower one. This might remind us of Frankfurt's distinction (section 1.3.3) between people and wantons. Was ibn 'Adī in effect warning us not to be wantons if we wish to be complete?

> [He also needs] to disdain money, ... to look upon it according to its deserts. ... In itself it is worthless ... When he has attended to his needs and has been sparing in his expenses and has settled his claims, he will ... review his situation. And if there is anything remaining of his money ... he will set aside a portion of it ... to which he can have recourse in misfortune, ... [after which] he will ... disperse [what is left] among the needy of his people, his neighbors, his relatives, and his friends. He will designate a portion of it for the weak, the poor, and the poverty-stricken – those who are overlooked. (Part 5, paras 8, 10)

Thus, part of how one should seek to become the best person possible includes acting well towards others (which we will discuss in section 5.2). But ibn 'Adī, I assume, would have seen this as flowing *from much else* within the complete person. It is not as if one could be lamentably incomplete yet *compensate* for this by acting well towards others.

That strict tone reflects these stirring almost parting words from ibn 'Adī (part 5, para. 26): 'How repugnant is deficiency in someone with the potential for perfection, and weakness on the part of someone well prepared to attain fulfillment!' Courtesy of ibn 'Adī, then, we have a picture, a conception, of how one should act towards oneself. He envisaged what he regards as an ideal. Presumably he hoped that readers would be inspired to apply his account to themselves. Was this an *argument* by ibn 'Adī for why they should do so? In a sense, yes: it was akin to a motivational talk, asking readers to imagine what being complete *would* be like – and to work towards *actually* being like that.

Readings for 5.1

For Confucius, see *The Analects of Confucius: A Philosophical Translation*, trans. R. T. Ames and H. Rosemont, Jr. (New York: Ballantine Books, 1998); quotations from pp. 85–6, 89, 90, 92, 152, 162, 188, 189, 190. For Aristotle, see *Nicomachean Ethics*, rev. edn, ed. and trans. R. Crisp (Cambridge: Cambridge University Press, [2000] 2014); quotations from pp. 11, 12, 194, 196, 197. For ibn 'Adī, see *The Reformation of Morals*, trans. S. H. Griffith (Provo, UT: Brigham Young University Press, 2002); quotations from pp. 5, 9, 15, 93, 95, 97, 101, 119.

5.2 Towards other people

5.2.1 *The Confucian* Great Learning

Manifesting what is special in being a person sounds splendid. That idea might motivate attempting to achieve such a state – being a Confucian sage, say, or attaining Aristotelian flourishing, or being a complete person in ibn 'Adī's sense (section 5.1). This might also point towards reasons for acting well towards *other* people.

We meet that theme in the classic Confucian text *The Great Learning* (*Ta-Hsueh* or *Daxue*). The text's dating is unclear (fifth/fourth/third century BCE?), as is its authorship, but it was one of the *Four Books* (the *Analects* was another: section 5.1.1) that long constituted the canon at the core of Confucian scholarship and education from neo-Confucian times. Here is the heart of its advice.

> The ancients who wished to illustrate illustrious virtue throughout the kingdom, first ordered well their own

> States. Wishing to order well their States, they first regulated their families. Wishing to regulate their families, they first cultivated their persons. Wishing to cultivate their persons, they first rectified their hearts. Wishing to rectify their hearts, they first sought to be sincere in their thoughts. Wishing to be sincere in their thoughts, they first extended to the utmost their knowledge. Such extensions of knowledge lay in the investigation of things. (Para. 4)

That describes a sequence of desired causal links – one thing being needed to cause another. So it is a sequence of *necessary conditions*. Doing A is needed for doing B, which is needed for doing C, which is needed for doing D, etc. – the ultimate goal being a successful kingdom, which is achieved only if each condition is satisfied in turn.

But even a lengthy sequence of necessary conditions might not *suffice* ('only if' is not the same as 'if'). One thing after another being *needed* does not ensure that, even if all of these are achieved, the original aim is achieved. Maybe more will be needed in a particular case. Still, that *is* what always happens here, we are reassured by *The Great Learning*.

> Things being investigated, knowledge became complete. Their knowledge being complete, their thoughts were sincere. Their thoughts being sincere, their hearts were then rectified. Their hearts being rectified, their persons were cultivated. Their persons being cultivated, their families were regulated. Their families being regulated, their States were rightly governed. Their States being rightly governed, the whole kingdom was made tranquil and happy. (Para. 5)

Thus, a progression is described as having occurred: A did lead to B, which did lead to C, which did lead to D, etc. And we are told that, once all of these conditions were satisfied, so was the whole. After which, we can survey that whole. What do we find?

> From the Son of Heaven down to the mass of the people, all must consider the cultivation of the person [as being] the root of *everything besides*. (Para. 6)

> It cannot be, when the root is neglected, that what should spring from it will be well ordered. It never has been the case that what was of great importance has been [only] slightly cared for, and, at the same time, that what was of slight importance has been greatly cared for. (Para. 7)

We were guided, in paragraphs 4 and 5, along a sequence of reasoning, each step describing a circumstance that is needed *and enough* for the next one. Now we conclude, in paragraphs 6 and 7, that this pattern linked each individual person with society as a whole. Take care of yourself – your knowledge, your thoughts, your heart. But do not do this purely for yourself. Do it for others.

Thus, each of us is part of a social whole, the health of which depends on each of us. But each of us, of course, is also a whole, with parts – including what one knows and thinks. Look within, and make these what they should be, so that you are properly cultivating yourself. Do this not only for yourself. Wider social worth flows from this.

It is difficult to know how to evaluate that thinking. Is it describing what will happen if each of us is as we should be? Or is it aspirational, envisioning an ideal way for an individual to contribute to an ideal social whole?

5.2.2 Immanuel Kant's ends-in-themselves
I am asking how we should regard, and act towards, other people. In his 1785 *Foundations of the Metaphysics of*

Morals, Immanuel Kant (1724–1804), from Königsberg in East Prussia (the city is now Kaliningrad in Russia, although Kant wrote in German), had this striking message:

> every rational being exists as an end in himself and not merely as a means to be arbitrarily used by this or that will. ... Beings whose existence does not depend on our will but on nature, if they are not rational beings, have only a relative worth as means and are therefore called 'things'; ... rational beings are designated 'persons' because their nature indicates that they are ends in themselves, i.e., things which may not be used merely as means. (428)

A person is deemed to be an end *in themselves*, with *intrinsic* moral value. And being a person is distinguished from being a *thing*. We can rightly use things – but not people – in effect as tools. Sometimes, as life unfurls, it feels as if one is indeed being treated like that. Kant proposed a way of understanding such actions as morally wrong.

Think of any action as having an *end* – what the action is 'aimed at', consciously or not. When someone does X in order immediately to achieve Y, her action's end – its direct point – is at least Y. Its end might also indirectly be something further: achieving Y can be intended as a step towards Z. But if Z is an end in itself, reaching it is not meant to achieve something else. For Kant, we must accord ourselves and others that ultimate status.

I used 'must' just now because it seems that, for Kant, morality was a matter of doing what *duty* demands. What kind of duty, though? Laws, parents, schools, and so on, might claim to be specifying duties. Is this all there is to morality? Doing what laws, parents, schools, etc., instruct us to do? Or did Kant see morality as reflecting a deeper duty, applying to anyone from any culture? He did: 'Act so that you treat humanity, whether in your own person or in that of another, always as an end and never as a means only' (429). This 'practical imperative' (as Kant called it) is like an order, although not a normal one. It is somehow *from* everyone *to* everyone. It is universally-to and universally-from. It was one version of Kant's idea of a 'categorical imperative'. To violate it is to act immorally.

Kant considered examples. The first concerns suicide. He highlighted 'the concept of necessary duty to one's self' (429). One must treat oneself as a person, not a thing: 'he who contemplates suicide will ask himself whether his action can be consistent with the idea of humanity as an end in itself' (429). How should that question-to-oneself be answered? Harshly (some will feel): one cannot treat even oneself, Kant thought, as a mere means; yet that is what one does in committing suicide.

> If, in order to escape from burdensome circumstances, he destroys himself, he uses a person [= himself] merely as a means to maintain a tolerable condition up to the end of his life. (429)

So, although I could think that I was respecting myself, Kant did not see it in that way.

> Man, however, is not a thing, and thus not something to be used merely as a means; he must always be regarded in all his actions as an end in himself. Therefore, I cannot dispose of man in my own person ... (429)

Even if I cause no hardship for others, that is not enough, on Kant's approach. I would be treating myself merely as a means – towards experiencing no further pain, say. I would not be finding ultimate value in myself, *as* a self.

What of Kant's categorical imperative and acting towards others? Famously, he was critical of all lying. We might have regarded this as at least sometimes morally reasonable (such as to save someone's feelings, even their life). But no:

> he who intends a deceitful promise to others sees immediately that he intends to use another man merely as a means .... For he whom I want to use for my own purposes by means of such a promise cannot possibly assent to my mode of acting against him and cannot contain the end of this action in himself. (429–30)

How would I not be respecting the other person's ultimate value? Maybe I would not be allowing her the opportunity to respond with rational autonomy, deciding for herself how to react to the relevant truth. (I would not be *telling* her the relevant truth.) I might think that I have spared her from awareness of an awkward truth. But I would have denied her the chance to respond as a freely rational being to such awareness.

Kant apparently thought that anyone must act (if they are to do it morally) in ways that could be 'universal laws', as if these had been *legislated* by purely rational beings – all of us – with no one acting on only her own desires. 'So act as if your maxims should serve at the same time as the universal law (of all rational beings)' (438): 'merely the dignity of humanity as rational nature without any end or advantage to be gained by it ... should serve as the inflexible precept of the will' (439).

Can we act as Kant is advocating? He has given us more of a theoretical analysis of morality's nature (what morality *is*) than practical-action advice (what to *do* if one is to act morally). Still, could I *try* according everyone inherent value as rational beings, not merely beings with desires? Not everyone is always clever or thoughtful; yet does everyone have a capacity for rationality that can freely guide their actions? This is a picture of what a person is, insofar as she is a moral agent at all – her having moral *standing*, even if not always acting morally well.

And would that picture enrich this book's early sections, where we asked *what a person is*? We did not talk about morality. Can we now say that being a person also includes *having* a moral nature (even if perhaps not always one that spreads joy)?

5.2.3 Mary Wollstonecraft's early feminism

A moment ago (section 5.2.2), I wrote 'she' when talking about 'a person' being 'a moral agent'. That should sound unsurprising, since we take for granted that women, like men, have moral agency. But philosophy's history has included individuals making substantial *arguments* for this.

One of those individuals was Mary Wollstonecraft (1759–97), in her 1792 *Vindication of the Rights of Woman*. An English philosopher (whose second daughter was Mary Shelley, the author of *Frankenstein*), she developed a feminist argument – not the first, but a notable one – before the word 'feminism' had arrived. She felt the injustice of how women had long been oppressed, in significant ways, by 'the tyranny of man'. She wrote especially about education, about lost opportunities for women's moral and intellectual development.

> To render women truly useful members of society, I argue that they should be led, by having their understandings cultivated on a large scale, to acquire a rational affection for their country, founded on knowledge, because it is obvious that we are little interested about what we do not understand. ... I have endeavoured to show that private duties are never properly fulfilled

unless the understanding enlarges the heart; and that public virtue is only an aggregate of private.

That passage mentions some of Wollstonecraft's favoured phenomena – understanding, knowledge, virtue, and their being cultivated. She argued that a woman's understanding should be cultivated through proper education – this being no different to a man's understanding being cultivated, since men *and* women are rational:

> cultivate their minds, give them the salutary sublime curb [= the supremely welcome rigour and discipline] of principle, and let them attain conscious dignity by feeling themselves only dependent on God. Teach [women], in common with man, to submit to necessity [= principles], instead of giving, to render them more pleasing, a sex to morals.

Encourage within women 'what deserves the name of intellect, the power of gaining general or abstract ideas, or even intermediate ones', a power that can come from reading 'history and moral essays'.

That is not merely a matter of making women more interesting, say. Nothing less than 'the improvement and emancipation of the whole sex' is at stake: if men, who had almost all of the relevant power within Wollstonecraft's society, 'will not improve women, they will deprave them.' This did not mean turning women into social outcasts (reflecting how we use the term 'deprave'). It meant limiting women to a lesser state than they could – and hence should be enabled to – attain. Such limiting involved keeping women 'in ignorance', since 'it is a farce to call any being virtuous whose virtues do not result from the exercise of its own reason':

> not only the virtue but the *knowledge* of the two sexes should be the same in nature, if not in degree, and

> ... women, considered not only as moral but rational creatures, ought to endeavour to acquire human virtues (or perfections) by the *same* means as men, instead of being educated like a fanciful kind of *half* being ...

How did Wollstonecraft argue for that view of knowledge as the same kind of thing in men and in women? She relied partly on viewing us as created in enough of God's image, especially with our capacity for reason.

> Reason is ... the simple power of improvement; or, more properly speaking, of discerning truth. ... More or less [of it] may be conspicuous [= evident] in one being than another; but the nature of reason [= the nature of reason per se] must be the same in all, if it be an emanation of divinity [= if it comes ultimately from God], the tie that connects the creature with the Creator; for, can that soul be stamped with the heavenly image [= be made in God's image], that is not perfected by the exercise of its own reason [= if it is not being used *as* reason]?

The power to know comes from God, each of us being at least *that much like* God. This is as true of women as of men. We can say something about what such knowledge looks like.

> The power of generalising ideas, of drawing comprehensive conclusions from individual observations, is the only acquirement, for an immortal being, that really deserves the name of knowledge.

That is worth stating, since there is a lesser alternative – using one's senses, *not* reason.

> Merely to observe [= via one's senses], without endeavouring to account for [= explain via reason] anything,

may (in a very incomplete manner) serve as the common sense of life; but where is the store laid up [= of suitable knowledge] that is to clothe the soul when it leaves the body [= when the senses are left behind]?

And Wollstonecraft argued that men restricted women to that lesser alternative. Men had denied almost all women opportunities to develop powers of reason, hence to gain real understanding: 'instinct, sublimated into wit and cunning, for the purposes of life, has been substituted in its stead' [= 'instead']:

> the very constitution of civil governments has put almost insuperable obstacles in the way to prevent the cultivation of the female understanding; yet virtue can be built on no other foundation.

Women had been '[c]onfined, then, in cages like the feathered race [= like birds]'. Until this changes, 'hereditary power [= being born as male in a society that gives power mainly to men] ... nips reason in the bud' (that is, it does not allow others' powers of reason to flourish). Most widely, *women's* reason is thus limited: 'the neglected education of my fellow-creatures is the grand source of the misery I deplore, and ... women, in particular, are rendered weak and wretched'.

Wollstonecraft saw a socially entrenched problem; have *we* fully solved it? If not, is *our* society as morally good as it should be?

5.2.4 John Stuart Mill's greatest happiness
Suppose, for argument's sake, that we can solve the problem described by Wollstonecraft (section 5.2.3): imagine men and women in general being equal participants in a society that is fully supportive of all. What would *then* make an action morally good within that society?

I will revisit John Stuart Mill (section 3.4.2). On his view of morality, happiness is central. We read a version of this with Aristotle (section 5.1.2); the idea was different in Mill's hands. His emphasis was on *anyone's* happiness, on there being as *much* of it as can be had. This was Mill's *utilitarianism*, a form of moral theory championed by others before him (notably, the English philosopher Jeremy Bentham: 1748–1832) and since.

Here is the central proposal from Mill's 1861 *Utilitarianism* (ch. II, para. 2).

> The creed which accepts as the foundation of morals, Utility, or the Greatest Happiness Principle, holds that actions are right in proportion as they tend to promote happiness, wrong as they tend to produce the reverse of happiness. By happiness is intended pleasure, and the absence of pain; by unhappiness, pain, and the privation of pleasure.

Should you do action A? Or action B? Which will cause more happiness and less unhappiness? Do that action, if either. That was Mill's main thesis – his 'principle of utility'. How did he argue for it? He began (ch. IV, para. 3) with an analogy between desirability and visibility (or similar qualities).

> The only proof capable of being given that an object is visible, is that people actually see it. The only proof that a sound is audible, is that people hear it: and so of the other sources of our experience. In like manner, ... the sole evidence it is possible to produce that anything is desirable, is that people do actually desire it.

Why was desirability Mill's focus? It is because an action's being morally good is its being relevantly *worthy* of being desired – in that sense, its being desir*able*. Mill added the idea that we should look to the action's being *desired*, either beforehand (in anticipation), or at the time, or afterwards (with people being consciously pleased that the action has been performed). So, *actual* happiness was Mill's key to moral worth – that is, even to moral desir*ability*.

But is that argument misleading? Was Mill mistaking a disanalogy for a helpful analogy? After all (on the following objection to him), 'visible' means 'can be seen' – whereas 'desirable', by meaning 'worthy of being desired', does not mean merely 'can be desired'. More simply, 'desirable' falls well short of meaning 'desired'.

I am unsure whether that objection succeeds. Mill was discussing *evidence* of what is morally worthy, not the *meaning* of moral worthiness. And what sort of evidence is possible? Can we observe action A's being *desirable*? Not directly. Can we observe its being *desired*? Perhaps so – which would be *some* evidence that A is worthy of being desired. What evidence beyond this is ever available? Maybe none. Our best evidence for applying the term 'desirable' might *be* uses of the word 'desired', as we observe people desiring action A.

How did Mill then infer his thesis about an action's wider desirability – for a population, say? He cited no evidence beyond instances of happiness in individuals. 'No reason can be given why the general happiness is desirable, except that each person, so far as he believes it to be attainable, desires his own happiness' (ch. IV, para. 3). Again, how did Mill reach his thesis about 'the general happiness'? He said this: 'each person's happiness is a good to that person, and the general happiness, therefore, [is] a good to the aggregate of all persons.' He seems to have been saying that happiness within a group is happiness within enough of the group's individuals: the more of it there is within the more of them, the better for the group itself.

Is that all we need in a theory of morality? 'Happiness has made out its title [= if his argument from a moment ago succeeds] as *one* of the ends of conduct, and consequently one of the criteria of morality' (ch. IV, para. 3). This might look as if Mill was conceding that happiness is *not* the only good. Not really, though. Yes, he acknowledged (ch. IV, paras 4, 5) that people do not always *overtly* desire only happiness. But he argued that, always, they at least implicitly desire it.

> They desire, for example, virtue, and the absence of vice, no less really than pleasure and the absence of pain. ... [T]he utilitarian doctrine ... maintains ... that virtue is ... to be desired disinterestedly, for itself. ... [And] in those who love it disinterestedly it ... is desired and cherished, not as a means to happiness, but as a part of their happiness.

This would make happiness complex. 'The ingredients of happiness are very various' (para. 5). Are they so various as to make Mill's theory unwieldy? 'It is better to be a human being dissatisfied than a pig satisfied; better to be Socrates dissatisfied than a fool satisfied' (ch. II, para. 6). Harsh words? Maybe. Is there truth in them? Mill continued: 'And if the fool, or the pig, are of a different opinion, it is because they only know their own side of the question. The other party to the comparison knows both sides.'

That is puzzling. I do not know what it feels like to be a pig, hence what a pig's pleasures are like *for* a pig. As a person, wallowing in mud has no appeal for me. But presumably pigs would feel no pleasure in much of what *we* do. Of course people prefer what people prefer, not what pigs prefer. Are people *absolutely* right to have those preferences? Who should say?

5.2.5 Nel Noddings's caring
Mill's theory (section 5.2.4) was built around the emotion of happiness. Is that the only morally significant

emotion? Nel Noddings (1929–2022), an American philosopher of education, placed *caring* at the heart of morality. She warned against becoming 'detached from the very heart of morality: the sensibility [= a general sensitivity] that calls forth caring.'

What *is* caring? I assume that it is at least a feeling, often expressed in actions. Noddings added helpful details, distinguishing *natural* caring from *ethical* caring.

> There can be no ethical sentiment without the initial, enabling sentiment [of natural caring]. In situations where we act on behalf of the other because we want to do so, we are acting in accord with natural caring. A mother's caretaking efforts in behalf of her child are not usually considered ethical but [are] natural. Even maternal animals take care of their offspring, and we do not credit them with ethical behavior.

So there is a difference. What *makes* that difference? What turns natural caring into ethical caring?

> This memory of our own best moments of caring and being cared for sweeps over us as a feeling – as an 'I must' – in response to the plight of the other and our conflicting desire to serve our own interests. ... I may reach toward this memory and guide my conduct by it if I wish to do so.

Ethical caring 'requires an effort that is not needed in natural caring'. That effort must be directed at what Noddings called a person's 'ethical ideal' – 'our best picture of ourselves caring and being cared for'. The word 'best' could be extremely demanding. But Noddings expected only a realistically 'best picture': 'it does not idealize the impossible so that we may escape into ideal abstraction' – which, in Noddings's view, amounts to *idle* abstraction.

> [T]here is a form of caring attitude natural and accessible to all human beings. ... But the ethic itself [= her overall care ethic] will not embody a set of universalizable moral judgments [= ones applying to *anyone* who fits some supposedly relevant general description]. Indeed, moral judgment will not be its central concern.

That matters, because much moral philosophy focuses on moral judgement – what form it takes, how it applies to us, how it motivates us. But we may rightly be wary of it. Think of how often we try not to be judgemental, worried about its making us less morally sensitive. So, Noddings focused on 'the moral impulse or moral attitude'.

I will mention two details. First, Noddings thought of caring as requiring not just one person to have a seemingly apt feeling. It is a *relation*, with two people playing a part in its being created.

> Caring involves two parties: the one-caring and the cared-for. It is complete when it is fulfilled in both. ... Suppose I claim to care for X, but X does not believe that I care for him. ... [I]f you are looking at this relationship, you would have to report, however reluctantly, that something is missing. X does not feel that I care. Therefore, ... the relationship cannot be characterized as one of caring.

Second, Noddings did not regard caring as merely a feeling. It involves a kind of commitment:

> at the foundation of moral behavior ... is feeling or sentiment. But, further, there is commitment to remain open to that feeling, to remember it, and to put one's thinking in its service.

With those details in mind, how did Noddings argue for our being able to bypass moral judgement?

We may legally punish one who has stolen, but we may not pass moral judgment on him until we know why he stole. ... The lessons in 'right' and 'wrong' are hard lessons – not swiftly accomplished by setting up as an objective the learning of some principle. We do not say: It is wrong to steal. Rather, we consider why it was wrong or may be wrong in this case to steal. We do not say: It is wrong to kill. By setting up such a principle, we also imply its exceptions, and then we may too easily act on authorized exceptions. The one-caring wants to consider, and wants her child to consider, the act itself in full context.

What mattered for Noddings was always 'the caring relation', which is 'ethically basic':

both parties contribute to the relation; my caring must be somehow completed in the other if the relation is to be described as caring. ... We want to be *moral* in order to remain in the caring relation and to enhance the ideal of ourselves as one-caring.

Philosophers often ask 'Why be moral?' Noddings offered a different form of theory to those of Kant (section 5.2.2) and Mill (section 5.2.4), in particular. Often, when considering why some action is wrong, I do try to imagine – and to care – how it does, might, or would feel for someone affected (such as an assault victim). Caring about caring can contribute to caring.

5.2.6 Martha Nussbaum's capabilities
We have been reflecting on apparently morally relevant feelings, such as happiness (section 5.2.4) and caring (section 5.2.5). But when are feelings inadequate indicators of moral worth?

I engage with that question via a proposal from Martha Nussbaum (b. 1947), an American philosopher known initially for work on ancient Greek philosophy before writing on much else, including social and political philosophy. I discuss her *capabilities* approach. It extends an earlier version, within economics, by the Indian economist and philosopher Amartya Sen (b. 1933), with whom Nussbaum has written about this.

Recall Mill's focusing (section 5.2.4) on an action's utilities. Nussbaum counters, in *Women and Human Development*, that 'reliance on utility ... does not even include all the relevant information.' It is true that 'we want to know ... how individuals feel about what is happening to them, whether dissatisfied or satisfied.' Yet 'we also want to know what they are actually able to do and to be.' What a person feels about an action's affecting her is part of the action's utility; Nussbaum urges us to look behind those feelings: 'We ask ... about what [a person] does, and what she is in a position to do (what her opportunities and liberties are).' Is the person being denied *opportunities* to act in ways expressive of who she really is or could be?

Nussbaum extends the point: 'we ask not just about the resources that are sitting around, but about how those do or do not go to work, enabling [the person] to function in a fully human way.' That idea of *fully human functioning* is reminiscent of Aristotle (section 5.1.2). A person's 'quality of life' is not better because there are 'resources ... sitting around'. They might be *out of reach* for her. She might not realise this, depending on how she has been encouraged or trained to think about herself.

Nussbaum's aim is feminist, too. *Women and Human Development* includes detailed discussions of India, especially of what was, or was not, realistically possible for Indian women. In a practical spirit, Nussbaum develops a list of 'central human functional capabilities':

- life ('being able to live to the end of a human life of normal length')

- bodily health
- bodily integrity ('being able to move freely from place to place; having one's bodily boundaries treated as sovereign')
- 'being able to use the senses, to imagine, think, and reason – and to do these things in a "truly human" way, a way informed and cultivated by an adequate education'
- 'being able to have [emotional] attachments to things and people outside ourselves'
- practical reason ('being able to form a conception of the good and to engage in critical reflection about the planning of one's life')
- affiliation ('being able to live with and toward others'; 'having the social bases of self-respect and non-humiliation')
- 'being able to live with concern for and in relation to animals, plants, and the world of nature'
- 'being able to laugh, to play, to enjoy recreational activities'
- having some '[c]ontrol over one's environment', both political and material

Two details should be noted for that final entry. Nussbaum does not mean, by *political* control, controlling other people. She means being 'able to participate effectively in political choices that govern one's life', having 'protections of free speech and association'. And *material* control involves abilities in practice to own property, to be employed, etc.

For Nussbaum, this is 'a list of *separate components*', each of 'central importance'. We cannot trade away the significance of some by increasing the role of others. Nussbaum links these with the idea we met when reading Kant (section 5.2.2). These conditions reflect the need to treat people as *ends in themselves*.

> We may thus rephrase our [Kantian] *principle of each person as end*, articulating it as a *principle of each person's capability*: the capabilities sought are sought for *each and every person*, not, in the first instance, for groups or families or states or other corporate bodies.

We saw Kant saying that acting morally towards someone involves treating her as an end, not a means. In Nussbaum's rephrasing, this means treating the person as someone whose full human potential should be respected and, where possible, accommodated. It is often helpful to formulate philosophical ideas in different ways, allowing us to notice various aspects and applications. Nussbaum's rephrasing seems to indicate how we could readily apply Kant's key idea.

How readily, though? This might depend on what roles Nussbaum is hoping that governments play. How do a government's actions affect citizens' real capabilities?

> [A] government that makes available only a reduced and animal-like mode of an important item such as healthy living, or sensing, has not done enough. All the items on the list should be available in a form that involves reason and affiliation. This sets constraints on where we set the threshold, for each of the separate capabilities, and also constraints on which specifications of it we will accept.

That idea of a *threshold* is significant within Nussbaum's theory. A government can do only so much; yet it should do enough. No one should be immorally cast aside, by anyone or by a government. Everyone should be allowed a realistic chance to live in a fully human way.

5.2.7 Charles Mills on the racial contract

Concerns (such as Nussbaum's: section 5.2.6) about groups of people being denied opportunities to participate fully in society take varied forms. For example, let us discuss some *racial* dimensions of that general worry. Charles Mills (whom we met in section 3.6.5) is again helpful.

Mills looked beyond individuals and whatever racially aggressive feelings they might – or might not – have:

> racism (or, as I will argue, global white supremacy) is *itself* a political system, a particular power structure of formal or informal rule, socioeconomic privilege, and norms for the differential distribution of material and opportunities, benefits and burdens, rights and duties.

Even within a racist system, people might not have consciously sought to make it racially unfair. Mills could say, however, that they *might as well* have done so. How did he argue for that interpretation? He adapted a venerable philosophical idea, of a 'social contract'.

> We all understand the idea of a 'contract', an agreement between two or more people to do something. The 'social contract' just extends this idea. If we think of human beings as starting off in a 'state of nature', it suggests that they then *decide* to establish civil society and a government. What we have, then, is a theory that founds government on the popular consent of individuals taken as equals.

The idea of a social contract is associated particularly with the English philosopher Thomas Hobbes (1588–1679). It is an *explanatory fiction*. It does not describe people having formulated a literal contract as a basis for a society's functioning. It is a philosophical move, not an historical one. It is interpretive. It imagines what *could* have occurred, *given* notable aspects of what we *do* observe: what *might* have produced what we are observing? For example, some political structures could be interpreted as functioning *as if* citizens had, at a vital time, agreed on relevant rules that proceeded to give shape and substance to those political structures. It might even be suggested that this is part of why we respect the structures: we react to them *as if* those rules had literally been part of how those societies were created, thereby giving the societies a form worth inhabiting.

What did Mills add to that older idea?

> [T]he peculiar contract to which I am referring, though based on the social contract tradition that has been central to Western political theory, is not a contract between everybody ('we the people'), but between just the people who count, the people who really are people ('we the white people'). So it is a Racial Contract.

The Racial Contract, said Mills, is an expression of 'white supremacy'. It reflects the historical fact that

> *non-white racial exclusion from personhood was the actual norm.* ... [W]hat has usually been taken (when it has been noticed at all) as the racist 'exception' has really been the *rule*; what has been taken as the 'rule', the ideal norm, has been the *exception*.

Many people do talk of racist realities, when these are highlighted, as deviations from what is mainly a racially fair society. But are those people misleading themselves (and others) by not noticing larger racist realities? Yes, if Mills was right:

> There is obviously all the difference in the world between saying the system is basically sound despite some unfortunate racist deviations, and saying that the polity is racially structured, the state white-supremacist, and races themselves significant existents that an adequate political ontology needs to accommodate.

What does that final sentence mean? An 'ontology' is a list of reality's basic categories (as we noted in section 3.6.3, with Longino). These are what there *is*, described in our most fundamental terms. This makes an ontology part of a metaphysics (such as we were exploring throughout chapter 1). A metaphysics *builds on* its contained ontology, seeking to understand those listed items and how they relate to each other as *parts* of an overall (and possibly larger) reality. A metaphysics might imagine how to construct *non*-basic parts of reality from those basic parts (the ontology): the metaphysics would be adding non-basic parts to basic parts in order to reach a total picture. Mills combined that sort of metaphysical urge *with political theory*. He was asking us to regard various racial divisions as having been used as political 'building blocks', functioning as parts of an ontology that have played (regrettable) roles for us, when we have been constructing our larger political world over many years. Following Mills in attending to those racial divisions, and those (unfortunate) roles that they played, could improve our *metaphysical* understanding of our political world.

What emerged, for Mills, from such theorising? He thought that we will be able to view societies differently, in a vital respect. On his portrayal, societies have always excluded some groups *on racial grounds*. This explains much. Our societies have thus been built around the Racial Contract, on Mills's view.

Have only some groups perpetrated this? Mills talked of its having been 'whites' who enacted, and who still enact, the Racial Contract. Yet (as he reminds us) it is not only people usually called 'white' who have taken such advantage of racially defined others. Should we expect to find instances of the Racial Contract occurring more widely across human history and geography?

Perhaps so. Mills's underlying point was not inherently about those white bodies (so to speak). It was as much about colonisation – hence power – as about physical race per se. Colonisation is not inherently reflective of physical whiteness, even if in practice it has often taken that form.

> *Race is sociopolitical rather than biological, but it is nonetheless real.* ... The 'Racial Contract' ... distinguishes between whiteness as phenotype/genealogy and Whiteness as a political commitment to white supremacy ... [It] decolorizes Whiteness by detaching it from whiteness, thereby demonstrating that in a parallel universe it could have been Yellowness, Redness, Brownness, or Blackness. Or, alternatively phrased, we could have had a yellow, red, brown, or black Whiteness: *Whiteness is not really a color at all, but a set of power relations.*

The basic point is that racial divisions have arisen – due to historical facts of colonisation and resulting exercises of power – where they need not have done so, and that many people have overlooked this – maybe preferring to think that all has been fair. It has *not* been fair. We must look harder to find how and where it has not been.

Marx, we saw (section 1.5.1), urged us to act, not merely to philosophise. Can we sometimes do both? Can an interpretation such as Mills's help us to act with philosophical insight? (And not only his interpretation; what of those that we read from Longino, Fricker, and Dalmiya, in sections 3.6.3, 3.6.4, and 3.6.6 – and from Mills himself in section 3.6.5?)

Readings for 5.2

For the *Great Learning*, see *Confucius: Confucian Analects, The Great Learning & The Doctrine of the Mean*, trans. J. Legge (New York: Dover, [1893] 1971); quotations from pp. 357–9. For Kant, see

Foundations of the Metaphysics of Morals, trans. L. W. Beck (Indianapolis: Bobbs-Merrill, 1959); quotations from pp. 46, 47, 48, 56, 57. For Wollstonecraft, see *A Vindication of the Rights of Woman* (London: Vintage Books, 2014); quotations from pp. 1, 28, 32, 53, 57–8, 78, 80, 81, 83, 266, 282, 292–3. For Mill, see *Utilitarianism, On Liberty, and Considerations on Representative Government*, ed. H. B. Acton (London: J. M. Dent, 1972); quotations from pp. 6, 9, 32–4. For Noddings, see *Caring: A Relational Approach to Ethics and Moral Education* (2nd rev. edn, Berkeley: University of California Press, [1984] 2013); quotations from pp. 3, 4–5, 27–8, 47, 68, 79–80, 92, 93. For Nussbaum, see *Women and Human Development: The Capabilities Approach* (Cambridge: Cambridge University Press, 2000); quotations from pp. 62, 71, 74, 78–80, 81, 82–3. For Mills, see *The Racial Contract* (Ithaca, NY: Cornell University Press, 1997); quotations from pp. 3, 122, 123–4, 126–7.

5.3 Towards non-human animals

5.3.1 Śāntideva's sentient beings
Humans are not the only beings that sense and – it seems – think. We are not the only ones, it also seems, with social lives. Does this imply *moral* constraints upon how we act towards some or all of those other beings – ones that we usually call 'animals'?

Not all philosophers have thought so. We saw Descartes dismissing animals as lacking minds, as more like clocks than clockmakers (section 1.2.4). Would that place animals beyond the reach of moral constraints? Maybe so, if they are akin to clocks. But are they?

Not all philosophers have believed so. A more welcoming view of animals has long been part of Buddhist thinking. I will present some thoughts from

Śāntideva, a North Indian monk (from the period 690–790) who, like Dharmakīrti (section 3.4.1), was based at Nālandā. One of his two major works was the Mahāyāna Buddhist *Training Anthology* (*Śikṣā-samuccaya*). It is mostly quotations seemingly meeting with his approval. For example, Śāntideva offered this, about '[s]omeone going for alms in a village, town, or city':

> as for those sentient beings who come into his field of vision, women, men, boys, and girls, *even including animals*, he should arouse thoughts of lovingkindness and compassion towards them all, thinking 'I should act so that all those sentient beings who come into my field of vision or give me alms will go to good rebirths.'

I added the *emphasis* to 'even including animals'. Śāntideva's use of 'even' suggests that advice beyond the glaringly obvious was being provided. Extending 'lovingkindness and compassion' to non-human animals was a move worth making – and worth highlighting.

Śāntideva continued with advice for performing those compassionate actions towards other people, before giving an example of how we might do so for other beings.

> While eating, he should arouse this thought: 'In this body, there are eighty thousand species of tiny animals. Through this [food], may they live feeling healthy and happy. Right now, I will bring them together through food. But when I have attained Awakening, I will bring them together through Dharma.'

Animals inside him are to be treated no less generously than people around him. In effect, he should eat for them, not only for himself. Not only for them, though; there are further beings to consider:

he should still eat moderately, let some of it fall to the ground, and then scatter some of the alms-food on top of a stone, thinking 'Whatever groups of wild animals or flocks of birds are looking for food, may they receive and eat this gift.'

Presumably, the aim was to treat those other sentient beings in a way that *they* would appreciate. But it was proposed as an element of one's own spiritual training. It was part of recognising and developing oneself in what, I expect, we would call a *moral* way.

Śāntideva was not providing an argument, in the obvious sense of premises or reasons being said to lead, by a process of inferring, to a conclusion emerging from them. Was he developing a different form of argument? It seems as if he was *drawing a picture* of how a person could choose to be in various settings – with this meaning her living in a morally inviting way. She would be living as a specific kind of person; Śāntideva was offering guidance for how to become that kind of person.

5.3.2 Peter Singer's liberated animals

Śāntideva's picture (section 5.3.1) may be read religiously. Can we find non-religiously philosophical ways of thinking that accord animals moral respect? One instance is from Peter Singer (b. 1946), an Australian philosopher, in his socially influential book *Animal Liberation*. He sought to persuade us to rise above

> the attitude that we may call 'speciesism', by analogy with racism. ... [It] is a prejudice or attitude of bias in favor of the interests of members of one's own species and against those of members of other species.

Singer begins by reminding us that people, including philosophers, had already engaged with analogous struggles, such as for women's political and social rights.

> When Mary Wollstonecraft [whom we met in section 5.2.3], a forerunner of today's feminists, published her *Vindication of the Rights of Woman* in 1792, her views were widely regarded as absurd, and before long an anonymous publication appeared entitled *A Vindication of the Rights of Brutes*. [It] ... tried to refute [her] arguments by showing that they could be carried one stage further.

That is a common argument strategy: show how an actual or imagined opponent's thinking can be applied more widely than she would welcome. Supposedly, this shows that her thinking is too strong for its own good: even if it provides the verdict that she wants in a particular case, it gives that same verdict where she would not want it. In which event, it is not a *form* of reasoning that she should trust. Thus, here is what Singer highlights as having been argued against Wollstonecraft.

> If the argument for equality was sound when applied to women, why should it not be applied to dogs, cats, and horses? The reasoning seemed to hold for these 'brutes' too; yet to hold that brutes had rights was manifestly absurd. Therefore the reasoning by which this conclusion had been reached ... must also be unsound when applied to women, since the very same arguments had been used in each case.

But (as Singer explains) that strategy is not decisive. We may respond by saying 'Thank you! Wollstonecraft's argument – for women being morally equal to men – was so good that it *should* be extended. Her style of thinking can deliver further truths about *more* than women – even about how we should treat other animals.' The anti-Wollstonecraft strategy would have backfired, by highlighting something that we would *welcome* once it has been brought to our notice. That is Singer's response (in my words). Wollstonecraft urged us to include women in our moral universe; Singer argues that animals have moral claims upon us: we have long treated them immorally.

Singer uses an insight from Bentham (mentioned in section 5.2.4), from his 1789 *An Introduction to the Principles of Morals and Legislation*. Bentham said, of 'a full-grown horse or dog', that 'The question is not, Can they *reason*? nor Can they *talk*? but, Can they *suffer*?' That was Bentham; this is Singer:

> If a being suffers there can be no moral justification for refusing to take that suffering into consideration. No matter what the nature of the being, the principle of equality requires that its suffering be counted equally with the like suffering – insofar as rough comparisons can be made – of any other being. If a being is not capable of suffering, or of experiencing enjoyment or happiness, there is nothing to be taken into account.

What is 'the principle of equality'? Singer offers analogies (as follows), so that we can understand this idea.

> Racists violate the principle of equality by giving greater weight to the interests of members of their own race when there is a clash between their interests and the interests of those of another race. Sexists violate the principle of equality by favoring the interests of their own sex. Similarly, speciesists allow the interests of their own species to override the greater interests of members of other species. The pattern is identical in each case.

These analogies, between speciesism and sexism/racism, begin the debate for Singer; they do not end it. He is not saying that dogs, for example, always have the same moral interests as people do, let alone greater ones. But he is saying that they *have* moral interests, ones that we should not 'override' simply because animals are not people.

In other words, that preliminary point from Singer welcomes animals into our moral atmosphere. After which, further challenges arise, of detail and application; but at least we can assess these with an eye on morality, not mere practicality (as in 'How can I best use these animals, perhaps to make money?'). Think of 'experimentation on animals' and 'rearing animals for food'. Singer's book explores 'these particular forms of speciesism' in empirically observable ways, citing real-world details of how animals' suffering receives no moral reflection and respect.

How does Singer's thinking compare or blend with other ideas in this book? I end this section with a comment on what he is doing, and one on what he is not doing.

His approach is *utilitarian* (section 5.2.4's moral theory, with Mill). What matters for Singer is that suffering be avoided, with happiness being available – not only for some beings (us!) who feel pain or pleasure, but for all such beings (including non-human animals).

Even so, Singer is not treating *caring* – in the sense of feeling pity – as morally central (section 5.2.5's moral theory, with Noddings). For Singer, that is beside the moral point.

> Nowhere in this book ... do I appeal to the reader's emotions where they [= the emotions] cannot be supported by reason. ... The ultimate justification ... is not emotional. It is an appeal to basic moral principles.

His main principle is about moral equality, explained in utilitarian terms of pain and pleasure. This does not require us to empathise with animals, in any way feeling their suffering. In the preface to his book's first (1975) edition, Singer explains that he and his wife 'didn't "love" animals. We simply wanted them treated as the independent sentient beings that they are, and not as a means to human ends.' Recall (in section 5.2.2) Kant's advocating that no person should be treated as a means to an end. Would Kant be happy to have his idea extended in that way, from people to animals? (I engage with that question in the next section.)

Here is another link with earlier discussions (this time, those of section 3.4, especially section 3.4.3 with Stein on empathy). *If* we cannot know that other people feel pain or pleasure, how can we know that other animals do so? I set this aside, however, since Singer is unworried about it in developing his moral philosophy: 'none of us has the slightest real doubt that our close friends feel pain just as we do.' Ultimately, we might try to blend epistemology – how to *know* other minds – with moral philosophy – how to *act well towards* other beings with minds. That is for another day, though.

5.3.3 Christine Korsgaard's fellow creatures

We have met Kant's idea (section 5.2.2) of treating people as ends in themselves. Christine Korsgaard (b. 1952), an American philosopher, extends that idea. She argues that (non-human) animals likewise should be treated as ends in themselves.

Korsgaard begins by focusing on the general nature of importance or value: 'nothing can be important without being important to someone – to some creature, some person or animal.' Her use of 'to' is the key here. But it does not yet imply that animals have value *in themselves*. Might animals have value only because of how we view them – hence value only *to us*?

We should therefore (urges Korsgaard) ask *how* animals could have value in themselves. And we can start by examining ourselves. Are we superior in value? How? Applying Korsgaard's use of 'to', these questions arise: 'To whom are human beings supposed to be more important [than animals]? To the universe? To God? To ourselves?' A similar question appeared earlier (section 5.2.4), with Mill's comments on Socrates and pigs. Can a *person* decide impartially whether *people's* happiness matters more to the world than does whatever brings joy to pigs? Maybe some things are important in an absolute way – being important-to every being for whom importance-to ever arises. But how can we show this? Maybe people are absolutely more important than non-human animals. Yet how can we show this, too?

> [W]hat we would have to show is that even from the point of view *of the other animals*, what is good-for human beings matters *more* than what is good-for those other animals themselves.

Is it more important-for a cat that her human 'owner' be happy than that she is? It is different. Is that *all*?

> [Even if] we human beings matter to ourselves, and value ourselves, in a way that is *different* from the way the other animals do … this does not have the implication that what happens to us matters *more* than what happens to our fellow creatures. … The fact that we matter more to ourselves, if it were a fact, need not be important to the other animals at all.

From those cautionary thoughts, Korsgaard derives a striking moral: 'I have not exactly been arguing that animals are just as important as people. I have been arguing that the comparison is nearly incoherent.' In other words, we should not even try comparing our importance with that of animals. This is not because of difficulty or impracticality. The problem is deeper.

> If everything that is important is important to someone – to some person or animal – there is no place to stand and make a comparative judgment, or at least one with any plausibility, about the comparative importance of people and animals themselves.

What might sound, to us, like a sensible comparing of our values with those of pigs is nothing of the sort. Indeed, Korsgaard deems the attempt to be meaningless. We can talk sensibly of what matters to people. We can also talk sensibly of what matters to pigs. *And that is that.*

I began this section by mentioning Kant. Korsgaard's reasoning extends his idea (section 5.2.2) of ends-in-themselves from talking of people to encompassing animals.

> The way that we value a creature for her own sake, rather than merely as a means, is by valuing what is good for her, in the final [= ultimate] sense of good, *for its own sake*, or *just because it is good for her*. ... [W]e value a creature's final good from a standpoint of empathy, because ... we look at the things that are functionally good for her from her own point of view, and so see them as the ends of action.

We can appreciate that view of Korsgaard's by also revisiting Singer's ideas (section 5.3.2). For him, what ultimately matters for an animal – as for a person – is pleasure and the absence of pain. For Korsgaard, the ultimate value is the animal (or person) *themselves*. For her, an animal is not being valued as an end in itself even when we remove its suffering – if we do this because we regard the removal of suffering as *itself* what ultimately matters.

So, how do we value animals as ends in themselves, as Korsgaard advocates? In a sense, she proposes, we defer to how animals value themselves. They 'necessarily set a value upon themselves'. They do this in how they function.

> A creature is a substance [= a thing] that necessarily cares about itself, a substance whose nature it is to value itself. The creature values herself by pursuing her own functional good and the things that contribute to it as the ends of action. Valuing ... is originally an activity of *life*, a feature of a sentient creature's relationship to herself.
>
> So, ... when we say that a creature is an end in itself, we mean that we should accord the creature the kind of value that, as a living creature, she necessarily accords to herself, and we therefore see her final good as something worth pursuing.

That is Korsgaard's Kantian step towards treating non-human animals as having value in themselves – hence not merely as a means by which *we* prosper. They have value as ends, not means. Saying this does not convey every detail about their value. But it reports their having value at all, along with the main reason why they do. If true, that is morally significant.

Readings for 5.3

For Śāntideva, see *The Training Anthology* of Śāntideva: *A Translation of the* Śikṣā-samuccaya, trans. C. Goodman (New York: Oxford University Press, 2016); quotations from pp. 125, 126 [= 128, 129 in standard citations; see p. xii of that book on this convention]. For Singer, see *Animal Liberation* (2nd edn, London: Jonathan Cape, [1975] 1990); quotations from pp. ii, iii, 1, 6, 7, 8, 9, 10, 22. For Korsgaard, see *Fellow Creatures: Our Obligations to the Other Animals* (Oxford: Oxford University Press, 2018); quotations from pp. 9, 11, 14, 15, 136, 137.

5.4 Towards nature

5.4.1 The Stoics' cosmos

We have discussed how, if possible, to act in morally good ways towards ourselves (section 5.1), other people (section 5.2), and non-human animals (section 5.3). What of nature itself? What of reality as a whole? Are there moral constraints upon how we treat it?

I return initially to the ancient world for potential guidance.

Stoicism arose, as a school, then tradition, in Athens around 300 BCE. Founded by Zeno of Citium, from Cyprus (c. 334–262 BCE), it was especially active for around five hundred years, spreading from Athens to Rome. Its influence persisted, sparking debates. We met one of those earlier (section 1.6.2), with Alexander of Aphrodisias commenting critically on the Stoic Chrysippus' views on causal determinism. Here I highlight another Stoic idea, about the nature of the cosmos – reality as a whole, including Earth and all else.

> Chrysippus in book one of *On Providence* [= *On Fate*, as per section 1.6.2], Apollodorus in his *Physics* and Posidonius say that the cosmos is also an animal, rational and alive and intelligent; an animal in the sense that it is a substance which is alive and capable of sense-perception. (Book 7.142–3)

Those words are from Diogenes Laertius (c. 300 CE), in his *Lives and Opinions of the Philosophers* (his *Vitae Philosophorum*), as are these.

> The cosmos is administered by mind and providence (as Chrysippus says in book five of his *On Providence* and Posidonius in book thirteen of his *On Gods*), since mind penetrates every part of it just as soul does us. But it penetrates some things more than others. For it

> penetrates some as a condition, for example, bones and sinews, and others as mind, for example, the leading part of the soul. In this way the entire cosmos, too, being an animal and alive and rational, has aither [= fire = one of the basic elements of reality] as its leading part, as Antipater of Tyre [says] in book eight of his *On the Cosmos*. (Book 7.138–9)

Why is that Stoic thinking relevant? We are asking how we should treat the wider world, including nature as a whole. What if that is a question about acting towards something *alive*? Should we think of the *cosmos* – the whole world, all reality – as alive, as a being? It is easy to regard parts of it (such as ourselves and animals) as alive, other parts as not. Yet is that selectivity misleading? Should we extend to *all* reality the moral sensitivity that some philosophers advocate having towards non-human animals, say (section 5.3)?

Diogenes mentioned the Stoic idea of the cosmos being literally part of us – helping to constitute, or be, aspects of each person. Should we therefore apply to *the cosmos itself* any philosophical proposals about acting well towards ourselves (section 5.1) and other people (section 5.2)? For that same reason, should a theory of morality-towards-persons *include* a theory of morality-towards-the-cosmos? If we and the cosmos are physically intertwined, must moral thinking about ourselves and others *encompass* the cosmos? Should we *therefore* act well towards it? We are within it. Is it within us?

While thinking about those questions, we might consider this further argument, also from Diogenes Laertius.

> For an animal is better than a non-animal; and nothing is better than the cosmos; therefore, the cosmos is an animal. And [it is] alive, as is clear from the fact that the soul of [each of] us is a fragment derived from it. (Book 7.143)

Is the cosmos literally alive, as animals within it are alive? Not every Stoic had this intriguing view. (Diogenes mentions Boetius as an exception.) But it was present in much Stoic thinking. It reminds me of how St Anselm (section 1.7.2) explained his conception of God. Anselm thought of God as unable to be improved upon, presumably better than anything else. Diogenes, we noted, said that 'nothing is better than the cosmos', as part of its being alive, on the Stoic thinking. God would be the ultimate Being. Is the cosmos the ultimate total-reality?

Diogenes is not our only authority on Stoic thinking. Here is an argument, from Zeno, reported by Cicero (Marcus Tullius Cicero; 106–43 BCE; a Roman statesman), who was not a Stoic but was sympathetic to some Stoic ideas. This is from his *On the Nature of the Gods* (*De Natura Deorum*).

> [Zeno] says, 'nothing which lacks life and reason can produce from itself something which is alive and rational; but the cosmos produces from itself something which is alive and rational; therefore, the cosmos is alive and rational.' (Book 2.22)

Zeno's reasoning was simple. Life comes only from life. We arise within and from the cosmos. It is thus alive – as alive as we are!

Again, *therefore*, do any moral obligations that we have towards each other extend to the entire cosmos? People often talk of how we should act towards Earth, or even Earth-plus-more (and soon we discuss examples of such thinking). We might want to read these Stoics as offering a *metaphysical* foundation for moral concern towards nature as a whole. They are not providing practical advice on how to act well towards nature. But are they describing a philosophical reason for *why we should wish* to do so? Can we combine their thinking about the *cosmos* with ideas about what it is to act well towards *ourselves* (section 5.1) or *other people* (section 5.2)?

5.4.2 Wang Yangming's one body

A similar motivation to that Stoic one (section 5.4.1) might emerge from the neo-Confucian Wang Yangming's 'Questions on the Great Learning'. We met him earlier (section 3.5.1), asking how knowledge links with action. Here, he responds to questions about the Confucian *Great Learning* (section 5.2.1). I present some of Wang's answers to the initial two questions.

Why was it 'appropriate' for a 'morally great person' to manifest the virtue that arises from their 'sagely learning'? Wang replied:

> Great [= morally great] people regard Heaven, earth, and the myriad creatures as their own bodies. They look upon the world as one family and China as one person within it. Those who, because of the space between their own bodies and other physical forms, regard themselves as separate [from Heaven, earth, and the myriad creatures] are petty [= morally small] persons.

Moral greatness thus involves a kind of uniting of oneself with reality as a whole. That is a way of respecting everything *beyond* oneself. What is the nature of that uniting? It is not a way of dominating. When Wang talked of regarding Heaven, earth, etc., as one's own body, he was not meaning that one possesses all of that (an entirety sounding like the Stoics' cosmos: section 5.4.1). Wang said that we are part of one 'family'.

He then strengthened that picture, with a detail about how the uniting occurs.

> The ability great people have to form one body with Heaven, earth, and the myriad creatures is not something

they intentionally strive to do; the benevolence of their heart-minds is originally [= naturally] like this.

Welcomely, Wang did not restrict that, at least in principle, to morally great people. 'Even the heart-minds of petty people are like this.' What is this 'this'? It is the 'benevolence' that one 'cannot avoid having' 'when they see a child [about to] fall in to a well', but also 'when they hear the anguished cries or see the frightened appearance of birds or beasts', and 'when they see grass or trees uprooted and torn apart', and even 'when they see tiles and stones broken and destroyed': 'they cannot avoid feeling a sense of concern and regret. This is because their benevolence forms one body with tiles and stones.'

Yet (we might wonder), if this benevolent uniting with the wider world is natural even for morally 'petty' people, why is great (moral) learning *needed*? Wang's reply would have been that the moral learning is important in order that one's heart-mind does not 'become cut off and constricted', or 'beclouded', through being 'moved by desires or obscured by selfishness'. *With* the moral learning, one's 'original state' – one's naturally 'bright virtue' – can guide one's living.

So, everyone *can* live morally well by '[m]aking bright one's bright virtue', 'forming one body with Heaven, earth, and the myriad things'. Wang then began listing details of how this unfolds, talking firstly of 'filial piety' and 'brotherly love'. He spread this pattern further: 'It is the same in regard to rulers and ministers, husbands and wives, and friends.' That covers our moral actions towards other people (section 5.2). But Wang continued, embracing also animals (section 5.3) and the wider natural world (our present focus):

> it is [also] the same in regard to mountains and rivers, ghosts and spirits, birds and beasts, and grass and trees.

It is only when I truly love them all and universally extend my benevolence that forms one body with them [= in this sense, uniting with them] that my bright virtue will be made bright in every respect, and I can really form one body with Heaven, earth, and the myriad things.

Like those Stoics writing on the cosmos (section 5.4.1), Wang was not clearly offering a how-to manual for acting towards nature – at least not towards it in particular. Might he have deemed such a manual a mistake, since in his view nature is not separate? (Thinking that it is makes one morally 'petty', with a 'beclouded' nature at that moment.) Should we therefore act towards 'Heaven, earth, and the myriad creatures' as we should act towards ourselves and other people, with all of whom we share 'one body'?

At the end of section 5.4.1, I asked whether we might want to extend one or more theories that we had met earlier (sections 5.1, 5.2). Wang himself was approving of *The Great Learning* (section 5.2.1). So, is that a base upon which we could build an environmental ethic (an idea that we are about to meet)? And what of Noddings's (section 5.2.5) theory of morality? It was based around caring, which we might align with Wang's talk of benevolence. As ever within philosophy, we must remain alert for expansive blendings and enlightening applications of ideas, questions, theories, and so on.

5.4.3 Arne Naess's ecosophy

Asking whether there are moral constraints on our actions towards the natural world (as the previous two sections did) leads naturally to questions within *environmental* philosophy. This branch of moral philosophy has gained momentum in recent decades, especially since the 1970s. (The term 'environmental ethic' was used, easily to our ears, a moment ago, in section 5.4.2.) One element of this movement comes from Arne Naess (1912–2009), a Norwegian philosopher. He distinguished 'shallow ecology' from 'deep ecology', initially in a 1973 article. (I will also look at his 1989 *Ecology, Community and Lifestyle*, based on a book in Norwegian published in 1976.) From the 1973 article:

> *The Shallow Ecology movement*:
> Fight against pollution and resource depletion. Central objective: the health and affluence of people in the developed countries.

Why is that 'shallow'? Naess means 'philosophically simple', I think – not 'practically unimportant'. On the contrary, this 'movement' is potentially significant in practical ways. It is even what some people mean when talking of 'environmental philosophy'. But Naess wants a *philosophically fuller understanding* of these issues. So, he offers a (compressed) philosophical overview, to accompany contributions to Shallow Ecology. Here is some of his overview.

> *The Deep Ecology movement*:
> (1) Rejection of the man-in-environment image in favour of *the relational, total-field image.* Organisms as knots in the biospherical net or field of intrinsic relations. An intrinsic relation between two things A and B is such that the relation belongs to the definitions or basic constitutions of A and B, so that without the relation, A and B are no longer the same things. The total-field model dissolves not only the man-in-environment concept, but every compact thing-in-milieu concept – except when talking at a superficial or preliminary level of communication.

This is philosophically challenging. What was Naess saying?

He did not provide an overt argument, laying down premises before explaining how they lead to a favoured conclusion. Instead (as has often happened in this book), we have a picture, this time painted with large brush-strokes, one that Naess apparently regarded as able to undergird and reinforce practical ideas and moves. Those brush-strokes *are* large, though, making the picture difficult to interpret. I will try, briefly, to capture its spirit.

It seems (for Naess) that we are among those 'organisms'. We are to think of ourselves as like 'knots' in a piece of wood – in effect 'the biospherical net', the natural environment. We are being encouraged not to conceive of people-in-a-natural-environment as a combination of two clearly *separate* things, each *fully itself independently* of the other – people over here, a natural environment over there. On Naess's picture, it seems, both persons and the natural environment *are* whatever they are, partly *by including* relations to the other. A person, on this Deep Ecology picture, is *fundamentally part of* a natural whole. This is a metaphysical blending, a harmonising.

What are its implications? In particular, should our sense of what things have value extend beyond people to the natural environment – if, *fundamentally and inescapably*, we are part of the natural world? Here is what Naess says next.

> (2) *Biospherical egalitarianism* – in principle. ... To the ecological field worker, *the equal right to live and blossom* is an intuitively clear and obvious value axiom. Its restriction to humans [= if we think that what matters is only *our* 'right to live and blossom'] is an anthropocentrism with detrimental effects upon the life quality of humans themselves. This quality depends in part upon the deep pleasure and satisfaction we receive from close partnership with other forms of life. The attempt to

ignore our dependence and to establish a master-slave relationship [= between us and nature] has contributed to the alienation of man from himself [= since he *is* part of nature].

(2) seems to reinforce (1)'s message of back-and-forth dependence, in a 'value-added' way. To deny our links to a natural environment is not to understand what we are, as people. By lacking such understanding, we lose some value. We are lessened.

In his 1989 book, Naess supplemented those thoughts with his 'platform of the deep ecology movement'. Here is the platform's first entry.

> The flourishing of human and non-human life on Earth has intrinsic value. The value of non-human life forms is independent of the usefulness these may have for narrow human purposes.

Naess's talk of 'intrinsic value' reminds me of Kant's view (section 5.2.2) of people as ends-in-themselves; similarly for Korsgaard (section 5.3.3) on animals. Was Naess encouraging us to treat the natural environment as if *it* is an end-in-itself, having that sort of moral value?

Naess's main concern was philosophical – with a practical dimension. He was developing his 'ecosophy', a personal philosophy of 'ourselves and nature': 'an ecosophy becomes *a philosophical world-view or system inspired by the conditions of life in the ecosphere.*' Once this philosophical picture is in place, any practical work – applying some 'shallow ecology' – that follows can be based on a conceptually deeper foundation, an expanded sense of how to *interpret* the nature, even the point, of the practical work.

5.4.4 Holmes Rolston's environmental ethic
We have been discussing some abstract theories, asking how they might offer a *metaphysical* base upon which

to build an environmental ethic. How may we do this? Holmes Rolston III (b. 1932), an American philosopher, offers possible assistance.

Vitally, he asks how values *reflecting* the natural world enter an ethic if it is genuinely environmental. We could begin by looking to ecology to inform us about nature. This will help us to form 'an ethic [not only] ... *about* the environment'. We want an ethic that is 'ecologically formed or reformed'. We do not want an ethic that is merely 'applied to but not derived from' what ecological science tells us. We want 'an ethic in which environmental science affects principles.' The principles – the ethic's intellectual core – are themselves to be shaped by ecological facts. In that respect, we need to think more radically than we might have anticipated doing.

> The ultimate [ecological] science may well herald limits to [economic] growth; it challenges certain presumptions about rising standards of living, capitalism, progress, development, and so on ...

Responding sympathetically to that sort of awareness could strike many of us as all that is needed within an ecological ethic. Not so, for Rolston:

> This realization of limits [= the kind quoted a moment ago], dramatically shift ethical application though it may [= if we do respond sympathetically to it], can hardly be said to reform our ethical roots ...

The reason for that is simple. That approach, though it might sound bold, falls short of being *deeply* ecological, *philosophically* ecological. After all, it

> remains (when optimistic) a maximizing of human values or (when pessimistic) human survival. All goods are human goods [on this imagined version of ecological

ethics], with nature an accessory [= not being accorded the primary value that human goods are treated as having]. There is no endorsement of any natural rightness [= values independently present in the natural world], only the acceptance of the natural given [= non-value facts about how the natural world functions, facts that might emerge from ecological science]. It is ecological secondarily, but primarily anthropological [= by applying human values throughout, even to the natural world].

The kind of theory to which Rolston is reacting (by deeming it insufficiently radical) seems akin to what Naess had in mind with his term 'shallow ecology' (section 5.4.3). Rolston seeks an ecological ethic built not just upon human values.

> Our ethical heritage largely attaches values and rights to persons, and if nonpersonal realms enter, they enter only as a tributary [= a means or pathway leading] to the personal. What is proposed here is a broadening of value, so that nature will cease to be merely 'property' [= existing with no potential value other than able to be possessed and used by people].

What might be an example of the more deeply ecologically valued ethic that Rolston is advocating? His aim is to motivate *and* begin a search for this. Those previous comments were motivational; after which, his search begins by looking to 'the holistic character of the ecosystem'. This, he believes, is needed in any ethic doing justice to that ecosystem's needs, with *its* values. Rolston welcomes the idea that a person 'operates in an environmental context where he must ground his values in ecosystemic obedience' – and hence 'morally ought to promote homeostasis', which is a kind of *state-of-balance* for a system's significant elements. He regards it as essential for dynamic ecological systems:

> Perhaps the paramount law in ecological theory is that of homeostasis. ... Systems [in nature] recycle, and there is energy balance; yet the systems are not static, but dynamic, as the forces that drive equilibrium are in flux, seeking equilibrium yet veering from it to bring counterforces into play. This perpetual stir, tending to and deviating from equilibrium, drives the evolutionary process.

'How does this translate morally?', asks Rolston. He cites a 1969 article by Thomas Colwell, 'a more venturesome [= bold, adventurous] translation of homeostasis into moral prescription', in which

> the claim seems to be that following [= knowing and being guided by facts about] ecological nature is not merely a prudential [= practical or useful] means to moral and valuational ends [that exist] independent of nature but is an end in itself ...

That thesis is highlighted from Colwell's article. Rolston continues, explaining it: 'or, more accurately, it is within man's relatedness to his environment that all man's values are grounded and supported.' Notice the 'all'. Rolston is tying *all* of our values to the natural environment. He acknowledges that,

> [i]n that construction of values, man doubtless exceeds any environmental prescription [= goes beyond what is forced by ecological details], but nevertheless his values remain environmental reciprocals [= they take into account, in a back-and-forth way, the ecological details].

Why is that reciprocity important? This leads Rolston to his main *structural* suggestion, reflecting ecological facts about homeostasis.

> They [= those ecologically reciprocal values] complement a homeostatic world. [A person's] valuations, like other

perceptions and knowings, are [thereby] interactionary, drawn from environmental transactions, not merely brought to it.

In other words, within this form of ethic, those values are not imposed on 'environmental transactions'. They are *created partly by* such interactions. When applying a fully ecological ethic, a person 'finds homeostasis a key to all values ... but one which ... informs and shapes his other values by making them relational, corporate, environmental.'

Rolston, we saw, endorses the idea that 'following ecological nature' is 'an end in itself'. We read Kant's idea that people should be treated as ends in themselves (section 5.2.2). Then we met Korsgaard's extending that Kantian idea to animals (section 5.3.3). Is Rolston applying that idea even more widely?

5.4.5 James Lovelock's Gaia

How far might we travel, along Rolston's ecological-ethic path (section 5.4.4)? I close this chapter with an idea associated especially with James Lovelock (1919–2022), an English scientist and inventor. He conceived of Earth as a kind of *living being*.

What kind? I present details in a moment (from his second book on this, following his 1979 *Gaia: A New Look at Life on Earth*). He called this living being *Gaia* – 'the name the [ancient] Greeks used for the Earth Goddess'. Thus an idea was launched. Lovelock offered it as an hypothesis – which became a theory, a scientific theory, open to being tested, hopefully able to explain much. 'Gaia theory gives a fair representation of the Earth.' This idea, it seems, was philosophical – but inspired by science and intended to fit well with science.

Gaia, explained Lovelock, is a *superorganism*. It has 'the capacity to regulate its temperature'. Superorganisms 'are bounded systems [such as a bee's nest] made up partly from living organisms and partly from nonliving structural material.'

> Through Gaia theory, I see the Earth and the life it bears as a system ... [with] the capacity to regulate the temperature and the composition of the Earth's surface and to keep it comfortable for living organisms. The self-regulation of the system is an active process driven by the free energy available from sunlight. ... Gaia had first been seen from space [thanks to the US space programme] and the arguments used [to interpret what was seen *as* Gaia] were from thermodynamics. I found it reasonable to call the Earth alive in the sense that it was a self-organizing and self-regulating system.

Does that make Earth itself alive?

> You also may find it hard to swallow the notion that anything as large and apparently inanimate as the Earth can in any way be said to be alive. Surely, you may say, the Earth is almost wholly rock and nearly all incandescent with heat. ... [But] the difficulty can be lessened if you let the image of a giant redwood tree enter your mind. The tree undoubtedly is alive, yet 99 percent is dead. The great tree is an ancient spire of dead wood, made of lignin and cellulose by the ancestors of the thin layer of living cells that go to constitute its bark. How like the Earth, and more so when we realize that many of the atoms of the rocks far down into the magma were once part of the ancestral life from which we all have come.

So, by analogy, we have reason – scientifically informed reason – to regard Earth as a living being. 'Geophysiology, the scientifically correct usage for Gaia science, is beginning to unite scientists in the common cause of a rational environmentalism.' The stakes are high. They concern the nature of life itself.

> In exploring the question, 'What is life?' we have made some progress. By looking at life through Gaia's telescope, we see it as a planetary-scale phenomenon with a cosmological life span. Gaia as the largest manifestation of life differs from other living organisms of Earth in the way that you or I differ from our population of living cells. ... Gaia is no static picture. It is forever changing as organisms and the material Earth evolve together ...

Lovelock has blended science and philosophy. Personally, I call this philosophy (while noting its also having helped to create Earth System Science)!

Hence, I have a philosophical question about it. Does Lovelock's conception of Gaia – Earth – as self-regulating also make Earth literally a *self* (in any of those senses discussed mainly in chapter 1)? We began the book by asking about one's personal self; should we now ask about the *Earth's* Gaian self? Does the idea of a self reach that far?

And in case it does, or even might, is that one more reason to act well towards Earth?

Readings for 5.4

On the Stoics, see *Hellenistic Philosophy: Introductory Readings*, 2nd edn, trans. B. Inwood and L. P. Gerson (Indianapolis: Hackett, 1997); quotations from pp. 133–4, 135 (for Diogenes Laertius), 144 (for Cicero). For Wang Yangming, see 'Questions on the Great Learning', in *Readings from the Lu-Wang School of Neo-Confucianism*, trans. P. J. Ivanhoe (Indianapolis: Hackett, 2009); quotations from pp. 160–3. For Naess, see 'The shallow and the deep, long-range ecology movement: a summary', *Inquiry* 16 (1973): 95–100, with quotations from pp. 95–6, and *Ecology, Community and Lifestyle: Outline of an Ecosophy*, ed. and trans. D. Rothenberg (Cambridge: Cambridge University Press, 1989), with quotations from pp. 29, 36, 38. For Rolston, see 'Is there an ecological ethic?', *Ethics* 85 (1975): 93–109; quotations from pp. 93, 95, 96, 97, 98, 99, 101. For the Colwell article discussed by Rolston, see T. B. Colwell, Jr., 'The balance of nature: a ground for human values', *Main Currents in Modern Thought* 26 (1969): 46–52. For Lovelock, see *The Ages of Gaia: A Biography of Our Living Earth* (2nd edn, Oxford: Oxford University Press, [1988] 1995); quotations from pp. xv, 3, 15, 27, 30–1, 39–40, 45.

6

Philosophical Viewing

6.1 Why be philosophical?

Chapters 2 and 4 described some ways in which philosophical *writing* and *thinking* function as philosophical *reasoning*. We are gaining a sense, I hope, of what being philosophical may include. Now we might want to ask this: *why* be philosophical? For enjoyment? Ideally so. To learn something? Again, ideally so. Yet *how* can we learn from being philosophical? And *what* might we learn?

We can answer those questions with some general ideas and suggestions. I begin by revisiting section 4.4's partial analogy between rhythmic gymnastics and philosophical reasoning. When a rhythmic gymnast completes her performance, what is the immediate result? It is her final pose. When a philosopher completes her 'performance' (her writing or thinking), what is the immediate result? It is a *view*.

Unlike the gymnast's parting pose, however, a philosophical view can be 'taken away' from the moment. It could be held in one's mind, for days, months, longer. It can be applied to claims, questions, or debates encountered later. It is an implement, a tool. It might literally be useful. (Maybe not in building bridges; but how often does *that* need arise for most of us?) Although the gymnast's performance could be remembered with pleasure, it cannot continue being *used*.

There is a vast diversity of tools. Some enable only a narrow range of movements: hammers are like that. Some philosophical views range widely, helping with many movements, be these physical or intellectual. Here is a brief taste of that variety. Views can be ...

- **about** X (I might think or talk *about* whether cockroaches are pretty)
- **on** X (I might have a view *on* whether cockroaches are pretty)
- **of** X (some views are like view*ings* – seeing, observing; I might have a view *of* a cockroach scuttling away)
- **over** X (some views are *panoramic*; I could have a view *over* a larger area where cockroaches thrive)
- **from** X (any view is *from* somewhere – in effect a lookout, a location for viewings; one can look out over a valley, say, surveying it).

This list might not be exhaustive. Even so, can it enrich our shared attempts in this book to understand *being philosophical*? Soon (section 6.2), I apply these remarks, while focusing on examples from chapter 5. First, though, note that the 'locatedness' – the '**from**' – of a view could sometimes be limiting. I am an Australian male, writing this book in Sydney. Are my philosophical views always constrained by that? In some cases, perhaps so. In others, possibly not. But I can never ignore that question. When being philosophical, we should *try* to find the best lookout available for forming a view.

6.2 Viewing the world philosophically

6.2.1 Contents

So, we should begin thinking more about what philosophical views are like, hence what they can accomplish. This first question concerns their *content*. In general, what are they *about*? When being philosophical, *of* what are we seeking to form a view?

The answer could seem obvious: philosophy seeks views of, or about, *the world*. All the more so if we use the term 'world' expansively, embracing anything that is, has been, will be, might be, must be, or even should be. This book has included a multitude of attempts to view aspects of the world in philosophical ways. We have met philosophical views *about*, *on*, *of*, or *over* the world and its potentially significant details. Thus (we ask), are there selves? What would they be like? Is there knowledge? What would it be like? Are there moral actions? What would they be like? And so on. (Those general questions gave us chapters 1, 3, and 5.) To make clearer that overview, here are some examples, from chapter 5.

Aristotle (section 5.1.2) Aristotle sought to uncover the nature of human flourishing. How did he do this? Did he discuss other people's *views* about this topic? No. He proposed ideas aimed *directly* at human flourishing and its nature. How should one act? One should act as an expression of how one has developed oneself as a human being. One should develop moral and intellectual capacities 'in accordance with virtue'.

Regardless of whether we agree with that Aristotelian view (which we might also think of as a theory), it was presented as being *of* or *about* an aspect of what it is to be a human being. So, it aimed to be directly of or about an aspect of *the world*. It was not a view about *how we would try to find* a view on such aspects, for example. That would have made it only *in*directly about those aspects of the world.

Mills (section 5.2.7) When Charles Mills advanced his idea of a racial contract, he offered an interpretation of aspects of our social histories. He surveyed various regrettable facts, hypothesising that they *might as well* have arisen through implicit adoption of a racial contract.

This idea from Mills was modelled on the older, more general, idea of a social contract – an idea that was itself a view (concerning how various social realities could have arisen). So, even when a view is offered on or about reality (in this case, social reality), it might be deliberately influenced by another view. This is not quite the same as being *on* or *about* that other view, though, which is why I mention Mills here.

Śāntideva (section 5.3.1) Less a theory than a picture, Śāntideva's view – his philosophical gaze – was directed at the world. He offered a view *of* an aspect of reality – what we might call a moral fact. He used others' views. He did this to paint a picture directly *of* how animals should be treated. This result was a view not *about* views themselves (even while being influenced by views) but *about* animals and morality, these apparent aspects of reality.

Stoics (section 5.4.1) The Stoic idea of the cosmos as a living being, indeed as alive within us, was a view directly *of* or *about* reality – reality as a whole. Was it also directly *about* moral aspects of reality – *about* how to act towards the cosmos? I am unsure. But possibly it had *implications* for such views: insofar as a view claims to tell us how to act towards other beings, must it take into account that Stoic idea about the cosmos?

If so, a view need not be *directly* of, or about, moral reality. It could be indirectly of, or about, this aspect of reality. This adds to what we should take into account when being philosophical: we must be alert to implications of our views, along with implications affecting those views.

Wang Yangming (section 5.4.2) Sometimes it is not fully clear whether a philosopher is seeking a view directly about *reality* or a view directly about *views* (which could themselves be directly about reality). A case in point is Wang's views in 'Questions on the Great Learning'. He responded to questions about *The Great Learning*. Was he also presenting views directly *about reality beyond* that book? I think so.

Wang was commenting directly, it seems, on 'great people' and their nature. These views from him then have implications for views expressed earlier in *The Great Learning*. But Wang was not arguing *from* supposed flaws in that book's approach *to* his views about great people. His reasoning went in the opposite direction, *from* his views on the nature of great people.

6.2.2 Attitudes

Are there specific *attitudes* that do, or should, accompany philosophical views (once these have been formulated with a specific content: section 6.2.1)? For example, must those views be advanced with a feeling of certainty, accepted as definitively and unquestionably true?

It seems not, judging by the diversity in this book's readings. They have been our companions and guides while wandering with philosophical intent, maybe along Parmenides' Way of Truth (section 2.2.3) or Confucius' Way, his *dao* (section 5.1.1). Time and again, we have happened upon new views. Philosophy began, inevitably, with new views; then ideas that were newer still arrived, refreshing it along the way; it *remains* rich in ever-newer ideas. When walking along a Parmenidean or a Confucian Way, we might regard some of those ideas as true. But nowhere along either Way are we obliged to experience *certainty* – being fully confident that *now* we have attained unquestionably true philosophical views.

At any rate, that is one possible message to take from this book's variety of views. The message could emerge from looking back at how philosophy has taken shape so far, with so many newer-new views replacing older-new views. That message of variety and replacement could be reinforced, too, by philosophy's imagined future. Might a Parmenidean or a Confucian Way – a Way of Truth or a Confucian *dao* – stretch, seemingly unendingly, before us and our philosophical descendants? Might they reflect upon us much as we are now looking back at our philosophical ancestors?

Those questions about future philosophical thinkers matter *even for what we are doing here and now*: if you cannot know that you have reached a Way's end, and if (as you peer ahead) you cannot notice such an end somewhere in the distance, how can you know *where you are now* along that Way? Do you even know *how far along* you are, compared to how far remains along the Way?

If not, how can you know whether what seems true, here and now, will *still* seem true once you are further along the Way? You see a horizon ahead – but it moves as you move: soon it changes into another, then another another, on and on. New horizons, new views, new assessments of earlier views – endlessly?

Are we therefore denied the chance to reach finally settled views of reality – until we reach the *end* of a Way? Perhaps only *then* can one turn around, perusing the Way along which one has travelled, and view – at last! – How Reality Is. Would we only *then* have reached philosophical knowledge of Reality? Would full philosophical confidence only *then* be apt?

And are we there yet?

6.3 Viewing views philosophically

In practice, many philosophers do not seek only views of, or about, significant aspects of *the world*. They also form views *upon views* – such as other philosophers' views, or their own earlier views, or imagined hypothetical views. (They evaluate whether so-and-so had *a good argument*, for instance, one that we should accept.) Some viewed views remain directly on, or about, reality *beyond* views – How Reality Is. But many views are *only of* views: they are Views of Views.

Why so? Can that improve one's being philosophical – *even* about the wider world? Can one think better about reality by thinking about other people's thinking about it?

Ultimately, I expect, most philosophers do wish for insight into significant aspects of reality: 'Today I will think about selves. What *are* they?' Can it therefore be distracting to discuss *other discussions*, such as *what other philosophers have written* about selves? We call this 'scholarship'. And sometimes, yes, it is distracting. When well done, though, it can improve our views of the world itself – the world *beyond* views. In many of this book's readings, we have found philosophers *thinking about thinking about* a topic or idea, say. But they might do this in order then to think *better* about that topic or idea itself: it is an *indirect* way to think about that topic or idea.

For instance, it is one thing to form a view that X is part of being moral; it is another to form a view *on how best to form a view about* what morality includes. Should a philosopher take 'time out' to do the latter if she wants to do the former? One philosopher's view is that 'X is needed for morality'; another's might be that 'Y, not X, is the key to being moral.' How can we choose *well* between those two? We might seek a view *on, or about, how to* reach a view that would resolve the clash.

So, discussing views and how best to reach them can help more broadly. It can be an *indirect* way to reach views about the world beyond views (such as about the nature of morality). This may be done in different ways.

- A philosopher might discuss directly *how we should reason* about some aspect of reality. Her stated aim could be to improve upon prior views, maybe applying them in a new way, perhaps adding important details, and so on. Her indirect – and ultimate – aim may then be to use these improved ways of reasoning in thinking directly about that aspect of reality.
- Sometimes a philosopher's focus on other views is less apparent. For instance, she might comment directly on *our concept* of some aspect of reality. Philosophers often claim to discuss 'our concept' of something. But a concept is what it is, partly by appearing in our views, being used by them.
- A philosopher may have a mixed strategy. She might blend (i) views directly of, or about, reality with (ii) views directly about views (including ones directly of, or about, reality). For instance, an argument for 'Free will is X, not Y' could be accompanied by questions directly about what Kant wrote on free will. Maybe his views point towards a better view – directly – of whether free will is X.

Here are two examples of how one might develop a philosophical view by engaging *directly with other views* (even when indirectly seeking a view about the wider world). These are from chapter 5.

Singer (section 5.3.2) I include Singer here (rather than in section 6.2.1) because he presents his view as an improvement upon how a prior view – utilitarianism – had been applied to the wider world. We might view his view as not *directly* about animals' moral needs. He highlights an analogy between speciesism and racism/sexism – these being *views*. He argues for applying utilitarianism – an existing *view* – to the plight of animals, so that we shelter these under the moral protection provided by respecting utilitarianism as a view about morality's reach.

Rolston (section 5.4.4) In seeking to view the natural world through the lens of an environmental ethic, Rolston asks whether we could build on earlier forms of ethical theory – these also being views, of course. Can we build ecological values into the general idea of an ethical theory from the outset, making it a better way of viewing the natural world? The *direct* aim is to form an improved view of how to view the natural world; the *indirect* aim is thereby to form a more deeply ethical view of the natural world. The ultimate aim is a better view *of moral reality*. But the immediate method involves a view *of a view* – hopefully finding an improved one, *en route to* that better view of moral reality.

6.4 Views, views, views

This chapter is discussing views, as what emerge from philosophical reasoning. What can they achieve? That is our guiding question about them: what do we hope will emerge from being philosophical? Towards answering that, we are asking, firstly, about what *forms* philosophical views take. And, since we have highlighted *reasoning* as the means by which philosophical views are reached, this question follows immediately: must philosophical views always be *considered statements of a thesis reached after a step-by-step argument*?

Maybe surprisingly, no, not always so – based on what this book has displayed.

Earlier (section 4.1), I listed several kinds of elements, some or all of which may help to constitute an instance of philosophical reasoning:

> Ideas. Concepts. Phenomena. Data. Interpretations. Theses. Reasons. Questions. Puzzles. Conclusions.

Now I am asking whether philosophical *views* (as this chapter has described them) must always be philosophical *conclusions* (the final entry in this list). The answer is apparently 'No.'

Think of the flexibility that we enjoy in talking of views. We saw (section 6.1) that they can be *about*, or *on*, or *of*, or *over* (and *from*; maybe more besides). This range allows us to look beyond seeking theses, let alone ones derived from a step-by-step inference. A potentially wider array awaits.

As we saw, for example, a view can be like a lookout, a place *from* which to form a view (one that is not itself a lookout) *over*, and *of*, a landscape. Forming that view could be a complex process, but the view reached *need* not be a thesis. Imagine forming questions prompted by what one sees – before answering some of those questions. The questions are views; so are the answers. The answers might be theses, even conclusions reached through step-by-step reasoning. The questions would not be theses, of course. Yet all of this – the questions *plus* the answers – can be a kind of view. It would be composed of other views, which themselves take different forms (questions, answers). So it is complex. And its complexity is like many cases of being philosophical where we form questions, offer answers, and maybe blend these. We have no guarantee that being philosophical will result in a *simple* view – let alone a simple thesis concluding a step-by-step argument. Nor need this worry us.

Being philosophical might not even result in a *finished* complex, such as final questions with accompanying answers, even provisional ones, let alone decisive ones. Being philosophical *can* leave one confused, puzzled, floundering – still seeking even good questions, let alone satisfying answers. One might feel as if one is drowning, not waving. One could be left only with questions – which need not yet feel like the *best* questions with which to think about the topic. The search may continue for *better* questions. For a start, one might still be seeking better *concepts*. And concepts are merely *parts* of a question, *parts* of a thesis. As our list from a moment ago reflects, concepts can be elements of philosophical reasoning – while being at most *parts* of conclusions, which either *use* those concepts or are *about* them. Some reasoning might be philosophically helpful simply by introducing a new concept.

And much the same can be said for the other elements in that list of possible elements of philosophical reasoning. I encourage you to rework the previous paragraph's remarks more widely, directing them not only at questions and concepts (from that list).

It seems, then, that we may readily adopt a generous view of philosophical views – what they are, what they look like, what we can do with them. We may be quite inclusive in the forms of thinking – the kinds of views – that we deem philosophical. A philosophical view need not be a thesis, a conclusion of step-by-step arguing. It could be a question. Or a puzzle. Or an idea. And so on. Philosophical views can take any of many forms. They might be ways of looking, of seeing, of thinking. They might be 'snapshots' – pictures perhaps of a landscape, possibly of a detail within that vista. Or they could be views – viewings – still being formed as we stand there, looking, reflecting, appreciating.

All of this occurs – I am supposing, in an investigative spirit – as you travel along a Parmenidean or a Confucian Way (or another kind). In contemporary terms, we might portray this Way as akin to a highway, fixed and even straight, solid and well repaired, easy to follow while ever we remain focused. And highways can spawn byways, branching off hither and thither, leading to ... sometimes it is clear, sometimes it is not. We saw Confucius, especially, welcoming the role of *questions*, which we may envision as like some of those potentially more mysterious byways. Imagine finding yourself – courtesy of questions and puzzles, say – following smaller roads branching off the highway to ... who knows where, until you have arrived there? That is a highly apt analogy: being philosophical *can* lead you back and forth, here and there, up and down – without your knowing in advance where you will spend the night. Even that does not prevent your continuing your journey along that highway, along that Way – so long as, somehow, the byways allow you, when need be, to *rejoin* the highway.

So, my philosophical advice here is simple. If you turn off a main road, exploring a byway, keep in sight a landmark – such as a key idea, a motivating question, an hypothesis being tested – with which to find your way back to that highway once you wish to return, perhaps having fully explored where that byway wended its own way. You need never lose direction and location. And if your journey takes longer, so what? Whoever would have *expected* that a philosophical journey – for this is what you would be on – must be completed in the most direct way possible? Speed is not a need in being philosophical.

6.5 Philosophy as experiment

I have used three main metaphors, as analogies, in asking about the nature of being philosophical.

- When being philosophical, we are travelling along a Way, perhaps Parmenides' Way of Truth or Confucius' *dao* (section 6.2.2).
- Being philosophical may be viewed as having striking similarities to rhythmic gymnastics, including the use of something odd or surprising as a distinctive part of the performance. In a philosophical performance, the oddity is an unusual idea, concept, question, etc. (section 4.4).
- Philosophical views take many forms, such as active viewings, or lookouts from which we survey a landscape, or elements within other views, including concepts, questions, theses, etc. (section 6.1).

Those metaphors are easily blended. At times, we could be wandering more, or less, purposefully along a Way – a Parmenidean one, a Confucian one, perhaps one not described in this book. We may make distinctively odd or surprising moves along the way, as a puzzle arises, a question is posed, a concept occurs to us, and so on. We might reach a lookout (perhaps a temporary resting place) – an opportunity for extensive viewing, perhaps resulting in an hypothesis, an interpretation, etc. Maybe we gaze back upon where we were, gaining a panoramic view of our thinking so far. Perchance we peer ahead: are we able yet to see where we are heading? Might we choose a path (even a byway) to follow next, in order to test our current view – the hypothesis or interpretation with which we are now surveying our surroundings?

Even that invitingly blended metaphor is not everything that we might need. It does not distinguish being philosophical from being scientific, say. After all, scientists also seek truth while using hypotheses and interpretations; and science includes many odd and surprising moments (although we might wonder whether some of those have been philosophical, a possibility raised in section 5.4.5 about Lovelock's idea of Gaia).

That cautionary thought persists even if we revisit another of this book's venerably pre-scientific ideas, from the *Mahābhārata*, about truth *as it is for us* (section 2.2.4):

> The forms that Truth assumes are impartiality, self control, forgiveness, modesty, endurance, goodness, renunciation, contemplation, dignity, fortitude, compassion, and abstention from injury.

Can being scientific embrace those qualities? Possibly so, such as by including sensitivity and caring. You might recall Longino's feminist discussion (section 3.6.3) of how scientific reasoning could be improved by not ignoring ontological heterogeneity – any fundamental variety in potential data. Truth should matter not only to being philosophical. *That* focus is not enough to mark off philosophy from all other ways of thinking.

I have another reason, too, for treading warily here. This book samples philosophy's vast variety, from disparate centuries and cultures. We have travelled far and wide, across time and space. Yet philosophy is even larger. Its history is extensive. Hence, even if we could find distinctive features shared by the book's readings, might we need to change our minds in the future about the nature of being philosophical – *upon reading even more philosophy*?

If so, we might profit from a further metaphor: maybe being philosophical is like *contributing to an experiment*. Could the history of philosophy be like a *very long-running* experiment? Is philosophy as a whole *a long-term* experiment – one to which all of us can contribute? Those are intriguing questions.

Think about experimental practices in science. Interim interpretations, of results gained from earlier stages, *may be overturned later*, by interpretations of results yet to arise. Could that sort of result occur within philosophy, such as from reading more widely? What had felt philosophically true would no longer do so, as we savour and digest previously unread ideas and challenges. Having built and shaped an interpretation, we might apply it and evaluate the result – before modifying or even replacing the interpretation. A changed view would emerge. Or we might remain with the initial interpretation, still applying it, still examining and testing. In any event, we are *working with* ideas, concepts, interpretations, questions, etc. – applying and testing, possibly modifying. This is part of being scientific. Is it also part of being philosophical?

Seemingly so. Let us therefore extend the analogy.

Scientific practice counsels us always to be flexible when positing and interpreting hypotheses, say. We may accept that they could be refuted upon further investigating. We would stand ready to replace an interpretation with an apparently better one. On and on this might continue – back and forth, living the adventure of scientific inquiry. Is that flexibility likewise present within philosophy, as part of being philosophical? I think so. It seems to me that here and now, reading this book, being philosophical, we are immersed in an experiment. In effect, philosophy can be treated as a long-term experiment in human inquiry. This is not to describe being philosophical *as* being scientific in all ways; to me, for instance, it also feels artistic. The immediate point is just that there seems to be at least that structural kinship with being scientific.

In which case, the following questions arise about philosophical practice (as similar ones do about scientific practice).

How long should our philosophical efforts continue before there is no risk of overturning our currently favoured views (including our sense of what philosophy even is)? *For how long* should we be doing philosophy if we are to gain real understanding of what it is and what it reveals?

Those questions are challenging, partly because (as mentioned in section 6.2.2) we might not really know *where* we are located in the 'fullness of philosophical time' along the philosophical Way that we are travelling. We are located somewhere 'inside' philosophy as it unfolds – before us, around us, after us. Are we now standing at its ultimate lookout, viewing its completed state, finally able to gauge its fully expressed nature and contents? Is Here-and-Now special in that way? I doubt it.

Is it possible that we are only at an *early* stage of philosophy – of philosophy-as-a-continuing-experiment with the potential to generate ever more ideas, questions, concepts, and so on? I suspect so. Might we view philosophy as having been 'running' as this kind of experiment for thousands of years, across a wide range of cultures? Maybe it has thousands of years – or longer – still to 'run' before – if ever – its nature will become fully apparent. Again I ask: *how* long-term an experiment is philosophy? Will we ever – will anyone, even far into the future – experience enough of it to know *what, ultimately, it is*? Until we view *what, finally, it has been*, do we fail to know – even now – *what, fully and deeply, it is*?

That might not be all. Until we view what, finally, philosophy has been, do we remain unable to know what its *best* views will have been? Could we know this only after the whole experiment has been completed – after philosophy's full potential has been expressed and appreciated?

And, once more, are we there yet?

6.6 Philosophy forever

What if the overall philosophy experiment never *can* be completed? Might philosophy be a potentially *endless* experiment – never exhausting its questions, ideas, concepts, and so on?

I am not asking whether, in practice, there will always be people reasoning philosophically. People ceasing to think philosophically, for example, would show nothing about the nature of being philosophical. For everyday reasons, people may walk away from being philosophical – parental duties, social responsibilities, professional demands, etc. And what of total human extinction? That would end all actual thinking. Yet it would reveal nothing distinctive about the nature of any philosophical views formulated prior to that cataclysmic moment.

What I mean by asking whether philosophy could be endless is the following. It is a kind of 'in-principle' endlessness. But *what* kind of in-principle endlessness would this be?

- Might philosophical reasoning always include, *implicitly within itself, ways of extending itself as reasoning*? Does whatever has been written or thought within philosophy *point to further* possible philosophical reasoning? Thus, will philosophy never have said all that, in principle, it can say?
- For example, can philosophical reasoning *always implicitly raise further philosophical questions*? (I say

'implicitly' in case no one has explicitly formulated those further questions.)

Here is an illustration of that. Suppose your friend claims that X is the final philosophical word on topic T: X is *the* view to adopt if you are to understand T. You are unconvinced. You reply: '*Why* is X the best? Are there other views, similar to X – perhaps almost-X – that would work as well as X does in telling us about T?' If your friend answers thoughtfully, then potentially *more* than X-on-its-own is being sought collaboratively by you and she. The best might now be a substantive X+, no longer quite your friend's X. It might be X-*plus*-her-explanatory-comments-responding-to-you.

This investigation could continue. Suppose that your friend says 'Even if X is not the final word, X+ is.' Still puzzled, you continue questioning, requesting explanation – *but now treating X+ as you previously treated X*. What close alternatives to X+ might there be? Why are they not as good as X+?

And so on. Will X+ lead to X++, then X+++, etc.? *Ever* more details, ideas, questions, concepts, etc.? This could happen, it seems. Does philosophical reasoning always include a potential for added details, ideas, questions, concepts, etc.? Maybe so. In which event, are there no *philosophically* final philosophical views? Is this *foreverness* inherent within any moment of being philosophical?

And could such foreverness reflect another intriguing possibility? Does it suggest that anyone's – yours, mine, even a group's – being philosophical is only *a passing moment in a potentially endless experiment*?

- Perhaps philosophy's potential can never be fully realised (completed or fulfilled) by anyone – no individual, no group.

- If so, anyone can only ever contribute – even at most – something small to philosophy as a whole.
- *How* small?
- *So* small: if philosophy is endless, then any potential contribution is only a finite contribution to an *infinity*.
- Would that amount, in mathematical effect, to making *zero* impact upon that infinitude? (Infinity divided by a finite number is zero.)
- Is that so, no matter how much philosophical thinking we and others will ever do on a particular topic?
- It could be so, since our actual philosophical efforts will remain finite even if they occupy the entirety of our individual or collective lives.

6.7 Philosophical progress

Should we feel worried by those thoughts? This might depend on whether we expect *progress* to occur within philosophy.

Wherever there is progress, there has been progressing. That point links well with our guiding metaphor of travelling philosophically along a Way: philosophical progress would be made by progressing along that Way. Yet section 6.6 proposed that our finite philosophical efforts never *lessen* whatever distance remains if, in fact, we are travelling an infinitely long Way. (No finite number of steps lessens the infinitude remaining.) In which event, how *could* progress – through actual progressing – ever be achieved along that Way?

Walking can *feel* as if one is making progress: steps are literally being taken, hopefully towards an intended destination. But that feeling could be misleading: if the steps are not moving one literally *closer* to the destination, how is there any genuine progressing? This could amount to walking on an unceasing treadmill – without realising that one is so 'trapped'. Is this akin to Sisyphus' apparent plight (in Camus's discussion of absurdity in life: section 1.7.3)? And then we must ask: are such steps-being-taken like our thoughts-being-thought? When thinking philosophically, say, is this like pushing a heavy rock unendingly – up an *infinitely* tall mountain? Is being philosophical like *that*?

Those questions concern progress and philosophy, and they might feel worrying. But need they be? Or are they inescapable? We might question, in reply, whether making progress *is* part of the point of being philosophical. Is being philosophical an *end in itself* (remember this idea from Kant, in section 5.2.2, and Korsgaard, in section 5.3.3)? Does being philosophical have *inherent* value, as a way to live? I am unsure.

Maybe I do not *need* to be sure. When I mentioned (section 6.6) the idea of an infinitely long Way, I offered it as a possibility, not as definitely actual. (I was musing, not concluding.) And maybe its negation is also possible. Perhaps there *is* a possible final destination for philosophical thinking, even if no one will ever reach it.

So, we have both of those possibilities to consider.

And one of them allows us the freedom to dream of making philosophical progress. *If* philosophical thinking is not endless, maybe we can still aspire to finding a final philosophical destination. That destination might even include some final answers.

But I did say 'if', 'maybe', and 'might' just now.

6.8 Xenophanes' opinion

Questions in that spirit (section 6.7) are far from new. They may also be seen as posed by Xenophanes of Colophon (c. 570–480 BCE). (Colophon was an inland Greek Ionian town at that time.)

> ... and of course the clear and certain truth no man
> has seen
> nor will there be anyone who knows about the gods
> and what I say about all things.
> For even if, in the best case, one happened to speak
> just of what has been brought to pass,
> still he himself would not know. But opinion is
> allotted to all.

Xenophanes was writing about inquiry in general, not specifically about being philosophical. But do we have any 'clear and certain' reason not to apply his thoughts to philosophical reasoning? Suppose that what he called 'the best case' arises from some clever philosophical reasoning. Imagine, as Xenophanes did, that one has thereby 'happened to speak just of what has been brought to pass', so that one's final philosophical proposal is *true*. Is some such combination all that we could have sensibly *desired* when being philosophical?

Xenophanes implies that, even then, one 'would not know'. One would have only 'opinion'. Although it might be philosophical in content and tone, it would remain opinion. It would not be knowledge. Hence, too, it would not be philosophical knowledge. Could it have philosophical value, even so?

Xenophanes was writing in the earliest days of recorded philosophy. Does that make a difference to what message we may take from him? Are we better placed than he was, thanks to millennia of subsequent philosophical writing, a multitude of options for what to seek when being philosophical? We have been grappling with that question in these final few sections of the book. Do those millennia make no difference at all, *if* – thanks to the potential endlessness of the long-term experiment that philosophy in general might be – we are *actually no closer* than Xenophanes was to reaching the end of what remains an infinitely long philosophical Way?

We have reached no definitive answer to that question. Yet this is as it should be, if Xenophanes was correct: maybe 'clear and certain truth' is not ours to have in such matters. Truth? Perhaps at times. Clarity? Also perhaps at times. But certainty? At times, possibly, a feeling of it. But what would that prove? A feeling might be only a feeling. Even when it is of utter confidence, it might be mistaken – *not* true. Xenophanes' doubt concerned something more potentially impressive. Can we ever have a definitively and rationally unquestionable and unrevisable acceptance? What of rationally ruling out all alternatives to what one is thinking? Is *that* ever possible when being philosophical? I doubt it, if this book is a good guide. I doubt it, too, if Xenophanes' words were true.

And were they?

Reading for 6.8

For Xenophanes, see *Xenophanes of Colophon: Fragments. A Text and Translation with a Commentary*, ed. J. H. Lesher (Toronto: University of Toronto Press, 1992); quotation from fragment 34, at p. 39.

6.9 Living philosophically

Should we be *worried* by the possibility of Xenophanes' words being true?

Surveying this book's readings, I wonder whether being philosophical could *be* partly a matter of living without certainty. Being better at being philosophical – developing and improving one's philosophical skills and sensitivities – could then include being better – more skilful and attuned – *at* living without certainty.

Yet that might not be *so* simple – just as this book has not been *so* simple. Nor need it be emotionally simple. Within philosophy (as we have found), the lack of certainty would accompany thinking about some humanly sensitive issues, including ones for which we could desire answers to enhance our day-to-day living, including how we feel about ourselves and the world.

But the challenge here is not only about living with feelings. Living with an uncertainty traceable to being philosophical need not include *feeling* uncertain – hesitant, unsure, tentative – or anything more disturbing as a result. It might do so; it might not. In talking of philosophically inspired uncertainty, I mean primarily that a *considered concession of a lack of rational finality* would be present, maybe calmly, maybe not. How one reacts emotionally to this would be a separate matter. One may, for example, aim to live unworriedly *even* while conceding that one has no definitively final answers to fundamental questions, due to not having reached the end of a Way of Truth or a Confucian *dao*.

In which event, would remaining philosophical keep one *perpetually* alert to that possibly humbling realisation about oneself? It might.

Questions, ideas, concepts, puzzles, interpretations, hypotheses – in profusion, jostling for attention, competing for acceptance, like balls floating, tumbling, being caught, being juggled (and sometimes dropped, again, and again). We will experience philosophy's potentially unending range. We will experience optionality and choice. We will experience intellectual alternatives. Directed at many topics, issues, aspects of the world – those discussed in this book; but not only those, if philosophy can expand and extend, finding further challenges and applications. Where will this finish? Honestly, I do not know.

But wait a moment. My impression is that some philosophers whom we have met in this book *have* written with feelings of certainty, arguing forcefully

– not expressing doubt – for their favoured views. Were they not *really* being philosophical?

That sounds harsh, and I would not insist on that view of them. For even what I am saying now about living without certainty is *itself* being proposed without certainty. It appears as an hypothesis, an interpretation. (So, let the applying, the testing, the reshaping of *it* begin.)

What I do now say with at least a feeling of certainty should be less contentious. It seems to me that being philosophical – such as with the vigour and variety displayed by our readings in this book – can be thoughtful and ordered and stimulating rather than random or hectic. Even an acknowledged lack of certainty can be thoughtful and ordered and stimulating rather than random or hectic.

It can be philosophical.

As can you. This book ends here and now. But your being philosophical need not. Where will that lead you? You will know, if ever, only by trying.

Index

action
  and knowledge 118, 184, 228
  see also American Indian knowledge-how; Anscombe, G. E. M.; Nyāya; Ryle, Gilbert; Wang Yangming, and knowledge
  and mind 27–8
  and morality 40–1, 45, 72–3, 184, 185, 189, 195–7, 201–3, 207, 223–4, 228, 243
  and will *see* causal determinism; Foot, Philippa; Frankfurt, Harry; Ullmann-Margalit, Edna; will, freedom of
Akṣapāda, Gautama 94
Alexander of Aphrodisias 55–7, 89, 225
al-Ghazālī, Abū Ḥāmid Muḥammad ibn Muḥammad *see* doubt, and al-Ghazālī, Abū Ḥāmid Muḥammad ibn Muḥammad
American Indian knowledge-how 142–5, 182
animals 19, 33–4, 40, 99, 102, 112, 189, 205, 209, 210, 225–7, 229, 233, 237
  see also Beasts; Descartes, René, and animals; Korsgaard, Christine; Mill, John Stuart, on moral action; Śāntideva; Singer, Peter
Anscombe, G. E. M. 139–41, 144
Anselm, St 64–6, 67, 70, 89, 227
Aquinas, St Thomas 139, 141
Aristotle 89, 112
  on free action 52–4
  on knowledge *see* Sanches, Francisco
  on personal flourishing 185–8, 192, 202, 208, 243–4

Index

Āryadeva 74–6, 89
Avicenna 21–3, 24, 42, 89

Beasts *see* Midgley, Mary
Bentham, Jeremy 202, 219
Berkeley, George 121–5, 126, 127, 147
  see also physical matter
Buddhism 8–11, 41, 89, 215
  Madhyamaka 35–7, 74
  Mahāyāna 36, 216
  Yogācāra 37
  see also Āryadeva; Dharmakīrti; Milinda, King; Nāgārjuna; Śāntideva; selves, versus no-selves; Vasubandhu
Burkhart, Brian Yazzie 142–4

Camus, Albert 67–9, 89, 260
caring 35, 220, 230, 254
  see also Noddings, Nel
causal determinism 47, 49, 55, 58–9
  see also Alexander of Aphrodisias; Foot, Philippa; Stoics; will, freedom of
certainty 30, 98, 109–10, 117, 120, 150, 261
  see also doubt; philosophy, and certainty; Xenophanes
character 9, 47, 58–9, 87, 146–7
  see also Aristotle, on personal flourishing; Confucian *Great Learning*; Confucius; ibn 'Adī', Yaḥyā; Noddings, Nel; virtues, moral
Chrysippus 55, 225–6
Churchland, Patricia 13–14, 89
Cicero 227
Colwell, Thomas 236
Confucian *Great Learning* 192–4, 228, 230, 245
Confucius 181–4, 245, 246, 252, 253, 263
  see also Confucian *Great Learning*; Neo-Confucianism; Wang Yangming
consciousness 9, 20–1, 36–7, 42
  see also Dharmakīrti; introspection; Locke, John; Mill, John Stuart, and other minds; mind–body dualism; souls; Stein, Edith; Vasubandhu
consciousness-moments *see* Vasubandhu
cosmos 57, 225–8, 230, 244–5
  see also environment

Dalmiya, Vrinda 159–61, 214
dao 182–3, 245–6, 253, 263
  see also Confucius
de Pizan, Christine 29–31, 78, 89
death *see* Epicurus; Lucretius
Descartes, René 89, 127
  and animals 25–7, 32–3, 215
  see also doubt, and

Index

Descartes, René; mind–body dualism
Dharmakīrti 126–9, 216
Diogenes Laertius 225–7
doubt
  and al-Ghazālī, Abū Ḥāmid Muḥammad ibn Muḥammad 109–12, 119, 172–4
  and Descartes, René 115–18, 119–21, 135, 136, 139
  and Sextus Empiricus 101–4, 107, 114, 118
  and *Zhuangzi* 98–101, 104, 168–70, 172
  see also knowledge; Nāgārjuna; other minds; Sanches, Francisco
dreaming
  see doubt, and al-Ghazālī, Abū Ḥāmid Muḥammad ibn Muḥammad; doubt, and Descartes, René
duty 85, 195–6

Earth System Science 239
  see also Lovelock, James
ecology *see* environment
empathy 160, 220–1, 223
  see also Noddings, Nel; Stein, Edith
environment *see* Lovelock, James; Naess, Arne; Rolston, Holmes; Wang Yangming, and moral action
environmental ethics *see* environment
Epicurus 62

epistēmē 93, 104, 154
epistemology 93, 104, 126, 143, 148, 150–3, 154, 170–1, 182, 221
essence, personal 23, 33–4, 45, 47, 49, 51, 52
  see also Fanon, Frantz; Marx, Karl; race
ethics *see* morality
eudaimonia see Aristotle, on personal flourishing
evidence 10, 25, 26, 31, 43, 50, 93–7, 115–16, 121, 128–30, 141, 149, 153, 154–5, 157, 159, 167–8, 171, 172–4, 202–3
  see also doubt; epistemology; knowledge; *logos*; memory; perception; virtues, intellectual
evil demon *see* doubt, and Descartes, René
external world *see* Berkeley, George; doubt, and Descartes, René

faith *see* Anselm, St
Fanon, Frantz 47–9, 89, 154
fatalism 53–4
  see also Aristotle, on free action; will, freedom of
feminism 198
  see also Dalmiya, Vrinda; de Pizan, Christine; Fricker, Miranda; gender; Longino, Helen; Nussbaum, Martha; Singer, Peter; Wollstonecraft, Mary

Foot, Philippa 57–9, 89
Frankfurt, Harry 33–5, 41, 52, 89, 190–1
free will *see* will, freedom of
Fricker, Miranda 154–6, 159, 184, 214

Gaia *see* Lovelock, James
gender *see* essence, personal; feminism; Haslanger, Sally
God *see* Anselm, St; Berkeley, George; doubt, and Descartes; René; Korsgaard, Christine; Dharmakīrti; Wollstonecraft, Mary
gods 187–8
government 201, 210, 211
  see also politics

happiness *see* Aristotle, on personal flourishing; Mill, John Stuart, on moral action; Singer, Peter
Haslanger, Sally 49–51, 89
hermeneutics 155–6
Hobbes, Thomas 211
human capabilities *see* Nussbaum, Martha
human nature *see* character; Marx, Karl
Hume, David 12–13, 14, 19, 39, 89

ibn 'Adī', Yaḥyā 188–91, 192
idealism *see* Berkeley, George; Dharmakīrti
inference *see* knowledge; reasoning

injustice *see* justice
intention *see* Anscombe, G. E. M.
introspection 12–13, 89
  see also Churchland, Patricia; consciousness; Hume, David; Mill, John Stuart, on other minds; Stein, Edith; Vasubandhu

justice 30, 155
  see also Confucius; feminism; Fricker, Miranda; Mills, Charles; Nussbaum, Martha; race

Kant, Immanuel 194–8, 209–10, 221, 223, 224, 233, 237, 248, 260
  see also Korsgaard, Christine
Kneale, Martha 27–9, 89
knowledge 84, 87, 194, 243, 247
  see also action, and knowledge; doubt; *epistēmē*; epistemology; evidence; introspection; knowledge-how; *logos*; memory; moral knowledge; Nyāya; other minds; perception; Plato, on knowledge; Russell, Bertrand; Sanches, Francisco; self-knowledge; testimony; understanding;

virtues, intellectual;
  Wang Yangming, and
  knowledge; wisdom;
  Wollstonecraft, Mary;
  Xenophanes
knowledge-how *see* action,
  and knowledge;
  American Indian
  knowledge-how;
  virtues, intellectual
Korsgaard, Christine 221–4,
  233, 237, 260
  see also Kant, Immanuel

Locke. John 39–41, 43, 89
logic 54, 126
  see also rationality;
  reasoning
logos 93, 95, 167
Longino, Helen 150–3, 154,
  170–2, 214, 254
Lovelock, James 237–9
lovingkindness 216
Lucretius 61–3, 88, 92

Mahābhārata 84–7, 89, 90,
  145, 254
  see also Dalmiya, Vrinda
Marx, Karl 44–7, 89, 214
materialism *see* physical
  matter
meaning, in life *see* Camus,
  Albert; death; faith;
  Wolf, Susan
memory 14, 41, 43, 117, 205
  see also consciousness;
  Locke, John;
  Vasubandhu
Menkiti, Ifeanyi 15–16, 47, 89
Meno 91–3, 95, 97, 135, 167,
  168, 170, 172

  see also Plato, on
  knowledge
metaphysics 47, 91, 123, 188,
  213, 227, 232, 233
  see also ontology
Middle Way *see* Buddhism,
  Madhyamaka
Midgley, Mary 32–3, 89
Milinda, King 12, 16, 88
  see also selves, versus
  no-selves
Mill, John Stuart
  on other minds 128–32
  on moral action 202–4,
    207, 208, 214, 220,
    222
Mills, Charles 156–9, 210–14,
  244
mind–body dualism 23–5, 27,
  115
mind–body problem 27–8
  see also Kneale, Martha
Montessori, Maria 145–8
moral knowledge 72, 144, 181
moral responsibility 41
morality *see* action,
  and morality;
  animals; character;
  Confucian *Great
  Learning*; Confucius;
  environment; feminism;
  happiness; justice;
  Kant, Immanuel;
  moral knowledge;
  moral responsibility;
  Noddings, Nel;
  virtues, moral; Wang
  Yangming, and moral
  action

Naess, Arne 230–3

Nāgārjuna 74, 103–9, 112
Neo-Confucianism 136, 192
  see also Wang Yangming
neuroscience see Churchland, Patricia
Noddings, Nel 159, 205–7, 220
Nussbaum, Martha 207–10
Nyāya 93–7, 98, 100–8, 112

ontology 151–3, 171, 212–13, 254
  see also metaphysics
other minds see Dharmakīrti; Mill, John Stuart, on other minds; Stein, Edith

Parfit, Derek 41–3, 60, 89
Parmenides 78–81, 84–7, 88, 90, 144–5, 164, 178, 245–6, 252, 253
  see also reasoning, poetry
perception 12, 94, 96, 97, 104–5, 110, 114, 132–3, 158
  see also al-Ghazālī, Abū Ḥāmid Muḥammad ibn Muḥammad; Berkeley, George; evidence; introspection; knowledge; Nāgārjuna; Nyāya; Stein, Edith
Perry, John 76–8, 89, 140
personal essence 45, 47, 51
  see also Fanon, Frantz; gender; human nature; race; species-essence
personal identity
  see Buddhism, Madhyamaka; Locke, John; Parfit, Derek; selves; Vasubandhu
persons
  constituted within nature see Naess, Arne
  as ends in themselves see Kant, Immanuel; Nussbaum, Martha
  and significance see meaning, in life
  versus automata 136, 140
  versus substances 40–1, 43, 224
  versus wantons 33–5
  see also essence, personal; human capabilities; human nature; personal identity; self-knowledge; selves; souls
Phaedo see Plato, on souls
phenomenology see Stein, Edith
philosophy
  and certainty 245–6, 262–4
  and interpretive charity 166
  and progress 102, 114, 239, 259–60
  as end in itself 260
  as endless 105, 166, 257–60, 263
  as experiment 253–9, 261
  self- 76–8
  selfless 74–6
philosophy reasoning 80–4, 163, 165, 172–5, 178–80, 248–51, 257–9
  and truth 80–4, 164, 178; see also Way of Truth

as dialogue 8, 17 30, 88, 126, 165–8
by allegory 89
by analogy 28, 76, 92, 100, 156, 175–9, 202–3, 217, 238, 241, 249, 252, 255; *see also* Lucretius; Mill, John Stuart, on other minds; Nāgārjuna; Nyāya; Vasubandhu
by fiction 88, 89, 161, 211–12
by hypothesising 12, 13, 14, 19, 130–1, 167–71, 237, 252, 253, 264
by interpreting 23, 38, 82, 164, 171, 211, 214, 244, 253, 255, 264
by picturing 6, 17, 39, 46, 55–6, 72, 76–7, 85, 87, 95, 96–7, 123–4, 136, 150, 156, 175, 182, 185, 191, 198, 205, 213, 217, 228, 232–3, 239, 244
by poetry 78–81, 88
by questioning 2, 9, 12, 14, 17, 36, 51, 55, 59, 67, 73, 81–4, 98–100, 142–5, 151, 156, 163, 168–70, 182, 222, 226, 230, 241–2, 245, 246, 248, 250–3, 255, 256–8, 260, 263
by thought experiment 21–3, 42, 89
inductively 129–31
structure 167–8, 172–5
see also evidence; understanding; wisdom

physical matter 20, 21, 28, 41, 125, 238, 239
see also Berkeley, George; external world; mind–body dualism; Wang Chong
Plato 52, 88, 89
on knowledge 91–3, 95, 97, 167–8
on souls 17–19
politics 50, 159, 209, 211–14, 217
see also government
privilege *see* Fanon, Frantz; gender; Mills, Charles
Pyrrhonism *see* Sextus Empiricus

race *see* Fanon, Frantz; Mills, Charles
rationality 32, 40, 60, 66, 93, 97, 98, 111, 112, 189–90, 195, 197, 198–200, 225–7, 238, 263
see also doubt; Reason
Reason *see* de Pizan, Christine; Midgley, Mary; Wollstonecraft, Mary
reasoning *see* philosophy reasoning
Rolston, Holmes 233–7, 249
Russell, Bertrand 96–8
Ryle, Gilbert 137–9, 140

sage 6, 8, 160, 182, 192
Sanches, Francisco 112–15
Śāntideva 216–17, 244
scepticism 39, 100–1, 135–7, 139
see also doubt

science 15, 28–9, 55, 156, 254–6
  see also Churchland, Patricia; environment; Longino, Helen; Lovelock, James; Montessori, Maria; Naess, Arne; philosophy, as experiment; physical matter; Rolston, Holmes
self-knowledge 23, 169
  see also Anscombe, G. E. M.; Avicenna; Dalmiya, Vrinda; Descartes, René
selves 73, 83, 87, 243, 247
  as moral 198
  as social 15–16, 29, 45–7, 48, 49–51, 154, 194
  inner substantial 12–13
  versus no-selves 8–11, 74–6
  see also Buddhism; Churchland, Patricia; de Pizan, Christine; Locke, John; Marx, Karl; Midgley, Mary; personal essence; personal identity; persons; self-knowledge; souls; Upaniṣads; Vasubandhu
Sen, Amartya 208
Sextus Empiricus see doubt, and Sextus Empiricus
Singer, Peter 217–21, 223, 249
Sisyphus, myth of see Camus, Albert

social constructivism see Mills, Charles
social contract see Hobbes, Thomas; Mills, Charles
Socrates 204, 222
  and knowledge 91–3, 94, 95, 98, 135, 167–8, 170
  and souls, 19–20, 24
  see also Plato
souls 8–9, 12, 24–5, 62, 101, 186, 200–1, 225–6
  see also animals, and souls; Avicenna; ibn 'Adī', Yaḥyā; mind–body dualism; persons; Plato, on souls; selves; Wang Chong
species-essence see Marx, Karl
speciesism see Singer, Peter
Stein, Edith 132–4, 160, 221
Stoics 225–8, 244–5
  see also Alexander of Aphrodisias; Chrysippus; Diogenes Laertius; Zeno of Citium
substance see Berkeley, George; physical matter; selves, inner substantial; Stoics; universal emptiness

testimony 94, 104
Theaetetus 91
  see also *Meno*; Plato, on knowledge
Timon of Phlius 101
truth see Kant, Immanuel; *Mahābhārata*; philosophy reasoning,

Index 273

and truth; Way of
 Truth
Ullmann-Margalit, Edna
 59–61, 89
uncertainty *see* certainty
understanding 51, 64, 73–4,
 79, 81, 106, 114, 122,
 134, 159, 165, 179,
 199, 201, 213, 231,
 233, 256
 see also Fricker, Miranda;
 Montessori, Maria;
 philosophy reasoning;
 virtues, intellectual;
 Zagzebski, Linda
universal emptiness 107–9
 see also Nāgārjuna
Upaniṣads 5–8, 88
utilitarianism 202, 204, 208,
 220, 249
 see also Bentham, Jeremy;
 Mill, John Stuart, on
 moral action; Singer,
 Peter

value, intrinsic 233
 see also Korsgaard,
 Christine; persons, as
 ends in themselves;
 philosophy, as end in
 itself
Vasubandhu 37–9, 40, 43,
 89
Vātsyāyana 94
Vedic texts 5, 93
vices, intellectual 148–9
 see also virtues, intellectual
virtues, intellectual *see*
 Dalmiya, Vrinda;
 Fricker, Miranda;

Longino, Helen; Mills,
 Charles; Montessori,
 Maria; Wollstonecraft,
 Mary; Zagzebski,
 Linda
virtues, moral *see* Aristotle,
 on personal flourishing;
 Confucian *Great
 Learning*; Confucius;
 Fricker, Miranda;
 ibn 'Adī', Yaḥyā;
 Noddings, Nel; Wang
 Yangming, and moral
 action; Zagzebski,
 Linda

Wang Chong 19–21, 89
Wang Yangming
 and knowledge 135–6, 137,
 184, 228
 and moral action 228–30,
 245; *see also*
 Confucian *Great
 Learning*
Way, Confucius' *see*
 Confucius
Way of Moral Truth 144–5
 see also Parmenides
Way of Truth *see* Parmenides
What Is *see* Way of Truth
will, freedom of 57, 61, 83
 see also action, and
 will; Alexander of
 Aphrodisias; Aristotle,
 on free action; causal
 determinism; Cicero;
 Chrysippus; fatalism;
 Foot, Philippa;
 Frankfurt, Harry;
 Ullmann-Margalit,
 Edna

wisdom 20–1, 25, 75, 84, 155, 187
  see also philosophy reasoning; sage
Wolf, Susan 69–70, 89
Wollstonecraft, Mary 198–201, 218–19

Xenophanes 260–2

Zagzebski, Linda 148–50, 159
Zeno of Citium 225, 227–8
Zhuangzi see doubt, and *Zhuangzi*